THE BRUSILOV OFFENSIVE

Twentieth-Century Battles

Spencer C. Tucker, Editor

General Aleksei A. Brusilov

THE
BRUSILOV
OFFENSIVE

TIMOTHY C. DOWLING

INDIANA UNIVERSITY PRESS

BLOOMINGTON AND INDIANAPOLIS

This book is a publication of

Indiana University Press
601 North Morton Street
Bloomington, IN 47404-3797 USA

http://iupress.indiana.edu

Telephone orders	800-842-6796
Fax orders	812-855-7931
Orders by e-mail	iuporder@indiana.edu

© 2008 by Timothy C. Dowling

The paper used in this publication meets the minimum
requirements of American National Standard for Information
Sciences—Permanence of Paper for Printed Library Materials,
ANSI Z39.48-1984.

Manufactured in the United States of America

Library of Congress Cataloging-in-Publication Data

Dowling, Timothy C.
   The Brusilov offensive / Timothy C. Dowling.
      p. cm. — (Twentieth-century battles)
   Includes bibliographical references and index.
   ISBN-13: 978-0-253-35130-2 (cloth)
   1. World War, 1914–1918—Campaigns—Eastern Front.
2. Brusilov, Aleksei Alekseevich, 1853–1926. I. Title.
   D550.D68 2008
   940.4'275—dc22

                                                                    2007044095

3 4 5   13 12

CONTENTS

MAPS

INTRODUCTION

In the west, the armies were too big for the land; In the east, the land was too big for the armies.

Winston Churchill, *The Unknown War: The Eastern Front*

There is a society devoted solely to the study of the Western Front during the First World War. Created in 1980, it has more than 6,500 members around the world who form a network for the discussion of topics related to the Western Front. It boasts a website, a magazine, and an online shop, provides reviews of books of interest to members, supports remembrance and research projects, and organizes many public events related to the First World War on the Western Front.[1] And the members of this association are certainly not alone in their fascination. The conflict in the west has been dissected, debated, and analyzed in almost unimaginable detail by scholars and aficionados of all stripes. The merits of almost every commander on the Western Front have been weighed, and it seems that every diary of every soldier on every side has been published with commentary. Full-length monographs explore the minutiae of nearly every major battle on the Western Front as well as many minor ones. Innovations in tactics and weaponry on the Western Front have been traced exhaustively.[2] Even casual students of the First World War are familiar with the First Battle of Ypres ("the slaughter of innocents") and the Somme, with Ernst Jünger and Siegfried Sassoon. *All Quiet on the Western Front* and the battle for Verdun are standards in textbooks on modern European history and even in histories of Western or world civilization. The trench warfare of the Western Front, in all its glory and horror, forms the most persistent and prevalent image of the First World War in the minds of most people.

Yet the First World War consisted of far more than just the Western Front. The opening salvos came in the Balkans, where Austria-Hungary sought to punish Serbia, halt the tide of nationalism, and preserve its empire. A second, equally infamous, campaign took place in the Dardenelles during 1915, when the forces of the British Empire attempted to exploit the "soft underbelly" of Europe at Gallipoli. Italy and Austria-Hungary combined to mount no fewer than fifteen offensives across the Isonzo River, despite not going to war with each other until mid-1915. There were land battles in Greece, Bulgaria, and Romania, and sea battles in the Mediterranean and North seas as well as the Atlantic Ocean; even Asia and Africa served as theaters of war to some degree.

It might be argued, with some justification, that these were all "side shows" that had little or nothing to do with determining the outcome of the war. It is impossible, however, to say that of the Eastern Front. Helmuth von Moltke, chief of staff for the German army, was so concerned with the Russian Front in August 1914 that he took five crucial divisions from the forces moving through Belgium toward Paris and sent them east. When the Schlieffen Plan failed to produce the quick victory in the west that Germany's political and military leaders were relying upon, they turned their attention to the east. There, where vastly outnumbered German forces had eradicated two Russian armies, it seemed possible to achieve victory. In the summer of 1915, the Central Powers thus launched an offensive on the Eastern Front that they hoped would decide the war. It did not, of course, but 1916 brought the Brusilov Offensive, which once again drew the attention of Austria-Hungary and Germany away from other adventures—including, to some degree, Verdun.

From October 1914 to February 1917, the struggle against Tsarist Russia thus occupied between one-fifth and one-quarter of Germany's army, in addition to some 2 million Habsburg troops. Several of Germany's leading military figures, including Paul von Hindenburg, Erich Ludendorff, August von Mackensen, and (later) Hans von Seeckt secured their reputations on the Eastern Front. Poison gas was first used at Bulimov in eastern Poland, and the "creeping barrage" was developed at least in part by German commanders there. Nearly 750,000 German soldiers lost their lives on the Eastern Front, as did almost a million soldiers from the Habsburg armies and more than 2 million Russians.

For all that though, developments on the Eastern Front during the First World War have received scant attention from the general English-speaking public. Scholarship on the topic has been, until recently, a niche reserved for specialists. Winston Churchill penned a fine narrative of the conflict in the east in the late 1920s, but it was not until 1975 that the first scholarly examination of the Eastern Front appeared in English.[3] Progress since then has been slow and, outside of Dennis Showalter's masterful exposition of the Battle of Tannenberg, largely unnoticed by the English-speaking public.[4] Scholars were forced by the destruction of German military documents during the Second World War, and by the breakup of the Habsburg Empire, to scour smaller archives in their attempts to correct and add to the politically unbalanced official histories published in Germany and Austria during the 1920s, '30s, and '40s.[5] Not until 1997, when Holger Herwig published *The First World War: Germany and Austria-Hungary 1914–1918*, were most of the relevant German- and English-language sources combined for a detailed, if still briefer than desirable, view of events on the Central Powers' side of the Eastern Front.[6]

The other side, unfortunately, has developed even more slowly. Contemporary journalists such as Stanley Washburn and John Reed provided glimpses of Russia and the Imperial Russian Army during the First World War, as did the French ambassador to Russia Maurice Paléologue, but none covered the entire conflict or had consistent access to primary documents.[7] British Major General Alfred Knox, an observer with several Russian armies during the conflict, kept extensive notes that he later extended into a complete history of the Russian effort; his access to primary sources was limited, however, and he naturally paid less attention to the actions of the Central Powers.[8] Norman Stone's much later work made extensive use of Russian-language sources based on primary documents, but most were unreliable or incomplete. As Stone himself wrote of one such "standard," Lieutenant General Nikolai N. Golovine's *The Russian Army in the World War*: "what is true is not new, and what is new is not true."[9] Stone had no access to the Russian (Soviet) military archives.

The official Russian history of the conflict, published under the title The Commission for the Research and Study of the Experience of the World War and the Civil War, appeared in seven volumes between 1920 and 1923.[10] The best single volume on the war is the 1924 work by the Russian military historian Andrei M. Zaionchkovski under the auspices of the Workers' and Peasants Red Army Military Academy of the U.S.S.R. It was republished in 1931, 1938, and 2000—but, like the official histories, it has never been translated.[11] A volume of maps to accompany the work appeared in 1924.[12] These histories, however, are at least as problematic as the official German and Austrian histories, though for slightly different reasons. Zaionchkovski, for instance, had served as commander of the Russian XXX Corps in 1916 and early 1917, and the portions of his work dealing with the Romanian campaign contain a clear bias. It is also true that he met with his German and Austro-Hungarian counterparts at least once after the war to discuss the writing of the conflict's history, and that his work bears marked evidence of western influences. Both the seven- and the single-volume summaries of the Russian war experience cite orders at length, but there are few references, and those citations that do exist are often to Western sources, usually memoirs of somewhat dubious veracity. Several Russian and Soviet histories of armies, campaigns, and individual commanders have been written as well—in addition to a volume by Zaionchkovski on the international run-up to the war—but few have appeared since the 1960s; most were produced in the 1920s and '30s. A short history of the conflict did appear in Russian in 1964, but it is of limited use for specialists.[13] Soviet military historians, including Peter A. Zaionchkovski, apparently preferred to deal with less ideologically charged times, as did participants in the conflict.[14]

Western historians, meanwhile, tended to blend the First World War into the Russian revolutions. They studied the officer corps and the army, but almost always with an eye to the disintegration of 1917 rather than out of concern for the war itself. The closest thing to an overarching, historical view of the Russian army's performance during the First World War yet produced in English is thus W. Bruce Lincoln's *Passage through Armageddon*, which, for all its brilliance and erudition, is more a political and social analysis than a military history.[15] The fact that within the past decade (in 1999) an international conference was held in St. Petersburg to discuss the memory and social aspects of the conflict in Russia, however, offers some hope that work on the topic will continue despite the financial troubles of many Russian and former Soviet archives.[16] It may indeed be possible, in the near future, to produce a comprehensive history of the Eastern Front.

Such an assessment is certainly beyond the scope of this work, which aims only to explicate the significance of the Eastern Front in a general sense, as seen through the lens of a single campaign. The Brusilov Offensive lasted nearly six months and was part of the same general strategy that the Russian Supreme Command had followed since August 1914. In broad outline, the Russians sought to separate the Germans from the Austro-Hungarians in order to bring their numerical superiority to bear effectively. The Southwestern Front was supposed to be a sideshow in the summer offensive of 1916, but it should not have been surprising that Russian forces met with success against the Habsburg armies. That had, after all, been the pattern of 1914 and 1915. The devastating Russian defeats in eastern Silesia in 1914 were countered by stunning Russian victories in Galicia and the Bukovina. The Central Powers' massive summer offensive in 1915, spearheaded by German forces, pushed the front eastward by nearly 150 miles, but it never broke the Russian armies. The Austro-Hungarian attempt to follow up on their own failed so miserably that it became known as the "autumn swinery" (*Herbstsau*) among the troops. Brusilov's master stroke in June 1916 erased the Central Powers' gains of 1915 to a large degree and forced the Germans to shift their attention to their southeast.

Originally planned in conjunction with the fateful Somme Offensive, Brusilov's strike was pushed forward because of French and Italian pleas for relief from the German and Habsburg campaigns at Verdun and in Tirol, respectively. Brusilov's attacks of early June 1916 caught the Central Powers unprepared and drove them back nearly 100 miles in some sectors in what was by most estimates the greatest Russian military achievement of the war. Habsburg positions deemed impregnable fell overnight as Austria-Hungary's forces were decimated, and in some cases driven from the field. Brigades disintegrated in the face of the meticulously planned and precisely executed Russian assault, and entire Habsburg corps—even armies—shattered. More than 350,000 Habsburg soldiers became prisoners of war.[17] Brusilov's armies regained all of the territory lost in 1915 and advanced once again to the Carpathian Mountains, where they threatened Hungary. Only rapid action by Germany's military leaders held the front together and prevented the collapse of the Habsburg Empire in 1916.

The results were astonishing in military terms, but the political consequences were perhaps even more significant. Contemporaries—and Brusilov himself—claimed that the offensive had relieved Verdun and rescued the British and French position in the west, saved Italy, and forced Austria-Hungary to consider a separate peace. While those claims are controversial, Brusilov's success undoubtedly brought Romania into the war, extinguished the offensive ability of the Habsburg armies, and forced the Austro-Hungarian Empire to accept German military commanders at the head of a unified force. Perhaps more than any other action, the Brusilov Offensive not only brought the Habsburg Empire to the brink of a separate peace, but also did a great deal to create the conditions for revolution within the Russian Imperial Army. It thus stands out in the military and political history of the Eastern Front as a turning point for both sides.

Brusilov's campaign was not characteristic of the Russian war effort in its planning and execution. Where most commanders relied on numbers and the bayonet, Brusilov created a primitive version of unified arms combat. Unlike the war in the west, the conflict in the east never settled into a pattern of stalemate and stagnation. While elements of trench warfare existed, armies on the Eastern Front covered large amounts of territory in sweeping movements. The flanking movements, encirclements, and dramatic breakthroughs envisioned but never realized in the west played out fully in the east. Given the vast expanses of Eastern Europe, commanders on both sides proved more flexible in their tactics and more willing to try new approaches. Brusilov's plan reflected the innovative, ever-changing approach to the war characteristic of the front, and the Brusilov Offensive was unlike any other campaign.

Certainly General Aleksei A. Brusilov himself, widely recognized as the best Russian commander of the war, was unlike most of the other Russian commanders. To begin with, he was not a graduate of the General Staff Academy, a bastion of conservative thought that produced the vast majority of Russian commanders.[18] Brusilov also had some experience with western military thought, having toured the German, French, and Austro-Hungarian cavalry academies, and he had analyzed the campaigns of the Russo-Japanese War in some depth. Perhaps as a result, he was less rigid in his thinking and more willing to consider new approaches. He borrowed liberally from tactics developed on the Western Front, drew heavily on the experiences of the Russo-Japanese War, and developed several novel tactics of his own. He made use of the old—cavalry and artillery—and the new—aviation and armor—in developing a coordinated system of warfare. Unlike other commanders on the Eastern Front, Brusilov adapted his approach to the terrain at hand and the available material to create opportunities where seemingly none existed.

The summer offensive of 1916 brought Brusilov both national and international recognition, but his performance as a commander both before and after also warrants attention. As commander of Eighth Army, Brusilov played a key role in the initial Russian successes in Galicia. His troops invested the key Habsburg fortress of Przemysl and drove to the Carpathians, endangering Hungary in autumn 1914. When the Gorlice-Tarnow Offensive threatened to shatter the Russian armies in the summer of 1915, Brusilov helped orchestrate an orderly retreat. When the tsar abdicated on 2 March 1917 (Old Style), Brusilov served the Provisional Government not just loyally, but with some enthusiasm.[19] Mikhail Rodzianko, president of the Duma and a prominent leader in the new Provisional Government, had served in Brusilov's Guards' regiment, and Brusilov—along with chief of staff General Mikhail V. Alekseev—had been among the first commanders to support the Duma's call for responsible government.[20] Brusilov saw in the February Revolution parallels to the situation in France in 1792, when patriotism had stirred the people to fight in defense of their nation. Brusilov was not alone in this; Admiral Aleksandr Kolchak, later renowned as a leader of the anti-Bolshevik forces in the Russian Civil War, also welcomed the revolution initially "as a chance to hope that it would rouse enthusiasm—as was in fact the case in my Black Sea Fleet at first—in the masses, and that it would make possible a victorious end of this war, which I consider as foremost and important, as standing above all else, above the construction of the government and political consideration."[21]

Though like Alekseev and the other, more conservative members of Stavka Brusilov believed it was vital to maintain military discipline in order to bring the war to a successful conclusion, he was more willing to cooperate with the new regime than most commanders. General Platon Letschitski, for example, resigned his post rather than work with the Provisional Government, while army commanders Nikolai V. Ruzski, Radko Dmitrev, and Nikolai N. Yudenitch were all relieved of their duties for their inability to adapt to the new situation.[22]

For Brusilov, it was a matter of duty. The army, he argued, could not get involved in politics. While the tsar remained in power, Brusilov had been organizing troops to put down the disturbances in St. Petersburg; when it became clear Nicholas II was going to abdicate, Brusilov had pushed for a quick and clean transfer of power.[23] On 24 March 1917, however, Alekseev sent his commanders a secret, coded letter in which he advised them that the Provisional Government was in reality powerless to rein in the more radical Petrograd Soviet and that they therefore needed to take steps to actively combat extremism at the front. Alekseev went so far himself as to request that the Provisional Government appoint a commissar to serve as a liaison to Stavka. Following Alekseev's suggestions, Brusilov organized committees in each army on the Southwestern Front to keep the troops informed of events in St. Petersburg and the policies of the Provisional Government.[24] He went further than many officers, however, by acting to reduce the number of officers serving on the committees at the higher levels and by excluding officers from company-level committees all together.[25] Working with the All-Russian Central Committee for the Organization of a Voluntary Revolutionary Army, moreover, he organized "voluntary revolutionary battalions for the formation of shock attack groups" on the

Southwestern Front. Brusilov also supported the formation of the 1st Russian Women's Battalion of Death founded by Maria Bochkareva and Valentina Petrova.[26] As was his wont, Brusilov still believed that the offensive spirit, coupled with the spirit of the revolution, could save Russia. Asked at the end of March 1917 if the army was prepared to undertake an offensive that spring, Brusilov replied in effusive terms.[27]

As unrest spread among the troops at the front and the power of the soviets grew, however, Brusilov revised his evaluation. By the end of April 1917, he noted that the situation at the front had "significantly turned for the worse," and Alexander Kerensky—then newly minted as minister of war in the Provisional Government—noted that during a speech at a meeting of delegates from the Southwestern Front on 12 May, Brusilov had painted the mood of the army as war-weary.[28] The general was particularly dismayed by the continuing decline in discipline and the government's inability—or refusal—to support officers in this regard. Brusilov had, in fact, talked of resigning already on 2 May when it became clear that Kerensky intended to publish a new order, "The Declaration of the Rights of the Soldier," that would further undermine officers' authority. His colleagues at Stavka, however, had talked him out of it, persuading Brusilov it would be better to wait and present a united front at a meeting with the representatives of the Provisional Government and the Petrograd Soviet scheduled two days later. When the time came, however, Brusilov gave a muted and somber picture of the state of the army, but still spoke in favor of the offensive. "We must not forget that we have no well-disciplined troops, that they are badly trained and that the officers have no authority," he said. "In these circumstances an enemy success may easily become a catastrophe. The masses must, therefore, be persuaded that we must advance instead of remaining on the defensive."[29] All of the other commanders spoke against the plan.

Kerensky, who already held a favorable impression of Brusilov from their earlier meeting, was now convinced that he had found the man to lead the revolutionary offensive that would save Russia. Believing that Brusilov was a "man of action" who had the support of the troops and could provide a buffer against the soviets, Kerensky dismissed Alekseev and appointed Brusilov as supreme commander on 22 May 1917. Though Kerensky approved the formation of shock battalions on the Southwestern Front—which Alekseev had opposed—Brusilov soon realized the true bleakness of the situation.[30] On the one hand, Kerensky insisted on going ahead with an offensive planned to launch in just three weeks' time. Regiments were to be reduced from four battalions to three, and corps were to increase from two divisions to three in order to provide greater flexibility.

On the other hand, the minister of war continued to replace commanders at all levels in an effort to placate the more radical factions within the Provisional Government. Four of the five front commanders were fired within a week of Brusilov's appointment and replaced with officers more acceptable to the soviets. Because of difficulties with rail transportation, the original plans to strike at Lemberg (Lvov) were altered so that the main blow would come further south, while the other fronts would mount delayed "demonstrations." This caused Brusilov to delay the launch by some two weeks; then, when he was ready, Kerensky asked for another two days to ensure the support of the All-Russian Congress of Soviets. "To tell the truth," Brusilov recalled, "the government itself did not know for certain what it really wanted."[31] Though he saw increasingly smaller chances for success, Brusilov carried out his duties as best he could.

When it finally began, the Kerensky Offensive of June 1917—sometimes incorrectly referred to as the Second Brusilov Offensive—met with some initial success. Provided for the first time in the war with adequate numbers of heavy guns and sufficient ammunition, Brusilov's forces opened two days of artillery preparation on 30 June 1917. On 1 July, the Russian Eighth Army, now commanded by Lieutenant General Lavr Kornilov, managed to break the Central Powers' front lines, opening a 48-kilometer gap in the lines of the Austro-Hungarian Third Army. As they had a year earlier, thousands of Habsburg soldiers simply threw down their rifles and fled. Within ten days Eighth Army had taken Stanislau and was threatening the oil fields at Drohobycz. The Seventh and Eleventh armies also made significant advances on the Southwestern Front, while in the north Deniken's Tenth Army captured the enemy's front lines and Fifth Army used its heavy artillery to smash the German trenches and take Dvinsk.

Once again though, Brusilov found that his supply lines and reserves were inadequate for the challenges posed by success. The Russian armies soon cracked under the strain created by inadequate preparation, and commanders lost control of their troops. General Erdelli, commander of Eleventh Army, reported that "despite our gains on June 18 and 19 (Old Style), which ought to have raised the spirits of the men and encouraged them to press on, no such spirit was noticeable in the majority of regiments, while in some there was a predominant feeling that they had done their stint and there was no point in going on with the advance."[32]

All along the line, the regular units of the Russian Army proved reluctant to follow the path blazed by the shock battalions. Troops that were ordered to attack elected committees to debate the order or simply refused it. Others went forward, seized the enemy trenches and then returned to their own lines even before a counterattack was launched. One regiment from the elite Guards Divisions actually retreated 18 kilometers rather than face the enemy.[33] "The army is on the run," one commander lamented.[34]

In an attempt to stem the tide, Kornilov deployed the "Battalions of Death" against rebels and deserters on the Southwestern Front, hanging the offenders at crossroads in the rear. Disheartened, Brusilov appealed directly to Kerensky for permission to reinstate the death penalty for deserters on all fronts. "It is time for us to come to our senses," he wrote on 11 July. "It is necessary to restore iron discipline, in the fullest sense of the term. [. . .] In case my demand is not satisfied by the government, I will relieve myself of all responsibility for the consequences and as Supreme Commander [. . .] I will not be in a position to further direct the military operations and to remain at my post."[35] This time, Brusilov meant it. At a conference held in Mogilev, he and the other generals—including Alekseev and Ruzski—firmly told the representatives of the Provisional Government that the army could not continue if the propaganda and unrest were not halted by whatever means necessary.[36] Sensing that the revolution had reached a turning point, Alekseev and several leading conservative members of the tsar's former general staff purportedly offered Brusilov the chance to lead a military government.[37] He refused, and when Kerensky replaced him with Kornilov on 18 July 1917—ironically for being too cooperative with the soviets—Brusilov went into retirement.[38]

He remained with his family in Moscow during the Bolshevik Revolution in November 1917, only to be arrested several months later on charges of supporting "the Russian imperialist bourgeois falsehoods of 'war unto victory'" and actively opposing the Bolshevik regime.[39] Released almost immediately because of a wound he had received while observing the shelling of the Guards Cavalry barracks in Moscow during the revolution, Brusilov was soon contacted by several of the monarchist generals fighting against the new regime. Alekseev, for instance, had created the so-called Volunteer Army in the Don Cossack region to fight the Bolsheviks, and both Kornilov and Denikin were also actively recruiting forces for that purpose.[40] He refused, however, either to join them or to emigrate. "It's time we all forget about the tri-color [the flag of the tsars]," he reportedly told one correspondent, "and united under the red banner."[41] When junior officers still serving in the army approached him for advice on what to do in February 1919, Brusilov opined that while governments came and went it was the duty of an officer to defend his country against external foes. The junior officers should wait, he said, until they could serve honorably again.[42] "Aristocrat that he was," one eminent Russian historian noted, "Brusilov could not share the Whites' belief that it was better to kill his countrymen than to allow them to live under Bolshevism."[43]

Not until the spring of 1920 did Brusilov act on his words though, and even then he did so somewhat reluctantly. On 18 April, he accepted a position with the Soviet Military Historical Commission to write the history of Eighth Army's opening campaign in Galicia during 1914. When the war with Poland broke out though, Brusilov wrote offering his services as a technical specialist to the new, Soviet, All-Russian Red Army Staff—the equivalent of the Imperial general staff. The government published Brusilov's letter with great fanfare, and, perhaps not surprisingly, a number of junior officers and his former comrades soon followed suit, including Klembovski.[44] Under Brusilov's leadership this group of former officers, called the Special Advisory Board, embarked upon a campaign of writing editorials for *Pravda* and other Bolshevik publications urging citizens to support the Soviet government. Copies of the articles were distributed among the units of the Red Army as well. When the conflict ended, Brusilov continued to serve as a technical specialist in the cavalry, where he worked with the future Soviet marshal Semeyon Budennyy in training cavalry cadres. "Governments change," he once explained, "but Russia remains. And all of us must serve her with the specialty we have chosen."[45] Brusilov eventually rose to become inspector general of the Soviet cavalry and a well-respected figure in Soviet military circles. He died on 17 March 1926, while on holiday at Karlovy Vary, in (then) Czechoslovakia. Two days later Aleksei A. Brusilov was buried in Novedevichy Cemetery in Moscow, the resting place of royalty and other great figures in Russian history, with full military honors.

Most military historians, including Soviet military historians, acknowledge that Brusilov was almost unquestionably Russia's finest commander of the First World War and deserves consideration as one of the outstanding military leaders in the conflict overall. His combination of practical experience and openness to new ideas led to striking success in 1914 and helped save Russia in 1915. He became a national hero for the achievements of his armies in 1916 and in 1917; "outside of the officer corps the new combination of Kerensky as Minister of War and Brusilov as Commander-in-Chief was hailed as though it was the answer to all of Russia's military problems."[46] In the early Soviet Union, his name was invoked as the outstanding example of a leader who placed his country above politics. Both Rostunov and Zaionchkovski credit him with laying the foundations for the later Soviet development of unified arms doctrine. To date, however, his achievements have merited only passing attention in English. Among the aims of this work is to correct that oversight, if only to a small degree, by bringing together sources in German, Russian, and English to provide a comprehensive view of one of the most politically and militarily significant events of the First World War, the Brusilov Offensive.

CHRONOLOGY OF
ALEKSEI A. BRUSILOV'S LIFE

19 August 1853:	Aleksei Alekseevich Brusilov is born in Tbilisi, Georgia.
27 June 1867:	enters the Corps of Pages school in St. Petersburg.
17 July 1872:	completes school and is assigned to the 15th Tver Dragoons as an ensign.
2 April 1874:	promoted to lieutenant.
29 October 1877:	promoted to staff captain (*stabskapitan*).
1 January 1878:	receives the Order of St. Stanislav, Third Class, for exemplary service in storming the Turkish fortress at Ardagan on 4–5 May 1877.
16 March 1878:	receives the Order of St. Anne, Third Class, for exemplary service rendered 23–24 August 1877 in the war against the Turks.
3 September 1878:	receives the Order of St. Stanislav, Second Class, for exemplary service in the attack on the Turkish fortress at Kars on the night of 6 November 1877.
7 October 1878:	awarded a place in the cavalry officers' school in St. Petersburg.
15 December 1881:	promoted to captain.

18 August 1882:   promoted to major ("riding master").
12 August 1883:   completes the officer's training course in St. Petersburg.
3 October 1883:   receives the Order of St. Anne, Second Class.
12 November 1883:   enters adjutant training.
29 November 1889:   begins training in horsemanship and horse breeding.
9 February 1890:   promoted to lieutenant colonel.
21 August 1890:   begins service as an assistant at the riding school.
30 August 1892:   promoted to colonel and assigned to the Guards Cavalry.
6 December 1895:   receives the Order of St. Vladimir, Fourth Class.
21 March to 30 May 1898:   tours cavalry schools, observes training and maneuvers in France, Austria, and Germany.
10 November 1898:   appointed as assistant commandant of the cavalry academy.
6 December 1898:   receives the Order of St. Vladimir, Third Class.
6 May 1900:   promoted to general major.
10 February 1902:   begins service as commandant of the cavalry academy.
6 December 1903:   receives the Order of St. Stanislav, First Class.
19 April 1906:   assumes command of 2nd Guards Cavalry Division.
6 December 1906:   promoted to general lieutenant.
5 January 1909:   assumes command of XIV Corps.
6 December 1909:   receives the Order of St. Anne, First Class.
15 May 1912:   appointed assistant commander of the Warsaw Military District.
6 December 1912:   promoted to general of cavalry.
16 March 1913:   receives the Order of St. Vladimir, Second Class.
15 August 1913:   assumes command of XII Corps.
19 July 1914:   assumes command of Eighth Army.

23 August 1914:	receives the Order of St. George, Fourth Class.
18 September 1914:	receives the Order of St. George, Third Class.
10 January 1915:	receives the Order of the White Dove with Swords.
17 March 1916:	assumes command of the Southwestern Front.
20 July 1916:	receives the Order of St. George with Diamonds.
22 May 1917:	appointed supreme commander of Russian army and fleet under the Provisional Government.
18 July 1917:	relieved of duty as supreme commander.
2 May 1920:	begins service as chairman of the special advisory board to the armed forces command.
8 November 1921:	begins service on the commission for the organization of the cavalry.
July 1922:	appointed inspector of the cavalry.
17 March 1926:	Aleksei Alekseevich Brusilov dies in Moscow.

THE BRUSILOV OFFENSIVE

CHAPTER ONE

RUSSIA IN THE FIRST WORLD WAR

The High Command of the Russian Imperial Army met at its headquarters (Stavka) in Mogilev on 14 April 1916 to discuss plans for the coming spring. In attendance were three commanders: General Aleksei N. Kuropatkin, commanding the Northern Front; General Aleksei Evert, in charge of the Northwestern Front; and General Aleksei A. Brusilov, who had recently replaced Nikolai Y. Ivanov on the Southwestern Front; along with the chief of the general staff, General Mikhail V. Alekseev. General Dmitri Shuvaev, the Russian war minister, Grand Duke Sergei Mikhailovich, inspector general of the artillery, and the chief of the Naval Staff, Admiral A. I. Rusin, were also present.[1] Tsar Nicholas II, who had assumed the post of supreme commander of the Russian armed forces at the end of August 1915, presided over the meeting, though he offered neither comment nor criticism. Few of the military leaders at Imperial Headquarters were in a positive mood, but the Russians were committed. Their representatives at the meeting of Allied commanders at Chantilly, France, in December 1915 had pledged a Russian attack in support of the British and French offensive on the Somme River planned for the following spring. The idea was to pin down the German forces on the Eastern Front and prevent their transfer to the west. This would, in theory, swing the balance of forces to the Allies and create the opportunity for a decisive breakthrough on the Western Front. The plan was largely the work of General Joseph Joffre, the French commander in chief, but the tsar had reviewed it in February

1916 and given his personal assurances to the Allies that they could count on Russian assistance to execute the design.

The Russian commanders were not so confident. A March 1916 offensive against the Germans on the Northern and Western fronts in the area around Lake Narotch, undertaken in response to French pleas for relief from the incessant German pressure on Verdun, had achieved little. Despite some initial success, 300,000 Russian troops had been unable to defeat 50,000 Germans or even force them to transfer reinforcements from the west. In the process, the Russians had suffered nearly 100,000 casualties—including 10,000 men who died of exposure. Kuropatkin and Evert argued that a renewed offensive against the Germans would be futile. A breakthrough was impossible. The Russian army, they contended, had not had sufficient rounds for its artillery in March, and it did not have enough now.

Alekseev insisted on going ahead. According to his calculations, once the new levies had been incorporated the Russian army would dispose of some 700,000–800,000 men along the sectors of the Northern and Western fronts by summer.[2] With these overwhelming numbers, he intended to launch a two-pronged offensive on a 20-kilometer front along the Dvina River in mid-May using the Russian Second and Tenth armies. The adjoining interior wings of the armies would drive on Vilnius; the northern and western wings, where the Russians figured to outnumber the German forces by five to one and six to one respectively, would hold their reserves to deal with any German counterstroke. Evert and Kuropatkin were not convinced and continued to argue against the action. Alekseev had to concede an additional two-month preparation period and promise to commit at least one thousand heavy guns to the offensive before the two commanders reluctantly agreed to the undertaking.

Then Brusilov spoke. He had been appointed as commander of the Southwestern Front only two weeks before; "with his mustaches twirled, his hair clipped short, and his body slim and straight, Brusilov still remained the dashing cavalry officer he had been during the Russo-Turkish War of 1877."[3] His predecessor, Ivanov, was present at the meeting, looking frail and shattered from the breakdown of late 1915 that had cost him the post. Brusilov offered, on his own initiative, to launch an offensive on the Southwestern Front to support the plan. It was a mistake, he said, not to take advantage of the numerical superiority the Russians held over the Central Powers by attacking on all fronts simultaneously. "I ask only the express permission to attack on my front at the same time as my colleagues," he said. "Should it be the case that I meet no success, I will then restrict my efforts to engaging the enemy forces; I will draw a portion of the enemy reserves and thus make Evert and Kuropatkin's task easier."[4]

The meeting was stunned into silence. Recovering, Alekseev warned Brusilov that he could expect no reinforcements and no additional material support for such an offensive. Brusilov replied that he expected none and that he would go ahead anyway because his troops felt an obligation to attack and to share the burden of their brothers to the north. Alekseev, though he personally thought the action of little use, approved the plan conditionally. Kuropatkin merely looked at Brusilov and shrugged his shoulders in pity.[5] One senior general, according to Brusilov, asked him after the meeting, "What made you expose yourself to such a danger? Had I been in your place, I would have done anything in my power to avoid taking the offensive."[6] Ivanov went so far as to approach the tsar in an attempt to countermand the offensive, but Nicholas II, typically, refused to make a decision. "I do not think it is proper for me to alter the War Council's decisions," he replied. "You'll have to take it up with Alekseev."[7]

Two days later, when Brusilov presented the proposition to his staff, the reaction was much the same. Faced with troop dispositions merely equal to those of Austria-Hungary and Germany on the Southwestern Front—about 135,000 men on each side of the front—Brusilov's subordinates expressed reluctance to attack. Only General Dmitri G. Scherbatschev of Seventh Army was even remotely receptive to Brusilov's proposal, and he thought that the offensive probably was not worth the risk. General Aleksei M. Kaledin, commander of the Russian Eighth Army, averred openly that the operation would not succeed. Scherbatschev then indicated his agreement with Kaledin.[8] No one, it seemed, wanted to carry the attack forward or expected much in the event they were forced to do so.

The Russian Army

This was not a reflection on Brusilov in particular. No one expected much of the Russian army in general after the first two years of the war—if indeed they ever had expected anything positive at all. A fairly typical assessment, published in 1916, had this to say: "The history of the Russian army justified the conclusion that the army of 1914 would prove inferior, man for man, to those of the other Great Powers of Europe; but much depended on the value of the experience in the war with Japan. Unless the lessons of that war had been well learned, unless there had been fundamental reforms, Russian arms were bound to be a disappointment."[9] The value of the Russian military had been brought into serious doubt by its defeat at the hands of the Japanese in 1904–1905—when Kuropatkin, not coincidentally, had led the Russian armies. Calls for reform echoed from every corner; the journal *Voennyi golos* (Voice of the Military), founded in January 1906, was dedicated to the issue of military reorganization. Over 1,500 books on military subjects were published in Russia in the years 1908–10 alone, and newspapers regularly carried articles and editorials on military affairs. Young, reform-minded officers (the so-called Young Turks) briefly formed a pressure group advocating the adoption of the "applied method" of teaching tactics in the Nicholas Academy of the General Staff. Even some members of the new Duma and of the War Ministry itself took up the cause of military renewal. The emphasis on maneuvers and war games as training tools gradually increased, and military education was increasingly a prerequisite for a field command by 1912.[10] Yet the pace of reform was slow, and most outside observers saw little change in the Russian military prior to 1914.

Much of the problem lay in the upper echelons of the Russian bureaucracy. In his capacity as minister of war, Kuropatkin had attempted to initiate some reforms even prior to 1904—most notably in the areas of artillery, supply, and the conditions provided for junior officers. Court intrigues and minister of finance Sergei Witte's economic plans for the Russian Far East, however, combined to block most of his designs. Kuropatkin's only limited success came in reducing the percentage of officers drawn from the nobility and increasing the percentage of officers receiving professional military training. Many of these programs were taken up again by A. F. Rediger, who served as war minister in the years 1905–1909. By 1912, for instance, 62 percent of all corps commanders and 68 percent of all infantry division commanders had graduated from the Nicholas Academy, and the budget for maneuvers and equipment increased significantly.[11] Factional politics mitigated against some of his more radical proposals, however, and Rediger was dismissed in early 1909.

Rediger's successor, Vladimir A. Sukhomlinov, achieved a bit more during his tenure, which lasted from 1909 to 1915. Though he would justly bear much of the blame for Russia's poor showing against the Germans in 1914 and 1915, Sukhomlinov had managed to bring the Russian army up to a reasonably modern European standard. The Russian artillery received Krupp 120mm quick-fire light howitzers as well as Schneider-Creuset

150mm quick-fire howitzers beginning in 1912. He introduced the modern artillery train to the army, integrated machine guns, sappers, and artillery more thoroughly with the infantry, and developed a new mobilization plan that allowed commanders to move battle-ready units to the front rather than filling out front-line units with reserves.[12]

The hardware to support these innovations, however, was lacking—largely because Sukhomlinov failed to organize production efficiently. He tended to protect the elites, often to the point of overlooking corruption and to the detriment of military efficiency, and was, according to one historian, "singularly uncommunicative with subordinates, cynically indifferent to criticism, and seemingly irresponsible in handling official business."[13] At the same time, however, Sukhomlinov was both deeply concerned about and actively improving Russia's military preparedness. He argued for the dismantling of the fortification system, for instance, and reorganized both the fortress troops and the territorial troops into front-line units. He streamlined mobilization planning, and did a great deal to modernize, if not numerically increase, the armaments of the Imperial Russian Army.

The Russian artillery of 1914 was mostly 76.2mm rapid-fire guns of the 1902 model, equipped with panoramic sights and steel shields; each infantry division was accorded six eight-gun batteries of these, while each rifle brigade was equipped with two six-gun 121.9mm Krupp howitzer batteries (1909 model) and eight machine guns. The Russian army's seven divisions of heavy artillery were in the process of changing over from two four-gun batteries of 106mm guns to 152mm Schneider guns when the war began. All told, each infantry division had only forty-eight field guns at its command, with seventy-five batteries of light howitzers serving as corps artillery and a further twenty-one batteries of heavy guns as army artillery. The Imperial Russian Army as a whole possessed only 620 pieces of heavy artillery.

Much of this artillery, along with a significant proportion of the funding for armaments, was still tied up in the series of fortresses along the borders with Galicia and East Prussia despite Sukhomlinov's best efforts. The standard German division, by way of comparison, was armed with nine twelve-gun batteries of 87.5mm guns, three howitzers, twelve machine guns, and two heavy (150mm) guns. The Habsburg armies fielded forty-two regiments of field artillery and fourteen regiments of field howitzers, along with eight divisions of cavalry artillery. The Russian cavalry had only two divisions of artillery and utilized the same artillery as the infantry in two six-gun batteries, despite the fact that it was generally considered too heavy for cavalry work. Thus the slightly larger Russian corps possessed more field guns than the average Austro-Hungarian corps, 108 to 96, but the French, with 120 field guns per corps, and the Germans, with 144, held a significant advantage.[14]

The experience of the Russo-Japanese War, however, had convinced the Russian general staff and the War Ministry—and many European observers—that the next war would be short and that the bayonet charge would still be the determining factor. Artillery had not played a great role in the Russo-Japanese War, and most planners assumed that both artillery and cavalry had been reduced to supporting roles by technological advances. Based on this notion, and the experience of 1905, Russian planners therefore provided for a stock of only 1,000 shells per gun in the period leading up to 1914. As ridiculous as that figure seems, it was 300 rounds per gun over the actual usage rates of 1904–1905, and generally still considered an adequate hedge in 1914. Most European armies thus found their supplies of shells as lacking in August 1914 as the Russians did, though the German army had at least allocated for nearly 3,000 shells per gun.

What was truly telling though was Russia's inability to produce munitions in sufficient quantity once the war began. According to prewar estimates made within the general staff, production of 300,000 shells per month would sustain the Russian artillery in combat. This worked out to about 1.5 rounds per gun per day—clearly inadequate under the conditions of the First World War, where usage ran about 80 shells per gun per day from the outset and could be as high as 700–800 shells per gun per day during an offensive. In December 1914 the Russian supreme commander, Grand Duke Nikolai Nikolaiovich, revealed that the Russian artillery had exhausted its ammunition reserves, having fired some 6.5 million shells since August. Confronted with this assertion by French ambassador Maurice Paléologue and by British Major General Alfred Knox, General Mikhail Beliaev of the Russian War Ministry confessed that Russian industry was capable of producing only 1,300 shells a day (about 35,000 per month) while the army was consuming around 45,000 a day. Russian shell production did not even attain the proposed, still-inadequate production level of 300,000 shells per month until March 1915, and the manufacture of munitions continued to lag well behind demand through 1916. At the end of that year, two out of every three shells—and the same proportion of bullets—fired by Russian guns had been produced outside Russia.[15]

The situation was similar in other areas. The Russian infantry was armed with the 1891 model Mosin 7.62mm repeating rifle, which was considered roughly equal to those of other European armies. German infantry, for example, carried an 1898 repeating Mauser, while Habsburg units were equipped with a .32-caliber model from 1895.[16] Yet the Russians suffered from a simple shortage of munitions here as well. In the early months of 1914, the Russian state rifle factory in Tula was producing no more than five rifles a month, though it had the capacity to produce 50,000. Supposedly, the army already had enough rifles at hand to supply 4.5 million men at that time; however, according to Lieutenant General Nikolai N. Golovine, who served on the Russian general staff during the war, in 1915 the entire Russian army disposed of only 650,000 rifles. On average, he claimed, the number of rifles supplied fell short by an average of some 35 percent over the course of the war.[17] The Russian quartermaster general, Iuri N. Danilov, reported that during peacetime instruction, soldiers were ordered to return their rifles to a comrade or noncommissioned officer if wounded so that another soldier might be armed.[18]

Things only got worse with the onset of war. By December 1914, even the tsar was well aware that reinforcements were being sent into the front lines without rifles, and Knox noted in early 1915 that the Russians had only 50,000–70,000 rifles to supply the 1.4 million recruits entering service that year. Only one in ten recruits was issued a rifle during training, and even these were outdated models left over from the Russo-Turkish War of 1877–78.[19] Even in January 1916 when the situation had improved—partly because Sukhomlinov had been replaced by General Aleksei Polivanov— the French ambassador reported that while Russia had mobilized some 5 million men in 1915, the Russian army had only 1.2 million rifles at the front, with another 700,000 in reserve.[20]

Had there been enough rifles though, it would only have made the munitions shortage worse. In August 1914, the Imperial Russian Army had about 2.5 billion rounds of small-arms ammunition in stock. During the opening campaigns of 1914, Russian industry produced nearly 59 million bullets a month. Yet a single regiment used 800,000 rounds (about 1.5 percent of the nation's total monthly production) in a single day of fighting in one instance. Given that the army contained 236 regiments, monthly production was hardly sufficient for a week's hard fighting—much less a sustained campaign—and what Russian planners had thought was a vast reserve was in reality hopelessly inadequate.[21]

Communications, transportation equipment, and technology of almost every kind were also sorely lacking. The Russian Second Army, for instance, had only twenty-five telephones and a few Morse coding machines available in 1914, and few men trained to operate them. Not until 1915 were Russian artillery brigades equipped with two telephones.[22] Russia did build up a numerically impressive air force in the years before the war—Second Army possessed forty-two planes, for instance—but it depended almost entirely upon foreign models and training. With only eight machine guns per regiment, Russia lagged far behind the Germans and French, who counted between twelve and fifteen machine guns per regiment; even the Habsburg forces counted nine of these new weapons per regiment in 1914. The majority of the Russian army's machine guns were 1910 Vickers-Maxim models, equipped with a shield and a lightened mount. Hotchkiss (France) and Colt (the United States) provided some machine guns as well, and the Russians produced their own version of the Maxim in an attempt to increase supply between 1910 and 1914. At the outbreak of the war though, the Russians had only 4,195 machine guns on hand, and many still lacked carriages. The Russian army thus had no readily mobile automatic firepower.[23]

Mobility was in fact another major problem for the Russians. Automobiles and trucks remained a rarity in Russia. Between 1910 and 1914, the Ministry of Trade and Industry had purchased 21,000 vehicles; the army received 259 automobiles and 418 trucks from that allotment.[24] Second Army thus had ten cars and four motorcycles for over 150,000 men in 1914.[25] Despite loans from France aimed specifically at increasing the military capacity of Russia's railroad network, moreover, only six double-track lines and two single-track rail lines ran from east to west along the front with Germany and Austria-Hungary in 1914. For every 100 square kilometers of territory in that area, Russia had 1.6 kilometers of railroad track, while Germany had 32. Russia's rolling stock was in any case of inferior quality, capable of moving at only about half the speed of German trains.[26] According to Golovine's calculations, the French—despite an army half the size of Russia's—employed almost fifteen times as much steam-driven horsepower as the Russian Imperial Army.[27] Knox, often noted as one of the keenest observers of the Russian army, summarized the situation thus: "For a long war, Russia was outclassed in every factor of success except in the number of her fighting men and in their mollusc-like quality of recovery after severe defeat."[28]

Throughout Europe though, a great deal was made of the overwhelming number of men Russia possessed. In times of peace, the Russian army numbered some 1.5 million men; on a war footing, this number would increase to nearly 6 million. Only France, which had about 1 million men serving during peacetime if territorial forces are counted, came anywhere close to matching that. Germany's standing army counted only 761,000 men, and the Habsburg Empire, beset by internal political problems, normally maintained fewer than half a million men-at-arms. Once war was declared the German army expanded to about 1.75 million men with military training on active duty, with another 7 million or so in the reserves, while Austria-Hungary could marshal some 2 million men into the front lines. German manpower, however, had to be divided between two fronts, and the Habsburg armies would likewise be spread over two fronts—three (Serbian, Russian, and Italian) after May 1915.[29]

The overwhelming numerical superiority of the "Russian steam roller" thus convinced a great many people—most notably the Russian general staff—that technological advances would play a minimal role. As Bruce W. Menning, one of the premier historians of the Imperial Russian Army, has noted that in the eyes of Russian military reformers after 1905, "Only the offensive promised both decision and all important retention of the initiative in warfare."[30] This was not unique to Russia by any means; the "cult of the offensive" dominated the thinking of most European general staffs in the first years of the twentieth century. The observations of the French general staff in Manchuria, for instance, led them to conclude that technology had rendered the defensive "impotent" and that offensive maneuvers would decide the course of modern wars. The bayonet charge, they wrote, remained "the essence of combat."[31] General Baron Franz Conrad von Hötzendorf, chief of general staff for the Habsburg Imperial Army and one of Austria-Hungary's most noted military theorists, was also an advocate of the offensive. Digging in, he warned in his widely read *Zum Studium der Taktik*, was bad for the fighting spirit and could cost an army dearly. "The moral factors," Conrad wrote elsewhere, "are the most decisive in battle."[32] Wars would be won, he believed, by courage, not technology. Firepower was certainly beneficial, but its effectiveness was limited, in Conrad's mind, just as it was in the thinking of most other European military strategists.[33]

It was in this same vein, and drawing on the lessons of the war with Japan, that Russian military training between 1906 and 1914 focused largely on cultivating "the spirit of the offensive," according to Knox.[34] Polivanov later noted sourly: "Before the war the general attitude of the higher commanding officers, the former Emperor, and the former Minister of War towards military technical improvements was one of contempt. The belief was then supreme that the most important thing in the army was its spirit, its aggressiveness and that the rest would follow."[35] This approach failed, above all, to account for the generally poor quality of Russian leadership and its importance in shaping the performance of the troops. While officers in the infantry—especially at the lower levels such as company commander or squadron commander—tended to be adequate, the levels of training and professionalism actually seemed to decrease with an increase in rank. As Menning notes, "Failure occurred more often than not at higher reaches of the command and organizational hierarchy."[36]

Despite the reforms of the Kuropatkin, Rediger, and Sukhomlinov eras, the Russian officer corps of 1914 remained drawn largely from the nobility. Of the 45,582 officers in the Russian army in August 1914, 51.3 percent were nobles—though only 40 percent of the infantry officers came from this social class. Nobles usually acquired rank more as a matter of social prestige than out of martial ardor, and they often were not subject to all of the "normal" requirements for advancement. Even regular officers, who underwent a seven-year course in the Russian Cadet Corps, earned promotion primarily on the basis of patronage and seniority. In his memoirs, General P. N. Krasnov recalled that as late as 1910 he had been forced to rely on connections even to obtain the relatively undesirable post as commander of the 1st Siberian Yermak Cossack Regiment in an isolated garrison near the Chinese frontier.[37]

There was no guarantee, moreover, that officers were well-educated no matter what their social class or training. By almost all accounts the training, habits, and performance of Russian officers lagged far behind those of their European contemporaries. In a survey conducted in 1906 on the problems of the Russo-Japanese War, several Russian officers indicated that their commanders had been completely unaware of basic tactics, or even the troop regulation manual.[38] An official British report of 1907 noted that "a very large proportion of Russian officers serve mechanically and apathetically and even dislike their profession."[39] Efforts to reform even general staff training, however, advanced slowly in the face of bureaucratic in-fighting.

This was especially true in the field; most of the officers who received general staff training after 1905 were found on district staffs in July 1914; at the corps and division level, it was unusual to have more than two or three such officers.[40] Knox, who accompanied several units in the course of his three-and-a-half years as liaison to the Russian army during the First World War, provides a rather damning evaluation of the Russian officer corps as he saw it:

[T]he bulk of the regimental officers of the Russian army suffered from the national faults. If not actually lazy, they were inclined to neglect their duties unless constantly supervised. They hated the irksome round of everyday training. Unlike our officers, they had no taste for outdoor amusements, and they were too prone to spend a holiday in eating rather more and in sleeping much more. [...]

The great majority of vacancies for regimental commander in the infantry and cavalry of the line were filled by officers of the general staff or Guard Corps, or by those who had been detached on extra-regimental duty. The natural result was that the men with a tendency to laziness consoled themselves with the excuse that it was no use working, and such men, though passed over repeatedly, were allowed to remain till they qualified for pension, meanwhile blocking promotion for their more capable and energetic juniors.[41]

Worse, the Russian chain of command was rigid, linear, and unidirectional, so innovative and energetic junior officers not only could not be promoted, they could not be heard. Communication at the top was not always clear either, however. The supreme commander of the Russian armed forces, usually a member of the imperial family, was endowed with far-reaching powers in the field and was answerable only to the tsar. Because Nicholas II, like his predecessors, viewed the army largely as his personal domain, members of the imperial family dominated the upper echelons. In addition to the Grand Dukes Nikolai and Sergei (supreme commander and inspector-general of the artillery, respectively), Grand Duke Konstantin Konstantinovich served as head of the main administration of military schools and Peter Nikolaiovich held the post of chief inspector of military engineers. Few of the Romanovs were actually qualified for these posts.[42] Their power lay in their person rather than in any military rank or training, and the bureaucracy was arranged accordingly. The Russian regulations provided for a headquarters (Stavka) and a staff that would oversee military and naval operations, yet they did not afford a supreme commander who was not the sovereign control over administrative matters such as the provision of rifles and shells. These remained the province of the war minister, usually a general himself, in consultation with the front commanders. Even for the supreme commander, the only channel to the tsar in matters of supply and technical support was through that minister.[43]

Because the appointments to these highest and most important posts were highly politicized and subject to court intrigue, moreover, the military leaders of the Russian Imperial Army were not always the most competent military men available. Sukhomlinov once boasted that he had never read a single book on military technology.[44] Grand Duke Nikolai Nikolaiovich, appointed as supreme commander in July 1914, was similarly ill-equipped for the task. According to Polivanov—who cites the grand duke as his source—"on the receipt of the Imperial order [to assume command], he spent much of his time crying because he did not know how to approach his new duties."[45] The grand duke's chief of staff, Nikolai N. Ianushkevich, had no field experience whatsoever, and even his background in military administration was mostly academic. According to Knox, his fellow officers saw Ianushkevich "as merely a Court nominee, as indeed he was."[46] Quartermaster general Iuri N. Danilov, on the other hand, had a great deal of planning experience, but tended to be "hidebound" rather than flexible in his thinking. Danilov was, in any case, usually kept busy looking after the grand duke's personal needs instead of supplying the armies.[47]

Many of the field officers were no better off, though they were generally more experienced in tactics and strategy. Neither General Iakov G. Zhilinski, the initial commander of the Northwestern Front, nor Kuropatkin had assembled a record of any note in 1904–1905, and both went on to fail spectacularly in the first two years of the war. Kuropatkin, in fact, had been in retirement since 1905 when he was called upon to replace General Pavel A. Plehve in command of the Northern Front. According to one historian of the Russian officer corps: "[Kuropatkin's] uninspiring personality might have rendered him yet another anonymous war planner but for his unexpected elevation to the war minister's seat at the end of the 1890s. The demands his emperor placed upon him there were well beyond his narrow technical background and limited strategic capability."[48] In short Kuropatkin was, as one Russian divisional commander put it, "a man who had been fully tried and found wanting."[49] Alekseev, according to one Russian officer, was "a second Kuropatkin, who could decide nothing."[50] Stone notes that Alekseev "worked himself into a continual migraine, and left himself no time to think things out," thus failing in the central task of a chief of staff: delegating responsibility.[51] Even Lincoln, who credits Alekseev with successfully regrouping the Russian army after the disaster of 1915 and seems to admire him as an administrator, admits that the tsar's chief of staff was too modest to exert much influence.[52]

Many of the remaining front commanders and army commanders had first seen action in the Russo-Turkish War of 1877–78 and spent the time leading up to the First World War working their way through a series of staff appointments and desk jobs in order to gain promotion. Knox wrote of General Pavel N. Rennkampf that "[he] might have been a Murat if he had lived a hundred years earlier. In command of an army in the twentieth century he was an anachronism and a danger."[53] This system generally encouraged sycophancy while discouraging innovation. The result was an overly bureaucratized force that moved sluggishly when it moved at all, which was unfortunate because, as Knox noted, "The Russian soldier requires leading more than any soldier in the world."[54]

This is not to say that the Russian solider was of generally poor quality. International observers and military experts had long noted the stubborn and determined nature of the Russian infantryman, particularly when on the defensive. Defeat in 1904–1905 led to improved and increased training in many areas—though the Russians apparently never practiced entrenchment. They had also created an experienced reserve.[55] What was lacking was precisely the forward impetus and initiative that the upper leadership was counting on. As one contemporary analysis put it: "The Russian soldier of the regular army has been patient, sturdy, devout, devoted to the Tsar and to Holy Russia. He has been always stubborn, sometimes heroic in defense, but he is handicapped by a lack of intelligence."[56] While in France no able-bodied male was exempt from military service, Russia regularly excused nearly half of its draftees each year. Despite this—or perhaps because of it—somewhere between 40 and 60 percent of the annual levy was either fully or functionally illiterate in Russia. Nearly 75 percent were peasants, drawn from rural settings and completely unaccustomed to the regimentation of military life. Roughly the same percentages held for reservists, though these figures do not include the Cossack cavalry regiments, which were raised separately and subject to special, separate regulations.[57] Nearly all of the Cossack cavalrymen were illiterate as well, and they had a reputation as undisciplined to the point that one observer labeled them "completely useless for offensive operations."[58] That same analysis, however, noted that "[t]here was no other army in Europe at the outbreak of the Great War that was likely to cause so many surprises as that of Russia. Its unprecedented numbers, equal to the combined forces of Germany and Austria-Hungary, gave it in the popular mind the character of invincibility. It was the only army in Europe that had met a first-class modern army on the field of battle. No other army had such a large number of veterans."[59]

When led well and vigorously, and adequately equipped at even the most basic level, Russian units were at least the equal of either the German or the Austro-Hungarian forces.

The Great War Begins

This was demonstrated quite clearly in the opening encounters of the war, particularly in Galicia and southern Poland. Along that 450-kilometer-long front from the Pripet Marshes to the Romanian border, six Russian armies—the Third, Fourth, Fifth, Eighth, Ninth, and Eleventh—faced only three Habsburg armies: the First, Third, and Fourth—supplemented by an army group commanded by General Baron Karl von Pflanzer-Baltin that anchored the right, southern flank. Conrad von Hötzendorf had originally intended to send his Second Army to the front as well, but last minute political maneuvering sent that force to aid in the invasion of Serbia initially. Because Russian divisions contained more battalions (sixteen) than either German (nine) or Habsburg (twelve) divisions, this meant that nearly 3 million Russians faced only about half as many Austro-Hungarian soldiers. Because the Italians had not entered the war, moreover, the Germans informed Conrad that five reserve divisions slated for the East would be kept on the Western Front. Despite this shortfall, despite the fact that the Germans—contrary to their stated prewar intentions—had also informed him that their troops in East Prussia would not launch an attack as part of a pincer against the salient of Russian Poland, and despite the fact that a series of miscalculations and transportation blunders forced the Habsburg armies to detrain some 150 kilometers behind their line of deployment and march to the front, Conrad pressed ahead with attacks on Lublin and Cholm. His aim was a sweeping encirclement of the Russian flank near Warsaw, using the fortresses at Lemberg (Lvov) and Przemysl to anchor his right wing. Habsburg cavalry units swept out an arc from the Dniester River to the Vistula River in front of the seventeen advancing infantry divisions. Despite heavy losses inflicted by Russian cavalry units, they were unable to locate the enemy.

The Russian commander on the Southwestern Front, General Ivanov, had divided his forces into two equal groups, sending the Fourth and Fifth armies via Lemberg toward Cholm and Kovel in the north, while in the south the Russian Third and Eighth armies moved forward via Dubno and Proskurov-Dunajevsky. Ivanov was one of those rare Russian generals who had risen through the ranks based upon talent, having seen combat in both the Russo-Turkish and the Russo-Japanese wars, and he had a reputation as an expert on modern warfare.[60] By moving aggressively against the ponderous Habsburg deployments, he hoped to achieve a double envelopment of both Austrian flanks while the Eleventh and Ninth armies waited in reserve.

The first engagements came in the north, on 23 and 24 August, when the Habsburg First Army under General Viktor Dankl defeated five divisions of the Russian Fourth Army at Krasnik. The Russian forces, commanded by Baron Aleksander E. Zalt'sa, had moved south from Lublin without a cavalry screen and were completely surprised to find the Austrians just 60 kilometers south. Casualties were heavy on both sides, as both sides preferred bayonet charges as their main weapon. Some Austrian infantry regiments suffered 40–50 percent losses; Zalt'sa's forces lost six thousand prisoners, thirty guns, and nearly 15 kilometers of territory. Zalt'sa was immediately relieved of command, and the Russian Fifth Army under General Pavel A. Plehve moved forward on the Austrians' left flank in support.[61]

Fifth Army met General Count Mortiz von Auffenberg's Fourth Army near Komarow on 26 August 1914. The Russians captured twenty field guns and almost four thousand Austrian prisoners during five days of murderous fighting, but ran out of ammunition and were forced to withdraw. Even as the main body of the Russian Fifth Army retreated though, Cossack cavalry discovered gaps in the Austro-Hungarian lines created by Conrad's overhasty and undermanned deployments. Plehve, now joined by the Russian Ninth Army under General Letschitski, immediately reversed direction, marching his forces between the Habsburg First and Fourth armies and threatening them with encirclement.

At the same time, the Russian Eighth Army under Brusilov and the Russian Third under General Nikolai V. Ruszki advanced resolutely against the outnumbered Habsburg forces in the south. Inexplicably, it was the Austrians who attacked near the Zlota Lipa River on 26 August. General Rudolf Brudermann, commanding the Habsburg Third Army, sent ninety-one infantry battalions, eighty-seven cavalry squadrons, and just over three hundred guns forward against what he thought was an isolated Russian corps. He discovered instead the whole of Ruszki's Third Army, with more than 180 infantry battalions and 685 guns.[62] The Russians counterattacked decisively, driving the Habsburg forces back more than 15 kilometers by the morning of 28 August. Brudermann attempted to make a stand at that point, deploying his forces behind the slight natural barrier of the Gnila Lipa River.

There the combined armies of Ruszki and Brusilov overwhelmed the Austrian Third with an attack on 29 August. The Habsburg Third Army still had 288 guns, but it was not enough. The Russians had over 400,000 men supported by more than 1,300 guns against Brudermann's force of fewer than 300,000 weary Austrians. Conrad nonetheless foolishly ordered a counterattack that broke against the Russian line on 30 August and gave way to a confused and panicked Austrian retreat. Nearly 20,000 Habsburg soldiers surrendered to the Russians, and the Austro-Hungarian forces abandoned one hundred locomotives and more than fifteen thousand railway cars.

Ivanov pressed his advantage. The Russian Fourth and Fifth armies pounded the First and Fourth armies of the Habsburg Empire relentlessly, while Brusilov and Ruszki pushed into western Galicia and threatened the Carpathian passes leading into Hungary. Only the heroic stand of the Silesian reserves kept the Austrian First from being wiped out at Tarnow. By 10 September, the Habsburg Fourth had lost 50 percent of its officers and 25 percent of the rank and file.[63] All told the Austro-Hungarian armies suffered more than 300,000 casualties and lost another 100,000 as prisoners of war. Roughly one-third of their total combat strength disappeared in these encounters. The Russian armies entered Lemberg (Lvov) unopposed on 3 September and continued westward, taking Krasnik, Komarow, Tomaszew, Rava Ruska, Halicz, Grodek, and Mikolajow in rapid succession and investing the key Austrian fortress at Przemysl. Both sides, however, were now exhausted, as even the victorious Russians had lost more than 230,000 men.[64] Thus when Conrad finally ordered a retreat behind the San River on 11 September, Ivanov halted as well. In just over three weeks, the Russians had taken more than 225 square kilometers of territory and brought the Habsburg armies to the brink of defeat.

Unfortunately, the Austrians were not the only opponent, and the Russian successes in the south were more than overshadowed by defeats against the Germans in the north. There the Russians played the role that the Habsburg forces had assumed in Galicia, combining inept leadership with inadequate technology to create an incredible disaster. Though the Russians' original war plans called for them to stand on the defensive against the Germans in East Prussia, during a staff conference in August 1911, Zhilinski had rashly promised that Russia would complete much of its troop concentrations fifteen days after mobilization. Factional disputes within the Russian general staff drove him to confirm and even enlarge upon this promise during a visit to Paris a year later. The prevailing Russian plan, in fact, was "to go over to the offensive against the armed forces of Germany and Austria-Hungary with the objective of taking the war into their territory."[65] The Russian Grand Duke Nikolai even gave General Joffre "categorical assurances" in conversations held during 1912 and 1913 that the Russian Second Army would invade East Prussia as soon as possible.[66] Article III of the Franco-Russian Military Convention signed in September 1913 contained an unambiguous Russian promise to send 800,000 men forward against the Germans in East Prussia fifteen days after mobilization had begun. Thus by 1914, the Russian army was committed to the invasion, though not fully prepared for it.

Faced with only one German army—the Eighth—in the field while having both the First and Second Russian armies at his disposal, Zhilinski developed a plan to trap the Germans between two prongs of the advance. Rennkampf's First Army would approach from the east, moving into East Prussia through the Insterburg Gap. The Russian Second Army, commanded by Aleksandr V. Samsonov, would march northwest and pin the German Eighth against Rennkampf's army in the area just west of the Masurian Lakes. It was an adequate if risky plan, requiring the two armies to maintain a considerable distance between them until almost the last moment due to the geography of the region. Neither Zhilinski nor his field commanders, unfortunately, possessed the equipment, skill, or determination to make it work.

Even before the offensive began, Zhilinski depleted his forces by ordering several divisions of infantry and cavalry, along with about two-fifths of the Second's artillery, to reinforce the fortresses on the flanks of the advance. The combined Russian forces still outnumbered the German Eighth by two to one, but where the Germans possessed 156 heavy guns the Russians now had only a handful—twelve, to be precise. Logistics were similarly neglected. While Rennkampf counted on the rail lines in the region of his advance for supply, Samsonov found himself moving through a region with neither rail nor road, and thus without any system of supply. Zhilinski's communications with Samsonov were conducted through the Warsaw General Post Office, where once a day a courier collected the incoming telegrams.[67] Russian wireless field communications most often went unencoded due to a lack of trained staff.

While the Russian colossus thus stumbled blindly forward, the German Eighth Army under General Maximillian Prittwitz had precise orders for offensive action, but wide latitude in developing specific operations. Stripping the Prussian border fortresses of every available man and gun, Prittwitz moved forward to meet Rennkampf's forces once they crossed into East Prussia. His plan was to draw the Russian First Army beyond its supply lines to the Angerapp River, defeat it in force, and then turn to deal with the slower-moving Second. The commander of the Germans' I Corps, Lieutenant General Herman François, had other ideas. Reporting to Prittwitz that the Russians were attacking along his entire front, François moved to engage them on 17 August 1914 at the small town of Stallupönen. Despite orders to retreat, François continued the action, taking three thousand Russians prisoner before retiring to Gumbinnen.

Stung, Rennkampf slowed his advance. Prittwitz, realizing the Russian Second Army might now reach his positions before he had time to deal with the First, accordingly shifted forward. Along with Lieutenant General August von Mackensen's XXVII Corps, François engaged the Russians again on 20 August. Covered by overwhelming artillery, François once again scored a tactical victory, nearly wiping out the Russian 28th Infantry Division. Mackensen chose to attack before his artillery could come up, however, and his unit was quickly pinned under a hail of Russian artillery and machine-gun fire. Where the Russians stood and died under similar circumstances, several German units broke and fled. By nightfall, the Russians could count a decisive victory. Shocked and reeling, the German commanders sounded a general retreat; Prittwitz issued orders to retire to the Vistula to save the Eighth Army.

Rennkampf, however, failed to follow up on this success. Instead of pursuing the fleeing Germans, he turned to besiege the fortress of Königsberg. The Germans, meanwhile, were changing direction. General Helmuth von Moltke, the German army chief of staff, cashiered both Prittwitz and his chief of staff, sending generals Paul von Hindenburg and Erich Ludendorff to replace them. In addition, going against German war plans and the recommendation of his new commanders on the Eastern Front, Moltke detached three German corps and a cavalry division from the Western Front and sent them east to augment Eighth Army. This decision proved crucial not in East Prussia, where Lieutenant Colonel Max Hoffmann—Prittwitz's first staff officer—had already altered the disposition of forces to account for a renewed German offensive, but on the Western Front. The loss of two corps weakened the critical right wing of the German advance on Paris and contributed to the failure of the Schlieffen Plan as a whole.

Even as these reinforcements moved east, moreover, the German Eighth Army resumed the offensive. Hoffmann, convinced that Rennkampf's forces had stopped their advance, had moved to concentrate against Samsonov and the Second Army. Leaving only a brigade of territorial troops and a single cavalry division as a diversionary screen in front of the Russian

First, the German Eighth Army now wheeled south on interior railway lines. Urged by Zhilinski to hurry north in order to cut off and eliminate the supposedly retreating Germans, Samsonov initiated a series of forced marches deploying little or no reconnaissance. The Russians were thus completely surprised when two German corps (XVII and I Reserve) struck their right wing near the village of Rothfliess on 26 August. Lieutenant General Aleksei Blagoveschchenski, commanding the Russian VI Corps there, lost his nerve and retreated nearly 30 kilometers without informing Samsonov. When François's heavy artillery crushed the Russian left wing the following morning, the Russians faced a double envelopment. Ludendorff pressed the attack all along the front. Samsonov's center held, but both wings fell back under fierce attacks.

The retreat quickly turned into a rout as the Russians discovered they were surrounded. Samsonov's soldiers acquitted themselves well—"The Russians fought like lions," one German general noted—but their position was hopeless.[68] German logistical superiority combined with daring leadership had created a ring of steel and fire around the Russian Second Army. With his army nearly destroyed, Samsonov shot himself on 30 August. The surviving soldiers of the Second Army—more than 90,000 men, mostly from the central XIII and XV Corps—surrendered on 31 August after several attempts to break out of the German ring failed. Another 50,000 Russians lay dead or wounded. Both Rennkampf and Zhilinski remained blissfully unaware of the scope of the disaster. Zhilinski, in fact, cancelled an order for Rennkampf to send two corps to Samsonov's aid only four hours after issuing it on 29 August, preferring to conserve his northern forces in their entrenched positions.

Amazed at the Russians' inactivity, the German Eighth Army wheeled again on its interior lines and deployed to confront the Russian First Army. Rennkampf, still expecting an attack from Königsberg, had focused four divisions there. Zhilinski had withdrawn another division to strengthen the Russian garrison at Grodno, over 100 kilometers away, on 23 August, so the remaining twelve divisions of First Army were strung out on a line of over 130 kilometers between the Baltic Sea and the Masurian Lakes. Against these forces the Germans sent fifteen infantry divisions, having left two-and-a-half divisions behind to guard against a Russian strike from the fortresses around Warsaw and having also been joined by the two corps from the west.

Once again, François's I Corps initiated the action, striking Rennkampf's left flank from the south on 9 September. The main body of the German

Eighth Army attacked that same day along the entire Insterburg Gap, but only François achieved any notable success. Supported by Mackensen's XVII Corps and two regiments of cavalry, I Corps routed the Russians at Soltmahnen and threatened to collapse Rennkampf's left flank. Over 30,000 Russians surrendered to the Germans, while more than 70,000 fell dead or wounded on the battlefields.

Faced with the prospect of an envelopment similar to that suffered by Samsonov, Rennkampf turned and fled. The Russian First Army retreated so quickly that it lost not only all contact with the Germans, but all communication with Zhilinski as well. Rennkampf's force covered 85 kilometers in the first fifty hours, and Zhilinski eventually relocated his defeated commander, sans army, well behind the Russian frontier at Kovno. Surprisingly, while Zhilinski was removed from his command in favor of General Nikolai V. Ruszki, Rennkampf survived an inquiry and retired in 1915. The situation on the Russian Northern Front remained bleak, however; Ruszki could think of no better plan than a general retreat to Kovno.

Fortunately for the Russians, the Germans had shifted their focus south in response to Conrad's pleas for assistance. Though the failure of the German Schlieffen Plan in the west precluded the massive transfer of armies envisioned prior to the war, the German general staff was well aware that the collapse of Austria-Hungary could be fatal as well. General Erich Falkenhayn, who replaced Moltke as chief of staff, therefore formed the Ninth Army around four corps of the Eighth Army and transferred it to the area around Krakow on the Austrian's northern flank in preparation for a renewed assault. The Russian high command, meanwhile, first argued whether to attack or retreat and then slowly began to gather its resources for a second offensive against Germany. The new plan, largely the brainchild of Grand Duke Nikolai, called for the Russian armies on the Northwestern Front to turn southward and strike into Silesia from the plain west of Warsaw.

Unfortunately for the Russians, German intelligence uncovered the grand duke's plan well in advance. Before the Russians could move their collected forces into the region, the German Ninth Army struck toward Warsaw on 29 September. Conrad's Austrian First Army attacked in support of the Germans the following day, and the remainder of the Habsburg armies went over to the offensive on 2 October. By 9 October, Ninth Army had pushed forward to the Vistula River, but there the tide turned. Rain and snow flooded the river and rendered roads impassable. Stavka nevertheless convinced Ivanov to order the Russian Fourth, Fifth, and

Ninth armies to attack across the river. Eighteen German divisions fought against sixty Russian divisions, and held them off for several days. Eventually the numerical superiority of the Russian forces won out; the III Caucasian Corps established a small bridgehead on the western bank of the Vistula that widened until the armies could engage in wholesale battle on 11 October. Threatened by the expanding Russian line on his own left flank, Hindenburg decided to withdraw on 13 October. At the same time Conrad's forces, which had lifted the siege of Przemysl on 7 October and then advanced to the San River, now met defeat at the hands of the Russian Eighth and Third armies. The Austrians rapidly fell back on Krakow while Hindenburg conducted a masterful retreat toward Czestochowa. It seemed that the "Russian steamroller" would win out at last.

Neither side, however, would succeed in establishing a clear-cut superiority in these opening campaigns. In the final battle before winter set in for good, from 11 to 25 November, the German Ninth Army drove a wedge into the left flank of the Russian forces around Lodz. The Russians were completely surprised. Five German corps broke through to Lodz, leading the Central Powers' commanders to hope for a repeat of Tannenberg.[69] Rennkampf's First Army narrowly escaped annihilation a second time, however, while the Russian Second Army struggled back to Warsaw. Faced with this disaster, Stavka canceled plans for yet another offensive in Silesia and ordered those troops to relieve the First and Second instead. When the Germans advanced toward Warsaw, therefore, they met Plehve's Fifth Army. In the ensuing battle of 16–25 November, the German Ninth barely escaped encirclement itself. Two weeks later, reinforced with four corps sent from the Western Front (II, XII, III Reserve, and XXI Reserve), the Germans finally succeeded in taking Lodz.

Each push of the Russian colossus found the more nimble Germans ready to deal a counterstroke. Each German thrust ran up against a wall of reserves. Russian forces consistently outnumbered the Germans by almost two to one, but casualties came in the same ratio. The Habsburg forces, while miserably led and sometimes of questionable military value, still provided enough of a counterweight in the south to prevent the Russians from concentrating even greater numbers against the Germans. At the same time, the weakness of the Austro-Hungarian armies increasingly forced the German High Command (*Oberheeresleitung* or OHL) to expend far more resources on the Eastern Front than they either planned or wished. "The Austro-Hungarian Army would have to be supported if it were not to be annihilated," Ludendorff wrote in his memoirs.[70]

Even as the Germans pushed the Russians back from Lodz, for example, the Austrians were once again teetering on the brink of disaster. The Russian Ninth Army, now commanded by General Letschitski, pressed the Habsburg Fourth Army back on Krakow on 16 November, while the Russian Third and Eighth armies advanced into the Bukovina against the Austrian Third Army. The two Austrian armies soon found themselves separated by more than 100 kilometers, and the Russian advance threatened to carry over the unprotected Carpathian passes and into Hungary. Only the ineptitude of the Russian leadership and the arrival of the German 47th Reserve Division allowed Conrad to stem the Russian tide at Limanowa-Lapanow.

It was a close thing. With Habsburg forces reeling, the Russians halted on 29 November. Ivanov, commanding the Southwestern Front, sensed the opportunity to drive Austria-Hungary from the conflict and perhaps end the war. Ruszki argued for a pause to regroup and replenish forces; the Russian artillery had only enough shell to supply ten rounds per gun per day.[71] While Stavka debated, Conrad struck, using the fresh German division as a spearhead. Four days of desperate fighting gained 60 kilometers and allowed the Austrian Third to establish itself in adequate defensive positions at the base of the Carpathians. Many of the Habsburg infantry divisions numbered only 5,000–7,000 men when the fighting ended, and a few companies reported having as few as 50 soldiers still fit for combat.[72] Of the 3,350,000 men who had been mobilized in August 1914, in fact, only 2,082,000 remained in the Habsburg armies. The officer corps alone had lost more than 25,000 men.[73]

1915: The Great Retreat

Conrad added to these numbers with an ill-advised winter offensive in early 1915. The primary objective, as far as Conrad was concerned, was the relief of Przemysl. This fortress was the jewel in the crown of expensive defenses the Austrians had laid out before the war; the Russians invested it in the early weeks of the conflict, and several attempts to lift the siege had already failed. Its loss would be a tremendous blow to the pride of the Habsburg Empire and to the prestige of the Austro-Hungarian military. Determined to prove the quality of the Habsburg forces, Conrad therefore sent the Austrian Third Army forward on 23 January 1915. A combined German-Habsburg force, the new South Army (Südarmee) under General Alexander von Linsingen, simultaneously would advance on Lemberg and thus remove the Russian threat to Hungary. The Austrian Seventh Army would feint toward Czernovitz and then support Linsingen's strike. Hindenburg's forces in the north—the German Eighth and Tenth armies—would also launch strikes to the east.

While the German efforts resulted in some tactical gains, the winter weather made operations difficult. The Central Powers' first attempt to use poison gas, at Bulimov, failed when the gas froze, for instance. Twice the German attack was stunted by driving blizzards, and the artillery found it required teams of ten or more horses just to wheel one of its guns into position. Fortunately the Russian command displayed its usual ineptitude, massing eleven divisions along a front only 10 kilometers wide and placing them all under a single commander. They were easy prey for the German artillery, and suffered 40,000 casualties in a single day. Further north the Russian commanders, complacent and almost completely unaware of the German troop dispositions, were caught by surprise when German forces appeared on the flank of the Russian Tenth Army on 25 January. The artillerists fled, leaving the infantry in the lurch; more than 90,000 men surrendered, and three hundred Russian guns were lost. Two weeks later, the German Eighth and Tenth armies nearly succeeded in encircling the Russian Tenth in the Augustovo Forest. The Russians lost over 200,000 men in the encounter. Only a heroic stand by Plehve's Twelfth Army during 12–14 February halted the German drive. Despite advancing nearly 100 kilometers to the east, the Germans had failed to break the Russian line and actually worsened their own position by extending their supply lines and the exposure of their southern flank.[74]

Things went no better in the south. The Carpathian passes were still clogged with ice and snow when the ill-equipped Habsburg troops began to slog their way forward. The weather was so bad that soldiers had to thaw their weapons prior to any attack, and the firing mechanisms on the field guns clogged repeatedly with ice. Dense fog and the occasional snowstorm usually prevented the Austrians from bringing their artillery to bear on the entrenched Russian positions in any case. Lacking artillery themselves, the Russians rolled barrels stuffed with explosives down on the struggling enemy. The Austrian Third Army took tremendous casualties. One regiment awoke to find that 28 officers and 1,800 men had frozen while they slept.[75] Colonel Georg Veith recorded the scene: "Hundreds freeze to death daily; every wounded soldier who cannot get himself back to the lines is irrevocably sentenced to death. Riding is impossible. Entire lines of riflemen surrender in tears to escape the pain."[76] Many soldiers committed suicide under these conditions. Progress in the mountains was measured in meters, and the objectives for the first day of the offensive were not reached until the end of January. By that time, Third Army had lost half its strength. One infantry division, the 2nd, went from 8,150 men to fewer than 1,000 in that time.

Conrad blithely paused to bring his forces back to strength and then renewed the attack, adding the Austrian Second Army in the center of the line. It lost 40,000 men—just under half its strength—without gaining any ground. Pflanzer-Baltin's Seventh Army managed to capture Czernovitz, along with some 60,000 Russian soldiers, but the general offensive was a failure. The Russians counterattacked on 5 February, driving the Habsburg troops back against the western Carpathians. Conrad renewed the offensive in a desperate attempt to relieve the fortress, but only incurred more casualties. The garrison at Przemysl, looking fit and trim by most accounts, surrendered to the Russians on 23 March 1915, turning more than 120,000 Habsburg soldiers into Russian prisoners. All told, the winter offensive cost Austria-Hungary another 600,000–800,000 men, including the last of its experienced officers at all levels.[77]

The Habsburg government passed extraordinary measures to make up the sheer numbers, allowing Gypsies to serve, extending the age span for military service from 19–42 to 18–50, and recalling the 2.3 million men who had been deemed unfit for duty in the previous decade. It could not, however, replace quality. Where the German officer corps had suffered roughly 16 percent missing and lost in 1914 and the Russians endured a 25 percent loss rate among officers, the Habsburg officer corps' losses— taking into account both killed and missing in action—totaled almost 50 percent.[78] For a force comprising at least fifteen different ethnic groups with as many languages, customs, and uniforms, the loss of field-grade officers was critical. Officers who had spent the prewar years teaching their units the so-called language of service—a basic vocabulary of about eighty to a hundred terms and commands in German—and learning the languages of their men in turn were now replaced by unfamiliar and poorly trained reserve officers.[79] The heart of the Austro-Hungarian armies was being torn out.

What was perhaps worse was that the head remained. Of the 3,200 Habsburg officers killed between August 1914 and January 1915, only 39 held the rank of colonel or above.[80] Austro-Hungarian military commanders, as with their counterparts in Russia, were more likely to be appointed on courtly than martial merit prior to 1914. General Oskar Potiorek, given command of the Habsburg forces in the Balkans in August 1914, had never commanded a unit larger than a battalion before. He managed to squander the lives of nearly 800,000 men in three unsuccessful invasions of Serbia before being replaced by the Archduke Eugen—who had been selected for the post largely because his name carried historic cachet. Archduke Friedrich, on the other hand, had been appointed commander in chief because the emperor was too old and his heir was too young.[81] Despite disheartening and downright embarrassing defeats, the general officers of the Austro-Hungarian Army remained by and large alive and in place. After the initial defeat in Galicia, Brudermann and Auffenberg were relieved of their commands along with several others, but Conrad refused to go further. Privately—and sometimes publicly—Conrad blamed the Germans for failing to bear their fair share against the Russian "hordes." The emperor also refused to blame his commanders, choosing instead to believe that they had merely been unlucky.

Others, however, noted that Habsburg flag officers were too frequently drunk, and that many had suffered mental breakdowns during the initial conflict. Conrad, according to his biographer, "clearly lost touch with the troops after the first weeks of the war."[82] There seemed to be no unifying goal for the campaign in Galicia, and yet he appeared unconcerned by the heavy casualties suffered by the Austro-Hungarian armies. Conrad confessed to his staff that if Franz Ferdinand had been still alive, the archduke probably would have had him court-martialed and shot. Instead, Conrad moved his headquarters back from Przemysl to the Archduke Friedrich's castle in Teschen. There he and his staff enjoyed three levels of table service, coffee houses, and tennis courts and, according to the German plenipotentiary, spent more time arranging for their wives and lady friends to shuttle back and forth from Vienna than prosecuting the war. The Austrian Military Chancery had observed much the same thing, and recommended sweeping changes in the staffing and appointments processes in November 1914. The recommendations had been studiously ignored, and archdukes, barons, and counts continued to cycle through the Austro-Hungarian command.[83]

The Russians were in no position to take advantage. Brusilov's Eighth Army was freezing in the Carpathians in March 1915, undermanned and undersupplied. "My regiments are from fifty to seventy-five percent under strength," he reported. "Replacements are arriving unarmed and there are no rifles to give them. Under the present conditions, even one or two days of not very intensive fighting would leave my army without bullets."[84]

The Russian Imperial Army was suffering from material shortages everywhere. Only 10 percent of the military's new recruits were issued a rifle in early 1915, and in many instances entire battalions trained without any arms whatsoever. Tsar Nicholas II nonetheless assured the French ambassador that plans for a general offensive in the spring remained intact. There was little question, however, that an attack on the Germans was out of the question, though Ruzski continued to insist that his front should be the focus of any offensive action. Austria-Hungary obviously had been weakened by the winter's activity, and Ivanov urged Stavka to take advantage of the opportunity since the fall of Przemysl had freed the Eleventh Army for an attempt to carry the war into Hungary. The grand duke accordingly announced his intention to shift the focus of operations in order to drive Austria-Hungary from the war: "The supreme commander now sees his main purpose as being to shift the entire Northwestern Front over to a purely defensive operation, and intends for the Southwestern Front to become the major focus of the campaign in the days ahead."[85]

The commanders of the Northern and Northwestern fronts, however, resisted the change and jealously guarded their reserves and supplies. Ruszki resigned rather than assume a subordinate, defensive posture in a weak position, and his replacement, Alekseev, simply refused the grand duke's requests to send his reserves to Ivanov. Two-thirds of the Russian forces therefore remained motionless north of the Pripet Marshes, though Alekseev did eventually surrender two divisions. Ivanov was forced to draw forces from across the Southwestern Front to assemble his strike force of some thirty divisions—only two more than the Habsburgs disposed of in the region.

The Carpathian offensive nevertheless moved forward for three weeks against the weak Austrian defenses. In a panic, Conrad began to lay plans for a fighting retreat all the way to Innsbruck and appealed to the Germans for relief. The Russians seized the strategic Dukla Pass, among others, and captured thousands of Habsburg troops, but that was the limit of their powers. Low on ammunition and with German troops—the so-called *Beskiden Korps* commanded by German Lieutenant General Georg von der Marwitz—arriving in the Carpathians to stiffen the Austro-Hungarian lines, Ivanov halted the offensive in early April.[86] "Fighting the Germans is quite a different matter from fighting the Austrians," Russian officers noted. "The German shell falls right into our trenches, and there is an extraordinary amount of it."[87]

The threat against Hungary had been enough to get Falkenhayn's attention though, and to change his thinking about the Eastern Front. Ludendorff had argued, since the end of January 1915, that a concentrated offensive in the east could end the war against Russia. Now, fearing that Austria-Hungary would, as Conrad had despairingly (and somewhat disingenuously) informed him, be unable to sustain itself against Russia if Germany continued to seek a decision in the west, the German commander in chief now decided to destroy the offensive capacity of the tsar's armies.[88] The Russians, he wrote, "threatened the Austro-Hungarian front in a way that could not be borne for any length of time on account of the decreasing morale of certain sections of the allied troops."[89]

This assessment was almost certainly correct, though perhaps not exactly as it was intended. There was a common perception on all sides that the Slavs would refuse to fight for Austria-Hungary in 1914. Brusilov, for instance, wrote in September 1914 that the Slavs of the Austro-Hungarian Empire seemingly sympathized with "their Russian brothers" and did not wish to fight, especially in the face of worsening conditions.[90] And there were concrete instances that supported this idea. Two battalions of the Czech 28th Infantry Regiment (IR) had surrendered to the Russians at Zboro in early April 1915, marching toward the enemy with banners flying and arms shouldered. The unit was disbanded, and the remaining Czech soldiers dispersed among four Austrian regiments. Throughout the Habsburg armies, rumors persisted that ethnically Slavic troops were abandoning their positions without resistance. A German liaison to the Habsburg forces noted pointedly "the unreliability of some nationalities."[91]

In reality though, poor morale and even desertion were widespread by the spring of 1915, and not just among Slavic units. Most of the "mass surrenders," where entire units went over without fighting, took place as part of a more general collapse. It would be foolhardy, for instance, to blame the loss of Przemysl on a lack of patriotism on the part of the Slavic units stationed there.[92] Morale was a problem throughout the Austro-Hungarian armies. Reports from the Austrian Second Army in the winter of 1915–16, for instance, noted that "the mood [of the soldiers] is very bad," and Ludwig Windischgrätz, an Austrian liaison officer to the Germans, noted that the Habsburg X Corps was "no good at all." Even among the Austrians at Conrad's headquarters, usually a bastion of self-deception, the general temper was said to be "below zero," and the German military plenipotentiary to Teschen believed that the Habsburg forces were entirely "rotten and decayed."[93]

Faced with this dilemma as well as with an unfavorable numerical balance on the Western Front, Falkenhayn decided to organize an elite and overwhelming force for what he hoped would be a decisive strike against the Russians in western Galicia. By taking the fourth infantry regiment of every division on the Western Front as well as a third of every artillery battery there, the Prussian War Ministry created four corps of battle-seasoned troops that were shipped east for the offensive. To this Falkenhayn added an additional eight divisions formed of new recruits and recovered veterans, along with a robust complement of artillery. When fully assembled, the strike force contained more than 350,000 troops with over 1,272 light guns, 660 machine guns, 96 trench mortars, and 334 pieces of heavy artillery. This was the greatest concentration of artillery yet seen on either front. Falkenhayn selected General Mackensen to command the force, now designated as Eleventh Army, and assigned Colonel Hans von Seeckt to serve as chief of staff.[94] The plan called for Mackensen to strike against the Russian Third Army on a front of some 35 kilometers between Gorlice and Tarnow, some 50 kilometers east of Krakow, and then drive north to pin the Russian forces against Hindenburg's Eighth Army just west of Warsaw. To support the offensive, the Austrian Third and Fourth armies would launch strikes on Mackensen's south and north wings respectively.

With only 219,000 men and fewer than 700 pieces of artillery—including only four heavy guns—the Russian Third Army was heavily overmatched. Because Stavka had decided in April 1915 to assemble the new Ninth Army in the Bukovina, moreover, the Russians had no significant reserves on hand. With the advance of Eighth Army and Eleventh Army toward Hungary, in fact, Third Army had been forced to extend its southern wing to cover part of the Carpathian Front. Only five and a half divisions from the eighteen and a half that made up Third Army were thus facing Mackensen's new force, and these were mostly second-line units. Even when intelligence reports revealed the German buildup the Russian commander, General Radko Dmitrev, took no action to strengthen that sector. Although Third Army had occupied its positions for months, the troops had not built any second- or third-line defensive positions, and even their forward trenches were relatively shallow. The Russian artillery remained dangerously exposed, where it had been the entire winter, and on the eve of the attack Dmitrev left his headquarters to attend the annual celebration of the Order of the Knights of St. George.

This carelessness, perhaps more than the numerical superiority of Mackensen's Eleventh Army, proved to be the Russians' undoing. Seeckt and the troops drawn from the Western Front had learned some important lessons from the early fighting there, and they brought this new style of warfare with them. Mackensen and Seeckt took care to try and camouflage their buildup of forces, in order to increase the odds of catching the Russians off-guard with their initial attack and to provide for adequate means of communication between the infantry commanders and the artillery. They had also learned the importance of the artillery; using air observers and data from the Austro-Hungarian troops that had occupied the positions previously, Mackensen's gunners were able to chart the location of the Russian guns and trenches with deadly precision.

At 9:00 PM on 1 May, Eleventh Army began to register its guns, firing phosphorus shells to chart ranges and determine points of impact. Over the next four hours, the German guns systematically destroyed the Russians' forward obstacles and cut their lines of communication. Then Mackensen's artillery began to focus on the trenches themselves, intensifying the barrage until more than one thousand shells rained on the virtually defenseless Russian infantry each minute. Lieutenant General François, commanding the XLI Corps at Gorlice, recalled the scene:

> The 12-cm. gun on Hill 696 gives the signal shot and all batteries, from the field guns to the heavy mortars, fire their first salvo on cue at the Russians. It is followed by thunder and booming, slamming and banging, as 700 guns open fire and hurl hissing iron and steel through the air. The shells explode in the ground on the other side, throwing earth, wood splinters, and other defensive works yards high into the air. [. . .] Trees break like matches, huge trunks are hurled through the air, the stone walls of houses cave in, fountains of earth rise from the ground.[95]

One Russian grenadier recalled that "there were shell craters on top of shell craters," and the German infantry were actually able to stand and watch the bombardment in the early morning hours.[96]

By the time the German infantry launched its assault at 10:00 AM, the Russian defenses had been obliterated. "All the Russians in the danger zone who were not killed or wounded were stunned or contusioned," one observer reported.[97] A single German corps quickly forced the interior wings of two Russian corps and opened a five-kilometer gap in the line; with no secondary positions, the Russians had to retreat over open ground, and the German guns simply mowed them down. The Russian X Corps lost 29,000 men over the course of two days; the III and V Caucasus Corps each lost 75 percent of their strength, while IX and XXIV Corps simply disintegrated. Within a week, Russian losses mounted to over 200,000. Stavka ordered its armies to hold the line and even categorically forbade retreat, but it was too late. The few, poorly armed Russian reserves that were available were quickly chewed up by the German offensive. Mackensen's forces advanced rapidly, covering between 6 and 12 kilometers a day as the Russians fled before them.

Within ten days the Russians had been forced back to the San River, where their commanders hoped to make a defensive stand. It was futile. What artillery the Russians could muster had only fifty shells per gun, and most of the armies' entrenching tools had long ago been sold by corrupt staff officers. When Dmitrev asked Stavka for additional supplies, he got a rebuke instead: "Your demands are in the impossible class. [. . .] It is essential that measures be taken to limit the vast expenditure of rifle cartridges that has occurred in recent days."[98] Though Alekseev now offered to send reserves from his front, the Russian railways were too overburdened to move them with the speed necessary. Fresh troops gathered at the rear assembly points, but few had either rifles or proper training in how to use them. According to Knox, the need for manpower was so great that raw recruits received—in theory—only four weeks' training before being sent to the front, while reservists got a six-week "refresher" course.

With only 40,000 men and fixed bayonets against the German artillery and machine guns, the Russian Third Army broke and fled once again. Thousands more Russian soldiers drowned or were machine-gunned as they attempted to swim across the river. Supported by the Austrian Third Army, Mackensen's Eleventh pushed across the San River in mid-May and advanced against Przemysl. The Austrians proved more of a burden than an aid in many instances, but Mackensen's momentum seemed unstoppable. The 11th Bavarian ID entered Przemysl triumphantly in the first days of June, and the kaiser elevated Mackensen to field marshal.[99]

The fall of Przemysl forced the Russians to withdraw their line in the south now as well, since the Central Powers might easily cut off the three Russian armies (north to south: Eighth, Seventh, and Ninth) that were pressing the hapless Austrians against the Carpathians. Indeed, after a short pause to bring Mackensen's shell and supplies up to capacity, the Central Powers now mounted a general offensive on the Eastern Front, designed to shatter the Russian armies. Their focus, however, was Galicia, not the Carpathians—which Falkenhayn considered out of danger. In the north,

Hindenburg and Ludendorff advanced against Riga and then turned their attention to the rail junction of Kovno, which they saw as the key to the Russian defenses.

Mackensen, meanwhile, turned his forces northward according to plan, hoping to catch the Russian forces in the Galician salient now created around Warsaw. His Eleventh Army, in conjunction with the Austrian Fourth, would drive on Lublin and Brest-Litovsk from the south while the German Twelfth Army under General von Gallwitz advanced southward from Tannenberg toward Warsaw. Prince Leopold of Bavaria's Ninth Army was to strike directly east from its position near Lodz to support the encirclement. Inside this ring lay three Russian armies (north to south: First, Second, and Fourth) and a line of fortresses (north to south: Rozan, Pultusk, Novo Georgievsk, and Ivangorod) on which the defense of Russian Poland rested. Inside the fortresses lay huge stocks of munitions, some nine thousand pieces of artillery, and nearly three-quarters of the Russian armies' forces (thirty of 49.5 corps). Rather than abandon Poland and withdraw to a more defensible line, however, Stavka decided to gamble on the strength of its fortifications.

The Russian citadels, once considered impregnable, proved no more defensible in 1915 than the Belgian and Dutch strongholds had been in 1914. For once, the commanders of the Central Powers cooperated, with Falkenhayn shelving his plans for an offensive against Serbia and Conrad putting his desire to crush the Italians (who had just declared war against Austria-Hungary in May) on the back burner in order to try and force Russia from the war. With the Austrian First Army covering his right flank, Mackensen launched his new strike on 13 July. He employed not the tactics of the Gorlice-Tarnow Offensive, but rather used his artillery to pound the Russians into submission in what was effectively a massive, primitive "creeping barrage":

"The heavy artillery would take up positions in places which were entirely—or almost entirely—beyond the range of the Russian field artillery, and the heavy guns would start to shower their shells on the Russian trenches, doing it methodically, as was characteristic of the Germans. That hammering would go on until nothing of the trenches remained, and their defenders would be destroyed."[100] The German artillery then moved forward and repeated the process against the next line of defense.

Progress was thus much slower than it had been in May. By 17 June, the Germans had moved forward by only eight kilometers. At each step, they encountered more Russian troops as Alekseev brought reserves to the theater. It took ten days to drive the Russians out of Cholm and more than twice that long to take Lublin, which fell on 23 July. Surprisingly, while the Russians continued to retreat without any general plan and each battle brought renewed chaos and mismanagement, their armies did not break. Knox reported that "[t]he Russian formations in the front line were merely skeletons, and their *morale* had been severely shaken by two and a half months of constant retreat. For instance, a report on July 17th from one corps stated that 'superhuman efforts were required to keep the men in the trenches.' The enemy was overwhelmingly superior in number of guns and in ammunition supply."[101]

On the orders of Grand Duke Nikolai, the Russians evacuated Warsaw at the end of July and withdrew further. Mackensen pursued them methodically eastward, inflicting heavy casualties at each encounter, and flattening the salient so that toward the end of August 1915, the front ran almost due south from Osoviec to Brest-Litovsk. Novo Georgievsk surrendered on 19 August; Kovel followed suit on 21 August. Five days later Kovno, Osoviec, and Brest-Litovsk itself were in the hands of the Central Powers; Grodno fell on 2 September, and Vilna (Vilnius) was captured two weeks later.

Still the Russians retreated, crossing the Polish border into their own territory and losing men and materiel at every step. "The retreat will continue as far—and for as long—as necessary," Tsar Nicholas II told the French ambassador, "until the day comes when we have enough rifles and munitions to mount a general offensive. The Russian people are as unanimous in their will to conquer as they were in 1812."[102] Though the tsar's words ring hollow to the modern ear, Knox's record of 5 August supports Nicholas's contention: "It was rumoured that Mitau and Lomja had been lost, but the Russians were quite happy. They said: 'We will retire to the Urals, and when we get there the enemy's pursuing army will have dwindled to a single German and a single Austrian; the Austrian will, according to the custom, give himself up as a prisoner, and we will kill the German.' The first part of the remark was strangely prophetic."[103]

As it had in 1812, nature eventually came to the defense of Russia, though this time it was simple topography and not winter that halted the invader. "It is not so much the enemy's strength as the complete impossibility of observation in terrain of this type," one German commander reported as his troops neared the great Pripet Marshes.[104] The depth and scale of the Russian retreat had, moreover, shortened the front so much by late August that the Central Powers simply could not bring all of their troops to bear. In addition, it was proving increasingly difficult to supply the various advancing armies as they moved further and further from the railheads of Germany and Austria-Hungary. Even the field railways—single tracks along which horses could drag loaded carts—went only as far as Lublin in mid-August; some of the more advanced units were 125 kilometers further east. It was difficult even to get enough food and water for the exhausted troops, as one German infantryman recalled:

> Exertions, privations, very heavy knapsack, neck and shoulder pain from the rifle and long, difficult marches; extremely tired feet and body. Bad roads—either uneven asphalt or deep sand—and always the uneven fields, marching up and down deep furrows. Often in double time, and usually no water or at best stinking water, no bread for days on end. When we do get food, it is little or bad, hardly any meat at all. Nothing but freezing and freezing, and back pains.[105]

Gallwitz had lost between one-third and one-half of his force during the advance under such conditions.[106] To Ludendorff, it was "obvious that Mackensen, Woyrsch [commanding Ninth Army in the center of the line], and Gallwitz [could] probably force the Russians to retreat, but not to a decisive end."[107] Hindenburg likewise recalled that "the Russian bear had escaped our clutches, bleeding no doubt from more than one wound, but still not stricken to death."[108]

Falkenhayn disagreed. The Gorlice-Tarnow Offensive and the "Great Retreat" of 1915 had inflicted nearly 2 million casualties on the Russian armies, and wrested Poland from the Tsar's grasp. He felt sure that Russia would now be ready to make peace, particularly if offered attractive terms, and he intended to offer Poland. For once, Conrad agreed with the German commander, declaring that "golden bridges" should be extended to St. Petersburg. Politicians on both sides, however, foiled his plans. Bethmann-Hollweg, the German chancellor, refused to enter direct negotiations with Russia for fear it would signal weakness to the Allies as well as alienating nationalist sentiment in Germany. There was, moreover, a strong and important circle in Berlin that wished to annex Poland as a *cordon sanitaire* against any future Russian designs. Nor was the Russian tsar willing to entertain even Falkenhayn's more generous offer.

Not only did Nicholas II inform a Danish intermediary that he would not renounce his pledge to stand by Britain and France, but he also personally assumed command of and responsibility for the Russian Imperial Army. Grand Duke Nikolai was pensioned off as viceroy of the Caucasus, and on 1 September 1915, Nicholas II formally took charge of Russia's armed forces with Alekseev as his chief of staff. Headquarters shifted to the town of Mogilev, and most of what Stone calls the "aristocratic furniture" was removed from Stavka in accordance with the tsar's expressed desire for an "apolitical" command. A core of qualified officers soon formed a working and reasonably efficient management team.[109] "I have to-day taken supreme command of all the forces of the sea and land armies operating in the theater of war," Nicholas II wrote in an order of 5 September. "With firm faith in the clemency of God, with unshakeable assurance of final victory, we shall fulfil our sacred duty to defend our country to the last. We will not dishonor the Russian land."[110]

Instead of inspiring confidence though, the move inspired fear and trepidation among most Russians. Knox reported that among the senior officers of the Russian Twelfth Army, "the one opinion regarding the change was 'bad.'"[111] Brusilov likewise reported that dismay was the prevailing sentiment in the trenches, and it was no better at the upper levels of society.[112] "I expect the most terrible consequences from this change in the high command," one minister confessed. "We are sitting on a powder keg. All we need is a single spark to set it off [. . .] the Sovereign Emperor's assumption of the army's command is not just merely a spark but a whole candle thrown into a powder magazine."[113] The Council of Ministers was so worried that it sent a collective warning: "[T]he decision you have taken threatens . . . Russia, You, and Your dynasty with the gravest consequences."[114] Nicholas II, as naïve and unconcerned as always, took no heed, though Alexandra saw such talk as evidence of a cabal. "May God's will be done," he is reported to have told his wife. "Perhaps a sacrificial lamb is needed to save Russia, and I am to be the victim."[115]

CHAPTER TWO

MAKING PREPARATIONS

Given the circumstances of early 1916, it is easy to see how Brusilov's offer to go on the offensive might have seemed suicidal. Over the course of the Gorlice-Tarnow campaign in the summer of 1915 and the subsequent "Yellow-Black Offensive," the Russians had suffered between 300,000 and 400,000 casualties per month. Over a million Russian soldiers were taken captive during the Central Powers' drive to the east, and many of those had surrendered without fighting. At some points, the Russian retreat covered 900 kilometers from their furthest westward advance. Many of the German and the Austro-Hungarian planners judged the Russians incapable of further offensive action. "The Russian armies have not been completely overthrown but their offensive powers have been so shattered that she can never revive in anything like her old strength," Falkenhayn had written the kaiser in December 1915. He assumed that any Russian attack was likely to result in the destruction of the tsar's armies, if not a complete revolution in Russia.[1] The Austrian staff planners on the Russian Front believed that the Habsburg forces had broken the enemy; one officer even opined that "it will soon be over." Conrad still expected the Russians to mount another attack, but at the same time he was so confident the Habsburg defenses would hold that he pressed ahead with a plan to pull two divisions from Galicia to assist with a spring offensive against Italy.[2] Ludendorff was so unconcerned that when rumors of a new Russian offensive began circulating in early March 1916, he dismissed them out of hand and took two days' vacation.[3] The

Russian failures around Lake Narotch only confirmed the judgment of the Central Powers' commanders. The Russian strikes, Falkenhayn wrote, "might, however, be described as bloody sacrifices rather than attacks." Russian power, he believed, was broken.[4]

Repairing the Damage

The problems in the Russian army were readily apparent and, at least numerically, seemed to justify Falkenhayn's assessment. By July 1915, the Russian army had suffered some 60,000 casualties among its officer corps—and there had been only 40,000 officers serving in August 1914. With an annual intake of only 35,000 or so officers, the Russian Imperial Army was effectively crippled in the first year of the war. Beneath the surface, however, lay grounds for hope. The retreat of 1915 had shortened the Russian lines, making supply easier, and by early 1916 Russian armaments production had reached respectable levels, producing almost 1.3 million rifles and 1.5 billion cartridges per year.[5] Improved connections to England and France, while still tenuous, had provided additional supplies as well. According to one estimate, the Russian army possessed 1.2 million rifles in its front lines in January 1916, and another 2 million were either already in Russian ports or due to arrive from abroad by April.[6] At the same time, foreign suppliers had shipped over 1,900 field guns to Russia, along with 355 mountain guns, twelve 4.2-inch guns, forty-three 4.8-inch howitzers, and sixty 6-inch howitzers, increasing the available artillery by between 60 and 70 percent from August 1914. The Russians also received nearly 5 million shells of various calibers to alleviate the shortages experienced in the first year of the war.[7] "We began to receive rifles—of various types and calibers to be sure—but in quantity and with sufficient cartridges nonetheless," Brusilov wrote in his memoirs. "Artillery shells, especially for light guns, also began to arrive in great quantities. They increased the number of machine guns, and organized in every unit so-called grenadiers who were armed with hand grenades and bombs."[8]

In his few short months as minister of war from July 1915 to March 1916, moreover, General Aleksei A. Polivanov had drafted an additional 2 million men into the Russian armed forces, reorganized recruitment to emphasize the physical fitness of the men, and reformed Russian infantry training. New recruits received far more combat training than previously, and they were often rotated into quiet sectors of the front lines prior to being deployed in combat. By the end of 1915, the Russian armies had almost 2 million men at the front, all with a rifle and an average of some 400 rounds, with ample reserves at hand.[9] The continued loss of officers during the campaigns of 1915 had also forced the Russian High Command to do what had been unthinkable prior to 1916: promote competent men from the ranks. Though few rose above subaltern positions, and there were still far too few officers overall, the skill level of field officers generally improved. The defeats of 1914 and 1915 had also served to weed out some of the more incompetent Russian commanders and changed the nature of Stavka. The tsar's assumption of command in September 1915, though purely nominal, at least brought a more professional military tone to the Russian headquarters, where previously the involvement of senior officers with military science had been considered the epitome of bad taste.[10] Ianushkevich and his courtiers gave way to the simpler, apolitical staff of Alekseev. Professional military officers concerned primarily with the conduct of the war, in other words, had finally succeeded to positions of influence.[11]

Brusilov fit this pattern perfectly. Norman Stone, the preeminent historian of the Eastern Front, notes that Brusilov was particularly intelligent and brought a crisp, simple, and direct style of command to the Southwestern Front. Stone contends that Brusilov, though he was married to a cousin of famed Russian politician Peter Stolypin and worked the promotions system adeptly, was in fact free of class prejudices and had a knack for choosing competent assistants without regard to their social standing. He visited the front lines frequently. His first act upon promotion to commander of the Southwestern Front, in fact, was to conduct a personal inspection of the front lines, and he demonstrated unflagging energy in his attention to detail and preparation.[12] Though he might have lacked the "common touch," his diligence in providing for his troops usually earned their loyalty. In both background and outlook, Brusilov embodied the qualities of the "new" Russian army that began to take form in the spring months of 1916, an army led by "modest and sensible technicians."[13] Brusilov brought many of the most competent technicians together on his staff and guided their talents ably. The youngest member of his staff, for instance, was Colonel Dmitri Karbyshev, who became an expert in fortifications and earned recognition as a "Hero of the Soviet Union" for his services in the Second World War.[14] Holger Herwig, an expert on the Austro-Hungarian operations, writes that "Aleksei Alekseevich Brusilov was probably Imperial Russia's best officer of the Great War."[15]

Born in Tbilisi, Georgia, on 19 August 1853, Brusilov came from a military family. His great-grandfather had served in the army of Peter I, and both his grandfather and father had continued the tradition. Aleksei was accordingly educated in the prestigious Imperial Corps of Pages and entered the military at the age of fourteen. One of his teachers, Staff Captain S. V. Peskov, wrote in an 1867 report that Brusilov possessed "a lively and even playful character, but [was] also direct and sincere, never concealing the plainness of his origins or boasting of his own goodness [. . .]. In conversation [he was] seldom coarse and shrill [but] well polished. [He has] good talent but loves idleness and thus will only meet with middling success."[16] When the English journalist Stanley Washburn met him later, just before the offensive in 1916, he painted a parallel portrait of Brusilov: "His hair has turned perceptibly and [. . . h]is face is deeply lined and his mien is sober and serious, while his sensitive mouth has grown stern and unyielding in its lines. Only the twinkle in his deep grey eyes shows the humour and the perpetual youth which are among the dominant characteristics of the man himself."[17]

Brusilov's initial posting in 1872 was as an ensign officer with the 15th Tver Dragoons, stationed in Tbilisi under the command of Colonel S. A. Shermetyev. He served nine years there, rising to lieutenant in April 1874 and regimental adjutant in the following year. Brusilov saw action in the Russo-Turkish War of 1877–78 as part of IX Corps, commanded by General M. T. Loris-Melikov, which stormed the Turkish fortress at Ardagan in May 1877. He received the Stanislav Medal for Gallantry when he was only twenty-five, and moved rapidly through the ranks thereafter, mingling with the more noble officers stationed in Tbilisi and their families. It was through such contacts that Brusilov met his future (second) wife, Nadezhda Zhelikovskaya, in 1880 and found his way to St. Petersburg, where he was sent to study at the cavalry officers' school. Upon completion of the course in October 1881, Brusilov became an instructor at the school and was promoted first to captain (December 1881) and then major (August 1882). He quickly earned recognition for his innovative teaching methods, particularly in the area of tactics, and became part of a circle of officers aiming to reform the school's curriculum.

He was promoted to lieutenant colonel in February 1890, and attained the rank of colonel in August 1892. Brusilov earned the four-star Vladimir Medal in 1895, and became deputy commandant of the Petersburg school in 1898 with the rank of brigadier general. One of his first duties was touring the staff and cavalry schools of Europe. The work took Brusilov to France, Austria-Hungary, and Germany, where he not only visited the various national military academies, but also observed several cavalry unit exercises and parades. The organization of field exercises in particular impressed him, and Brusilov became a firm advocate of practical training thereafter. In 1902 he became commandant of the cavalry officers' school with the rank of major general. He instituted regular field exercises, and reorganized the curriculum for the systematic preparation of cadres on the lines of the general staff school.

Soon after the war with Japan started in 1904, Brusilov transferred to a divisional command. His steady service during the Russo-Japanese conflict of 1904–1905 earned him promotion to lieutenant general in 1906, and he was given command of the 2nd Guards Cavalry Division of Eighth Army, stationed in the Kiev Military District. Though no longer directly connected to academia, Brusilov remained concerned with the scholarly aspects of war. He read widely on both Russian and foreign military affairs, and published several articles on tactics in the new journal *Vestnik Russkoi Konnitsi* (Russian Cavalry Messenger). He concerned himself, as did so many junior officers who experienced the Russo-Japanese War, with "the lessons of 1905" and particularly with the role of the officer in modern warfare. Brusilov believed that marksmanship and thorough knowledge of tactics and organization were among the most important traits for an officer to cultivate. "Modern combat," he wrote, "demands broad horizons and capabilities, the independence to draw his own conclusions and to take decisions based upon them without prompting."[18] He also advocated regular physical fitness for officers, particularly skiing: "It is very desirable that some of the imperial officers also become lovers of that beautiful winter sport."[19]

In January 1909 Brusilov was appointed commander of XIV Corps, Eighth Army, stationed in the Warsaw Military District. He quickly developed a reputation as a commander who paid close attention to detail and looked out for the well-being of his troops regardless of branch. Upon discovering that his staff officers did little or no map work, for instance, Brusilov instituted monthly staff meetings on tactics and geography to rectify the situation. He personally led several field exercises and war games, including those of 7–12 February 1911, where he commanded the "northern forces" against the "southern forces" simulating an Austro-Hungarian incursion. Though he always preferred to attack, Brusilov was no wide-eyed acolyte of the cult of the offensive. He was careful to note that "offensive" did not always indicate moving forward, for instance, and he insisted upon realism—to the degree possible—in all field exercises and games. Brusilov thus earned promotion to the rank of general of cavalry (full general) in 1912 and served as commander of XII Corps—also part of Eighth Army—in 1913 before rising to command of Eighth Army and being stationed again in the Kiev Military District during the crisis of July 1914.

Brusilov therefore had detailed knowledge of the Galician Front and the Russian units stationed there when the war began, having served there since 1906, and his service certainly reflected this. During the opening Russian drive, Eighth Army met almost unchecked success, and Brusilov's handling of the troops earned a commendation from Stavka. He quickly realized the shortcomings of cavalry in this new type of warfare and began to emphasize artillery and machine guns—again drawing on his experience of 1904–1905—even during the initial campaign against Lemberg (Lvov) in August 1914. "An artillery commander must direct his fire in much the same manner as a conductor directs an orchestra," Brusilov wrote, "and his role is of the greatest importance."[20] Brusilov earned both the three-star and the four-star George Medal for his efforts, but the performance of Eighth Army was overshadowed by the disasters of Tannenberg and Masurian Lakes.

After taking Lemberg on 3 September, Brusilov assumed command of an army group comprising his Eighth Army, the Third Army, and the newly formed Russian Eleventh Army. These troops initially invested Przemysl and then pressed forward to seize the Lupkow Pass, threatening Budapest. This strike forced Conrad to divert troops from his abortive offensive into the Warsaw salient. When Stavka failed to direct cover to the flanks of his forces, Brusilov staged a tactical retreat. The army group maintained the siege of Przemysl long enough to accept the surrender of the garrison in March 1915. A combined Austro-German counterattack retook the fortress in May 1915 as part of the Gorlice-Tarnow Offensive launched by the Central Powers in the spring of that year. According to the records left by Russian Major General Anton I. Deniken, then in command of the 4th Infantry Division in Eighth Army and certainly no friend of Brusilov, however, Brusilov's forces gave a much better account of themselves than Russian armies elsewhere:

> For eleven days the Fourth Rifle division fought stubbornly [. . .] eleven days during which, with increasing roar, the German heavy artillery swept away whole

lines of our trenches, and their defenders with them. Our regiments, although completely exhausted, were beating off one attack after another by bayonet or by short-range fire. Blood flowed unendingly, the ranks became thinner and thinner, the number of graves constantly multiplied. [. . .] Two regiments were almost annihilated merely by gun fire.[21]

Denikin blames Brusilov for the "excessive" casualties, claiming the army commander continued to attack even though the Russian artillery had no shell with which to answer the German bombardment.[22] In the end, the ammunition shortage finally forced Brusilov to abandon the fortress on 21 May 1915, but even then Eighth Army retreated in good order along a solid defensive front and managed to retain the strategically important Dukla Pass. In the estimate of British journalist Stanley Washburn, who accompanied the Russian armies in 1915 and 1916, Brusilov was "of the very highest intellect and the ideal of a soldier who is equally good at attack or defence."[23]

Part of this, certainly, was due to Brusilov's continuous study of the tactics of warfare and his willingness to entertain new ideas. Just as he had been willing to abandon cavalry for artillery and trenches in the first two years of the war, Brusilov now took a radically different approach in planning the offensive set for June. The war of position that had developed on both the Eastern and Western fronts had stymied commanders on all sides, as vastly superior firepower rendered frontal assaults suicidal and the network of trenches left no flanks to be attacked. Russian doctrine nonetheless emphasized infantry assaults as the primary tactic of offensive warfare. Both the cavalry and the artillery were granted only limited, supporting roles as observers and pursuers. This approach relied on numerical superiority and, thus far, had produced only incredible numbers of casualties.[24]

The Germans, on the other hand, had found a partial solution to these problems by using massive artillery attacks to blow holes in the Russian lines and create "artificial flanks." This had proven effective in 1915, but the concentration of troops, artillery, and supplies it required allowed the enemy to predict the location of the strikes and prepare a defense. Mackensen had then developed a primitive version of the "creeping barrage" known as the "Mackensen Wedge," which rendered such intelligence useless under massive barrages of heavy artillery that moved forward to provide cover for the advancing infantry. This had led Falkenhayn to develop a second variant, the so-called Verdun Strategy, which again relied on a massive concentration of artillery against an important position, but now intentionally drew the enemy forces into a war of attrition.

A New Type of Attack

Neither form of barrage was really an option for Brusilov. His forces did not control a point of strategic or national significance that might draw an unending stream of Habsburg forces into a crucible of fire, and even if they had, Brusilov could not have marshaled the artillery required. According to studies of the Russian offensives of December 1915 and March 1916, it required either 400 heavy shells or 25,000 light ones to blow a 50-meter gap in a belt of three-strand German barbed wire. By 1916, the Central Powers had entrenched themselves behind three belts of eighteen- or twenty-strand wire along most of the Eastern Front.[25] Even had Brusilov possessed the artillery to carry out such a plan, he believed that the gaps in the wire thus created were insufficient for a successful frontal attack. Troops entering such a small attack zone were vulnerable to enfilading fire and could not push through in large enough numbers to overwhelm the defenders. The tremendous Russian losses of March had proven this.

Brusilov therefore looked elsewhere for answers in how to balance the requirements of surprise and preparation in an offensive without overwhelming artillery support. He hit upon a twofold solution. The first part of his strategy involved the adoption of tactics the French had developed for their campaign in Champagne in September 1915. The French had forsaken the doctrine of concentration of forces in favor of preparation, creating holding areas for the reserves close to the front lines (*places d'armee*) and then sapping trenches exceptionally close to the German lines to reduce the time between the artillery bombardment and the infantry assault. The bombardment would in any case be relatively brief, lasting only one or two minutes, but concentrated—a process known to the Germans as *Trommelfeuer* (drumming fire), which forced the defenders to take cover just before the assault. This approach—known as the "Joffre attack"—proved effective in small-scale engagements with limited aims, and the French had sent instructors to Russia to encourage them to adopt the approach. Most Russian commanders declined to employ the French tactics on one ground or another: the ground was frozen or soggy; the spaces of the Eastern Front did not allow such limited assaults; Russian troops were not disciplined or reliable enough to prepare adequately.

Brusilov, however, thought that the French tactics could be used successfully on the Southeastern Front in June. He had in fact ordered Eighth Army to undertake such preparations nearly a month before he was elevated to commander of the entire Southwestern Front.[26] His particular genius though, was to apply these small-scale measures on a broad front. This, he believed, would create surprise not by concealment—which the broad, open spaces of the east denied—but by overwhelming the Austro-Hungarian forces with information and options. By having all four of his armies engage in similar preparations along the entire front, Brusilov hoped to prevent the Austrians from concentrating their reserves as well as to prevent them sending assistance to the Germans once Evert attacked. "I considered it absolutely vital to develop an attack at many different points," Brusilov wrote.[27] His first directive to his army commanders, issued on 19 April 1916, therefore, informed them that the offensive would be carried out along the entire 450-kilometer front from the Styr River in the north to the Pruth River on the Romanian border, regardless of the numerical disposition of forces. The main objectives would be the railroad junctions at Lutsk and Kovel. Preparations were to be completed by 11 May, though the Allies had not yet agreed upon an exact date for the summer offensive.

While the Russians' numerical superiority on their Northern and Western fronts was overwhelming, Brusilov's forces were much closer in strength to those of the enemy. His four armies—north to south: Eighth, Eleventh, Seventh, and Ninth—contained 40 infantry divisions to go along with 15 cavalry divisions. The Austro-Hungarians disposed of 38.5 infantry divisions and 11 divisions of cavalry within four armies (from south to north: Seventh, the so-called South Army [Südarmee], Second, and Fourth) and Army Group Archduke Friedrich, located on the northern end of the line. The balance of artillery was nearly equal, with the Russians having 1,770 light guns and 168 heavy guns at their disposal while the Austro-Hungarian forces possessed 1,301 light guns and 545 medium and heavy guns. Overall, Brusilov figured on an advantage of some 132,000 men, but the disposition of forces varied such that the Russian Eleventh Army was actually numerically inferior to the Habsburg forces opposite in every category.[28]

Knowing he would not receive significant reinforcements or supplies, Brusilov relied upon preparation to give the Russians the advantage. As a first step, the reserves of each army were brought forward and put to work. This had several advantages. It created a unified, long-term command, and it increased the manpower at the front without giving away the location of the pending offensive. It also provided additional manpower for the tasks at hand. These consisted largely of digging. All along the line, the Russian soldiers dug *places d'armee* about 300 meters long and 90 meters wide, using the dirt from the excavations to create broad earthen ramparts that would hinder direct observation by the enemy and provide some shelter from incoming artillery. They then dug communications trenches to the front and, when that task was completed, began sapping trenches toward the enemy lines. For the first time, the Russians actually dug tunnels under their own defensive obstacles to facilitate the attack. Brusilov wanted the point of departure for the Russian infantry assaults to be no greater than 100 meters, and he preferred that the distance be 60 meters or less.

While the soldiers' spades flew, Brusilov set other preparations in motion as well. He sent fliers specially instructed in aerial photography over enemy lines with specific directions to reconnoiter rear areas as well as the defenses of the first line. Where qualified personnel were lacking, the aerial unit commanders were instructed to train mechanics to perform double duty.[29] The resulting photographs were combined with intelligence gleaned from defectors and POWs to give a picture of the Austro-Hungarian Front that was in many cases as accurate as the maps the Austrians themselves possessed. Using these maps and the accompanying information, the four army commanders were to select one sector of their respective fronts on which to focus the attack. According to Brusilov's instructions, the area was supposed to be 15–20 kilometers wide, though it could be as narrow as 10 kilometers or as wide as 30. Beyond that, each commander was free to select the sector of the front he thought would prove most advantageous in consultation with Brusilov's staff of technical experts. General Dmitri Scherbatschev, commander of Seventh Army, for instance, selected a small salient in the southern section of the South Army's line. The terrain there gave the Russians an observation point from which to monitor the approach of reserve units, provided adequate cover for their infantry, and yet allowed their artillery clear lines of fire on all sides. Almost as importantly, Russian intelligence reports indicated that the area was held almost entirely by Slavic units, which were supposedly more prone to surrender than units of German, Austrian, or Hungarian heritage. While this may not have been entirely true, it certainly provided the Russians with cause for optimism.

Once the point for the breakthrough was chosen, the Russians constructed a model of the Austrian lines in the rear of their own position and practiced taking it again and again. According to Brusilov's general directive, attack groups were to be no larger than five divisions. An assault on a 15-kilometer front, for instance, would ideally be carried out by two corps, with each corps reinforced by one brigade. Attacks were to be divided into at least four waves, each with a specific goal. The first wave would be equipped with hand grenades; its goal was to push into the enemy's front trench and take out any flanking guns the artillery attack had missed. A second wave, also armed with hand grenades and bombs, would follow two hundred paces behind and move directly to an attack on the second line of trenches. "We have to consider that our opponent normally places the strength of his defense in the second line, and therefore troops halting in the first line only serve to concentrate the enemy's fire," Brusilov wrote.[30] Once the breakthrough was secured, the third wave would bring the Russian machine guns forward and, along with the fourth wave, set about expanding the breach. The Russian cavalry was then to pour through the gap and into the enemy rear.

Russian artillery units also used the models of the Austrian positions to gain familiarity with their targets. Rather than simply raining shells on the front wire, Brusilov wanted each gun to have a specific set of tasks. French and Japanese artillery veterans were brought in to instruct the Russian gunners.[31] The light artillery would be under the direct orders of the infantry commander in the front lines. As the attack opened, the light artillery was to create at least two holes 4.5 meters wide in the enemy wire, and then concentrate on destroying the enemy's machine gun emplacements. The heavy artillery was to focus on destroying the communications trenches of the opponent, and only then worry about bombarding the front lines. All of this would be accomplished with ten to twelve minutes of rapid fire rather than the two minutes of "drumming fire" recommended by the French. Brusilov, in fact, forbade the Russian heavy artillery to engage in drumming fire. Instead, he adopted the creeping barrage tactics developed by the Germans at Lake Narotch, where a brief, accurate barrage had covered the infantry's advance.[32]

Once the infantry assault began, the Russian light artillery was to focus on silencing the enemy's heavy guns while the Russian heavy artillery pounded the rear trenches to prevent the rapid advance of reserves. For this reason, Brusilov directed the army commanders to station their heavy guns no further than four kilometers from the enemy's forward trenches. This would also allow the Russian artillery to engage the Austro-Hungarian field guns and shield the attacking troops from enfilading fire as they sought to widen the breach.

With the exception of General Nikolai Sakharov, in charge of Eleventh Army, Brusilov's commanders had little faith in these new tactics. General Platon Letschitski, commander of Ninth Army, argued that his forces would be doomed by a lack of heavy artillery; the Russian Ninth had fewer than fifty heavy guns while their Habsburg opponents possessed at least three times that number. General Aleksei M. Kaledin, in charge of Eighth Army, complained that the defenses of the Austro-Hungarian forces facing him were simply too well built for an attack on them to succeed. In response, Brusilov cited figures assembled by his chief of staff, the intriguingly named Vladislav Napoleonovich Klembovski. These showed not only that each army had more shells per gun than had been available to the Russian armies in March 1916 but also that this number was more than sufficient to accomplish the tasks at hand, if the artillery was used properly. Brusilov further threatened Kaledin with dismissal, reminding his subordinate that he had once been in command of the Eighth and knew the front well enough. Brusilov had never wanted Kaledin in command of Eighth Army in any case; he had nominated Klembovski as his successor, but the tsar had decided otherwise—just one more instance where politics mitigated against an effective command structure.[33] Nonetheless, when Kaledin appeared to be on the verge of a nervous breakdown during the preparation phase, Brusilov made several trips to Eighth Army headquarters at Kovno to reassure the man.

This was typical of Brusilov; he drove himself as hard as he drove his troops, and he displayed his concern through personal attention to detail. In the single month between ordering and launching the offensive, for example, Brusilov visited each sector of the front several times to inspect the preparations and to encourage the troops. Major Blair, an English liaison officer with the Russian High Command, noted that Brusilov was regarded "as a man of the greatest energy and rapidity of action," and that his officers—if not his generals—were exceptionally fond of him.[34] Morale among the soldiers, moreover, appeared higher than ever.[35]

The commanders of the Central Powers could hardly help noticing the activity on the Russian side. Contrary to normal practice, Brusilov took no special care to hide these preparations from enemy intelligence or aerial observation. It was, in fact, part of his plan to overwhelm the Central Powers with information and possibilities to prevent them from shifting forces to deflect a single attack or from focusing their defensive energies on a single point. To confuse the enemy further, Brusilov mounted a counterintelligence campaign, sending false instructions over the radio and by messenger while specific instructions concerning the offensive were relayed verbally. He instructed his commanders to construct false artillery batteries where possible, for instance, in order to confuse and mislead the enemy's aerial observers. The real batteries were brought to the front lines

Table of Rank Equivalencies

American	British	German	Austro-Hungarian	Russian
Five-Star General	Field Marshal	General Feldmarschall	Feldmarschall	General Feldmarschall
None*	Colonel General*	General Oberst	General Oberst	None*
Four-Star General	General	General der Kavallerie General der Infanterie General der Artillerie	General Feldzugmeister (artillery)	General der Kavallerie General der Infanterie General der Artillerie
Three-Star General	Lieutenant General	Generalleutnant	Feldmarschalleutnant	General Lieutenant
Two-Star General	Major General	Generalmajor	Generalmajor	General Major
Brigadier General	Brigadier General	General	General	General
Colonel	Colonel	Oberst	Oberst	Polkovnik
Lieutenant Colonel	Lieutenant Colonel	Oberstleutnant	Oberstleutnant	Podpolkovnik
Major	Major	Major	Major	Major

* This rank did not exist in either the British or the Russian army; it was created by the Austro-Hungarian High Command in 1915 in an attempt to resolve a dispute over command on the Russian Front. The German High Command followed suit shortly after, continuing the dispute. The British "equivalent" is given here for purposes of translation only.

only the night before the attack, and even then Brusilov instructed his commanders to leave one gun from each battery to fire from its previous position in order to confuse the enemy. Another ploy suggested that the Russian II Corps was being relieved by the 3rd Turkestan Division, when in fact the 3rd was coming forward to reinforce II Corps.[36] This kind of deception was particularly important because Austrian and German analysis, having noted the Russian reliance on mass infantry assaults, equated large Russian troop movements with a coming offensive. Falkenhayn wrote that he saw no reason at the time, for instance, why the Habsburg forces could not hold against any impending Russian move in the south, particularly as the Russians had not shifted any additional troops in that direction and thus held only a slight numerical advantage.[37]

The Defenders

Such confidence was characteristic of the German command, but rather unusual for the Habsburg forces. The Austro-Hungarian record on the Russian Front was a mixed one at best, and Conrad had been pleading for German aid against the "overwhelming" Russian forces since 1 September 1914, at latest.[38] Conrad's adjutant, Colonel Rudolf Kundmann, acknowledged in his diary on 20 December 1915 that "the Russians prefer to attack us and not the Germans" because the Austrians were perceived as vulnerable.[39] Yet when it became clear from the activity on the front that the Russians were preparing an attack, Kundmann exhibited little concern. He speculated first, on 19 May 1916, that the Russians were not moving because they were "not materially prepared"—that is, that they had not yet moved troops to the front. Nearly a week later, on 27 May, Kundmann blithely dismissed what he now saw as an impending attack by the Russians as doomed to failure. "They attack stupidly, in thick masses," he wrote. "They can do no more because they have no training."[40] The Central Powers' successful offensive of 1915, combined with the dismal Russian performance around Lake Narotch in March 1916—where they had fought the Germans, and not the Austro-Hungarian forces—had raised the confidence of the Habsburg commanders to unjustifiable levels.

In part, the Austrians followed the Germans in believing the Russians to be incapable of another serious offensive, though Conrad and Kundmann remained clearly unconvinced of the truth of this at heart. Conrad told the German High Command in October 1915 that the Austrians had learned their tactical lessons from the war and that the Russian Front would henceforth be stable, for instance. Yet he was also quick to remind Falkenhayn at a 23 May 1916 meeting in Berlin that if a Russian offensive was forthcoming—he expected the Russians might be ready to attack after another four weeks' preparation—the Habsburgs expected assistance from their German allies.[41] The greater part of the Habsburg commander's "confidence," however, stemmed from his preoccupation with launching an offensive against Italy.

Nominally an ally of the Central Powers in August 1914, Italy had declined to enter the war on grounds that the alliance was defensive in nature while the Germans had taken offensive action. The Italians then entered protracted negotiations with both sides, seeking territory in the Tirol and on the Dalmatian coast in return for a military commitment.

In May 1915, Italy, France, and Great Britain reached agreement on these terms, signing the Treaty of London, which committed the Italians to fight with the Entente. Italy thus immediately became the archenemy of the Habsburgs and the bête noire of Conrad in particular, who devoted considerable energy thereafter to schemes designed to punish the Italians for their betrayal. When the forces initially delegated to this task bogged down on the Isonzo Front and the Germans—on the technical grounds that the Italians had not declared war on Germany—refused to send aid, Conrad began to pull troops from the Russian Front. Already in October 1915, Conrad detached the Austrian XIV Corps, in addition to the 8th and 6th infantry divisions, from the Austro-Hungarian Second Army on the Russian Front for service on the Isonzo, replacing them in the line with reserve units. When the Russian Front "stabilized" that winter, he began planning an offensive in the Tirol in earnest.[42]

In the initial discussions of December 1915 the Austrian High Command envisioned taking "only" two more divisions from the Russian Front for the offensive against Italy. By January 1916, however, Conrad's plan had grown to include three divisions from the Russian Front and two from the Balkan Front. To replace the former Conrad requested at least three German divisions from the northern half of the Russian Front, along with thirty German heavy artillery batteries. Falkenhayn, already focused on what would become the "Verdun strategy," had withdrawn eight German divisions from the Eastern Front for operations in the west since November. He therefore refused Conrad's request flatly, leading to a breakdown in relations, already strained, between the commanders of the Central Powers' forces. When Conrad officially declared his intention to go forward with the Tirolean offensive during a meeting with Falkenhayn on 3 February 1916, the German commander warned against such a move. He further indicated that not only would Germany not send troops south to reinforce the Habsburg forces, but if there were any increase in the Russian troop deployments in the northern sector the German forces remaining in the south (particularly the 1st and 22nd IDs serving with the Südarmee) would be recalled.

Though he professed concern for the security of the Russian Front, Conrad took little heed of Falkenhayn's warnings. Four divisions (the 10th Infantry Division, part of the Austrian Fourth Army; the 22nd Infantry Division from the Austrian Second Army; and the 34th and 43rd infantry divisions from the Austrian Seventh Army) were withdrawn from the Russian Front in March 1916 and sent to take part in the Tirolean offensive now planned for May. In addition, Conrad weakened other units on the Russian Front by diverting individual battalions, including some of those with the greatest combat experience, and nearly all of the Habsburg armies' heavy artillery—some fifteen batteries—to the Tirolean Front. The Habsburg quartermaster general, Feldzugmeister Franz Kranik, pointed out after touring the Eastern Front that the Russians had certainly noticed the Austro-Hungarian troop movements and were likely to act accordingly, but Conrad ignored him as well. He knew well that the Russian disposition of forces was heavily weighted to the north, where forty-seven German divisions and two Habsburg divisions faced some eighty-five Russian divisions. By Conrad's estimate, this left only about 600,000 Russian troops along the 450-kilometer front south of the Pripet Marshes, where the Austro-Hungarians had 570,000 men, including 13,000 Germans. "With this relation of forces," he wrote in late March 1916, "a Russian attack would have to be considered pointless."[43] In Conrad's view, any Russian offensive would require, given their normal mode of operations, at least thirty additional divisions, and he was certain that such a movement of troops would alert the Central Powers in time to react.[44]

Conrad's conclusions rested largely on the results of battles with the Russian army in December 1915, but had been confirmed by the Central Powers' experiences in the Lake Narotch campaign in March 1916. On 27 December 1915, the Russian Ninth Army had launched an assault on the positions of General Baron Karl von Pflanzer-Baltin's Austro-Hungarian Seventh Army and in the Bukovina. Letschitski, the Russian commander, employed the usual, problematic tactics; long, densely packed columns of infantry approached the Austrian positions from a distance of nearly two kilometers over open ground. They were completely exposed to the Habsburg artillery at a distance, and things only got worse as the Russians reached their opponents' front lines. Entrenched machine guns mowed down the massed Russian lines, aided by flanking fire from field artillery and grenade launchers. After two days of attacks the Russian Ninth Army withdrew, and the newly formed Seventh Army of Scherbatschev took up the cudgel. The initial wave of two Russian infantry divisions and a second wave comprising three divisions were repulsed by the Austro-Hungarian artillery before they even reached the Habsburg positions. When the Russians finally called a halt on 26 January 1916, they had lost over 70,000 men, while the Habsburg forces had suffered only 30,000 casualties.

The Habsburg commanders drew the conclusion, not entirely without warrant, that their Seventh Army had hit upon "the method" for defeating the Russians: well-prepared positions defended by artillery. Conrad accordingly issued a directive for the method to be replicated all along the Austro-Hungarian line.[45] "The Experiences from the Russian March 1916 Offensive against the German Tenth Army" (*Erfahrungen aus der russisch März offensive 1916 gegen die deutsche 10. Armee*), issued by the Austrian High Command on 21 May, contained what were thought to be the only instructions necessary for defeating any further attacks. It noted that the Russians had, in fact, carried out extensive reconnaissance for up to four months before attacking, and that "deserters" carrying false information had been employed. Habsburg commanders were instructed to take note of the Russians' tactical use of cavalry to exploit any gaps created in the lines and to disrupt communications before an attack. Other signs that an attack was pending included in the report were the bringing up of reserves and munitions, an increase in Russian patrol activity, diversionary gas attacks in other sectors, and the removal of sections of the Russians' obstacles where they did intend to strike.

Given all this, the report concluded, it would be easy to fend off any Russian strikes. Russian officers, it was noted, did not participate in the attacks but hung back to make sure their unreliable troops went forward; Russian machine guns were not used on the offensive, but to prevent their own troops from fleeing. The Russian infantry, according to this view, was nothing to fear. The frontline soldiers were said to be untrained youths, while the reserves were "weak momma's boys who immediately began to cry when attacked sharply."[46]

The winter and early spring of 1916 thus saw the Habsburg forces concentrating on construction rather than on any active defense against the Russians. Recruits sent to the Russian Front as replacements for the veteran troops diverted to the Tirol were put to work extending and strengthening the positions established at the end of the Yellow-Black Offensive in September 1915. The basic defensive position of the Austro-Hungarian troops consisted of three positions comprising three lines each. Each line was to be not less than fifty but not more than 100 meters distant from the other, in order to provide a "firing gap" for the Habsburg machine guns and artillery. The bulk of the infantry strength was to be located in the rearward positions, where huge, concrete-reinforced dugouts provided shelter from enemy artillery. Field artillery, the so-called *Sturmabwehrartillerie*, was to be placed directly behind the first line, not further than 3,000 meters from the enemy trenches. Some artillery was placed as close as 300 meters behind the first trench. The trenches in the forward line were deep, were topped by earthen berms, and contained concrete-reinforced positions designed for machine guns to provide enfilading fire, as well as timbered dugouts for the forward observers. "They were," according to one observer, "beautifully constructed of great timbers, concrete and earth. In some places, even steel rails had been cemented into place as protection against shell fire."[47] Ahead of these positions were two or, more often, three strips of barbed-wire obstacles, with each strip being 6–10 meters deep.

Because the December 1915 experience of the Austrian Seventh Army, whose front lines were most developed because they had moved the least since May 1915, showed that forward artillery strength was most important, the Austro-Hungarian High Command instituted several improvements in early 1916. The most significant of these was the extension of the system of foxholes (*Fuchslocher*) for the troops occupying the forward trenches—a response to the notably higher rate of Russian artillery fire noted in January 1916. Dug to a depth of three or four meters and reinforced to withstand artillery shells up to 18cm in caliber, these foxholes were designed to alleviate the feelings of claustrophobia that often drove men out of the dugouts and into the trenches. To prevent the men from being trapped, each foxhole was provided with two entrances.

As an additional measure, the Austrian High Command recommended the construction of concrete-reinforced lookout positions to allow the armies' forward observers to direct defensive artillery fire even during the enemy barrage. To increase the effectiveness of the field artillery, the Austrians introduced a 37mm gun, stationed its artillery officers in the forward lines to improve communication, and created mixed infantry defense units (*Infantriegeschützabteilungen*). Each Habsburg corps was to include at least one of these mixed units, though in reality only a few were formed prior to the opening of the Brusilov Offensive in June 1916. The Austrian Fourth Army, for instance, had only five mixed units, each with a total of ten 37mm guns, spread across eight infantry divisions. The complement of the Austrian field batteries was now raised to include twenty-four field guns, thirty-six field howitzers, and four heavy howitzers, in part to make up for the heavy artillery sent to the Italian Front.[48]

Thus the Austro-Hungarians came increasingly to rely on the strength of their forward position as the best, and sometimes the sole, means of defense, as a description of the Austrian Fourth Army's defenses from 4 June 1916—the day on which Brusilov launched his attack—clearly demonstrates:

The Eastern Front
June 1916
Frontline 4 June

Forces
German 9TH
Austrian 7TH
Russian 4TH

I. Position: 1st lines of all corps are completely capable of defense, [with] strengthened defensive trenches, [or] in the case of II Corps in swampy terrain, wooden breastworks erected. Sufficient traverses with concrete and stone positions built in exist. [. . .] The forward zones are well-flanked by machine guns. To combat the mining attacks of the enemy seven mine systems have been installed at predetermined points. The rolls [of wire] reach up to 106 meters forward from our own lines. Communications trenches to the rear are, for the most part, constructed as to be defendable.

The construction of the positions has been damaged by subsequent enemy artillery and grenade fire, and the work required to improve them has also been severely hindered in this fashion.

The second and third lines of the first position of the X Corps and Corps Szurmay are thoroughly prepared, [but in] II Corps only the strong points of the second line are present [and] the third line has barely been started.

Battle strong points for the commanders as well as observation points are present or under construction. In Corps Szurmay, there are four command strong points in the area of the 7th ID alone, and one in the area of the 70th ID.

II. Position: thoroughly defensible trenches with built-in strong points exist for X Corps and Corps Szurmay; II Corps has only strong points.

III. Position: those of the 41st, 2nd, and 70th divisions are completely ready; those of the 4th ID 60 percent and those of the 37th ID 90 percent ready. The 7th ID, however, does not have a third position.[49]

Along most of the line, the Central Powers had really only completed the front line of the first position by the beginning of June 1916. The Austrian Fourth Army reported on 1 May 1916 that the bridgehead positions on the Styr River near Lutsk remained incomplete because most of the troops had been sent to work on the forward positions.[50] Brusilov, because he had ordered extensive aerial reconnaissance, was well aware of such developments and altered his plans to take advantage. The commanders of the Central Powers, however, gave little or no thought to their rearward lines. On a visit to the sector of the front held by II Corps, X Corps, and Corps Szurmay in late May 1916, Linsingen had had nothing but praise for the defensive preparations.[51]

The narrow focus on creating a strong front line caused the Austrian commanders to neglect other aspects of their defensive strategy as well, namely training and active defense. Numerically, to be sure, the strength of the armies remained almost the same between January and June 1916; but as experienced units were drawn to the Tirolean Front, the general level of competence in the Habsburg armies declined.[52] On 14 February 1916, the Austrian Fourth Army, for instance, sent the 3rd Infantry Division—a unit with a decent fighting reputation made up of mostly German-speaking Austrians—to the Italian Front; in return Fourth Army received the 70th Honved (Hungarian Reserve) Infantry Division, a unit whose battle readiness was questionable, since it had never come under fire. Other experienced units were broken up, with battalions sent to serve as a "core" for new divisions of incoming recruits.

Not only did this weaken the units from which battle-hardened officers were drawn, it also failed to provide career officers in sufficient numbers for the new units to operate with confidence. When the Austrian Fourth Army amalgamated the 70th HID, for instance, it assigned three staff officers from each of three units (the 7th Infantry Division as well as the 37th and 41st Honved infantry divisions) to the new troops. This left each regiment of the with between one and four career officers—an average of one-quarter of an officer per company in the best case. The 7th Infantry Division was hardly better off; most regiments counted one career officer for every two companies. By the winter of 1915–16, the vast majority of officers in the Austro-Hungarian 8th Cavalry Division were young and untrained. They lived in trains behind the rearmost lines, where card parties complete with pastries and alcohol were the order of the day. One Austrian officer described it as "a regular Potemkin village" where war-weariness and rumors of a separate peace abounded.[53] The Austrian defensive doctrine, however, relied on "energetic officers" to roust men from the dugouts and foxholes at the appropriate time in case of an attack.[54]

The measure might still have been sufficient, however, had the Austrian commanders focused on training the new troops. The Austro-Hungarian armies upgraded their artillery considerably in the early months of 1916. The Austrian Fourth Army, for instance, increased its artillery complement by 45 percent, while the number of guns assigned to Army Group Linsingen (then part of Südarmee) rose from 578 to 748 in the first six months of the year. Many of the guns were of new manufacture, and the Austrian command had procured ammunition beyond previous supply levels. The spring levies also brought troop strength up considerably, transfers to the Tirolean Front notwithstanding. In the six months preceding the Brusilov Offensive, the Austro-Hungarians sent over 800,000 new troops to the Russian Front, along with nearly 16,000 new officers, while losses totaled only 206,455 men and just over 4,000 officers. In addition, over 38,000 German troops and 400 German officers were incorporated in the lines south of the Pripet River—though here again the quality of the troops was somewhat lower than normal, as the best German troops had been drawn off to fight at Verdun. By June, the sheer numbers of weapons, ammunition, and men on the Russian Front were at peak levels, and the health and supply for the troops was reported to be "satisfactory" almost without exception.[55]

For the most part, however, the new units were given little training. Instead, they were formed into labor groups and put to work strengthening the forward defenses. According to Lieutenant Alphons Bernhard, the six-week training course for reserves of the Austro-Hungarian 8th Cavalry Division consisted mostly of rifle drill, parades, and snow shoveling. They were given almost no training with hand grenades or live fire.[56] This had the dual effects of tiring the troops and establishing nonmilitary activity as the "norm" on the front lines.[57] In Trostinec, where the Austrian II Corps was stationed, a decidedly nonmilitary domesticity was the result:

> In front of all the houses were enclosures made of birch, portals, well-maintained entrances, order and cleanliness overall. Wooden sidewalks, wooden roads. In comparison to the earlier, Russian version of Trostinec it was a treasure. Many residents (700–800) had apparently returned. In the officers' mess building there was a fresco signed by RP Hirschenhauser on one wall of the breakfast room (others by Liebenwein) featuring a young Russian peasant girl at the spinning wheel.[58]

Most of the Habsburg commanders reported that this type of activity built morale and that they were "satisfied" with the training level of the troops under their command, but often this was a justification rather than a realistic evaluation. The commander of the Austrian 10th Cavalry Division, for instance, reported his troops as "fully trained for combat" in mid-May 1916, despite the fact that they had not been either in combat or training for combat for several months. Likewise Feldzugmeister Sellner registered at one and the same time his satisfaction with his troops, particularly the Austrian 2nd Infantry Division, and his doubts about the attack readiness of the battalions in the front lines.[59] An inspection report of the Austrian Second Army from 13 May 1916 is typical:

> The troops are healthy and look good; one notes in each and every one the caring influence of the officers, the military doctors, and the higher command. The construction of the front shows exceptional industry, understanding and determination. One sees everywhere the striving to bring the rearward lines and positions up to the same strength as the forward ones. [. . .] The effort to decorate the dugouts is also a welcome sign of the good spirits.[60]

This offers a clear reflection of the Austro-Hungarian attitude; they were not worried about offensive capability, but concerned primarily with the strength of their defensive positions. On 2 June 1916, Colonel Stoltzmann, General Linsingen's chief of staff, dismissed the chances of a Russian offensive. The Russians, he noted, lacked sufficient numbers, relied on "stupid" tactics, and thus had absolutely no chance of success—not even "beginner's luck"—against what he saw as the Central Powers' "formidable positions."[61]

Preoccupied with the Italian offensive and confident in their defensive preparations, the Austrian commanders almost completely discounted Russian preparations despite overwhelming evidence that Brusilov was preparing for a different kind of assault. Conrad considered the Russian Front only insofar as it might provide him with more and better troops for the Italian campaign, and Emperor Franz Josef supported this assessment. Falkenhayn, for his part, was both absorbed by the Verdun campaign and disgusted by Conrad's insistence on proceeding with the Italian offensive against the German's advice. As a result, he largely ignored developments on the Eastern Front.[62] This left the German general von Linsingen in charge, nominally, of the Central Powers' forces on the southern half of the Eastern Front.

Linsingen's authority was far from complete, however; the Habsburg Archduke Joseph Friedrich, in command of the Austrian Fourth Army stationed near Kovel, steadfastly refused to acknowledge the German as a superior. Though Conrad thought little of him as a commander and had even hoped to be able to dismiss him after the disasters of 1915, the archduke—who also happened to be the godson of the German emperor—had been elevated to the newly created rank of "colonel general" in February 1916 on the grounds that having a German in command of Habsburg troops was an affront to the imperial prestige. The German High Command had responded by elevating Linsingen to the same rank—and backdating the command so that the archduke had never, theoretically, been solely in charge of the front.[63] Communication between Linsingen and the Austrian Fourth Army took place exclusively by telegraph thereafter.[64] This kind of political competition, both between the supposedly allied staffs and within the Habsburg command itself, where rivalries were rife, provided ample distraction from the "meaningless" activities of the Russians during the last of the winter months.[65]

The individual Habsburg commanders nevertheless were well aware of both the increasing Russian activity in the spring of 1916 and the new tactics the French had pioneered in the Champagne Offensive the previous autumn. Officers of the Südarmee noted an increase in Russian aerial reconnaissance as early as mid-March, while Brusilov was still commander of the Russian Eighth Army; a downed Russian flier had informed them of a program to train aerial observers.[66] In the first half of May 1916, units in the Austrian Second Army reported that the Russians were sapping trenches forward persistently.[67] A circular from the command of the Austrian Fourth Army dated 6 May 1916 informed the troops that a Joffre attack would be preceded by the creation of *place d'armees*, an increase in aerial reconnaissance, and the sapping of multiple trenches toward their own front lines.[68] The Austrian Second Army informed headquarters on the 13th that "[r]ecently the enemy has been striving to bring his positions closer to our obstacles along the entire army front. The same process has also been observed by other armies. The aim of this activity is presently unclear."[69] During 18–19 May, Corps Szurmay in the Austrian Fourth Army relayed reports from Russian deserters that an attack was pending at the end of the month and that the Russians were sapping trenches forward opposite the Austrian 2nd Infantry Division.[70] On 21 May, reports from Second Army noted that the Russians had begun to dig foxholes in forward positions, and were even at work on underground passages.[71] By the 23rd, it was clear to Army Group Benigni (part of the Austrian Seventh Army) that the Russians were preparing to attack on the sector of the front held by the 42nd Honved Infantry Division and the Austrian 3rd Cavalry Division.[72] On 2 June, Second Army noted increasing troop movements, and the following day observers noted that the Russian units had cut their wire obstacles. Reports of continued Russian sapping were constant and increasing.[73] All the signs that a Russian attack was pending, as noted in the bulletin of 21 May, were present.

The Habsburg field commanders took what might be deemed reasonable countermeasures, shifting reserves to areas that appeared most threatened and attempting to disrupt the Russian preparations.[74] The Austrian 2nd Infantry Division sent a patrol on the night of 31 March–1 April 1916 to destroy the Russian sapping trench.[75] Patrols became larger and more frequent as the Russian activity increased. On the night of 28–29 April, for instance, the Habsburg 7th Infantry Division sent several companies out to destroy new Russian forward positions; the action captured nearly two hundred prisoners but cost the Austro-Hungarians more than seven hundred casualties when the Russians counterattacked. A second attempt to halt the Russian sapping on the following night cost the 7th Infantry Division another seventy-five men, including three officers.[76] Given the reigning doctrine of the superiority of the Central Powers' defenses, however, many Habsburg officers doubtless regarded such measures as either futile or unnecessary.[77]

Attempts to dislodge the Russians using artillery proved nearly as futile, in part because Habsburg field commanders felt obliged to save munitions. When Linsingen reported that his commanders needed more shells to effectively combat Russian sapping and forays into no-man's land in early April, for instance, the Austrian High Command replied that "the use of munitions for aimless firing and so-called registration fire has been restricted, but not that for important tasks."[78] Requests from the Second Army for more howitzer shells found a similarly confusing response. This abdication of responsibility made it difficult for officers in the field to judge which tasks would be important enough to warrant artillery fire, especially while the Habsburg offensive in Italy was in full swing.[79] When ordered to destroy the forward Russian trenches with artillery fire on 2 June 1916, for instance, the commander of X Corps replied that "[t]he necessity of such measures is well-known [. . .] but the necessary munitions are lacking."[80] Other parts of the Austrian Second Army, however, reported frequent skirmishes and grenade battles.[81] Units of the Austro-Hungarian Fourth Army also engaged in regular, indeed almost nightly, artillery actions intended to destroy Russian trenches and disrupt further sapping throughout April and May.[82] Subsequent studies have revealed that the Austro-Hungarian artillery almost doubtless possessed sufficient munitions to disrupt the Russian activity had the commanders chosen to do so.

The indifference of the Austrian High Command, however, combined with a defensive doctrine that placed its faith in established positions defended by concentrated artillery fire, created a false confidence. Even as reports of Russian troop movements increased and indications that an attack was imminent mounted, the Central Powers remained relatively unconcerned. When Conrad and Falkenhayn met at the German headquarters in Pless for the last time before the Brusilov Offensive, on 23 May 1916, the situation seemed to be well in hand. They deemed the possibility that Romania would enter the war remote, and neither commander saw any reason why the Austrians could not hold the front against the Russians as things stood.[83]

Last-Minute Complications

The Russian commanders, on the other hand, grew increasingly agitated as the date for the offensive came nearer. For one thing, the success of the Austro-Hungarian offensive in Italy created intense pressure to bring the timetable for the attack forward and cast the Russian preparations in doubt. On 19 May, only four days after Conrad had launched his attacks in the Tirol, the Italian representative at Stavka requested that the planned offensive go forward immediately to relieve the Austrian pressure on Italy. Tsarina Alexandra arranged a private meeting with Brusilov to inquire—without result—if the offensive was ready to go forward. A second, more urgent request came on 23 May. Alekseev protested that the fronts were not yet prepared, and both Kuropatkin and Evert agreed, stating that they could do nothing to advance the timetable. Brusilov said he would be ready to attack on 1 June. Believing that he would be unable to ensure adequate supplies for all three fronts in such a short time, Alekseev proposed that the offensive be staggered, with Brusilov attacking on 4 June and Evert following suit ten days later. The Russian chief of staff also pleaded with Brusilov to reduce his front in light of these developments. Brusilov's subordinates—Kaledin, Letschitski, and Scherbatschev—added their voices to that of Alekseev. The Southwestern Front, they argued, was merely a sideshow.

Brusilov agreed to wait the three additional days to attack on the condition that Alekseev (and presumably Evert) would ask for no more delays, as that would imperil his design. Alekseev agreed and, after the tsar approved the revised plan on 26 May, issued the directive for the attack on 31 May 1916. He also sent the V Siberian Corps to augment Brusilov's forces, hoping to make the blow strong enough to divert German troops from the north prior to Evert's attack there. His attempts to convince Brusilov to alter his tactics, however, were unsuccessful. The main attack on the Southwestern Front was to be carried forward by the Russian Eighth Army in Volhynia. All four of the army's corps plus its entire mobile reserve—148 battalions in all—would strike northwest from Dubno toward the railway junction at Kovel, supported by twenty-four batteries of heavy artillery. In the south, the Russian Ninth Army would attack along the Dniester River near the Romanian border, while in the center the Russian Eleventh and the Russian Seventh would aim at Sapanov and Tarnopol, respectively. In accordance with Alekseev's plan, Brusilov declared that there was no strategic aim to the attacks; the bulk of the Russian forces, therefore, were to concentrate on simply destroying the Austro-Hungarian forces.

Unhappy with this declaration, and perhaps driven by news that the Italians appeared to be stabilizing the Tirolean Front, Alekseev made one last attempt to persuade Brusilov to change his plans. On the evening of 3 June 1916 Alekseev telephoned Brusilov to ask, purportedly on behalf of the tsar himself, that he postpone the attack and reassemble his forces for a consolidated attack at a later date. Brusilov refused, and offered to resign rather than undermine the confidence of his troops at such a late hour. Alekseev hesitated, claiming that he could not wake the tsar to ask for a decision on the matter, but Brusilov insisted. Reluctantly, Alekseev gave in; "God be with you," he said. "Act according to your own judgment. I will inform the Tsar of our conversation in the morning."[84]

CHAPTER THREE

THE OFFENSIVE BEGINS

General Brusilov issued the order for the offensive to begin at 1 AM on 4 June 1916. "It is time to drive out the dishonorable enemy," he wrote. "All armies on our front are attacking at the same time. I am convinced that our iron armies will win the victory."[1] The basic plan remained intact: the main thrust—which was still intended as a diversion from the central action against the German forces in the north—would be carried out by Eighth Army. The attacks by the Seventh, Ninth, and Eleventh armies were to pin down the Habsburg forces on the remainder of the front and prevent reinforcements from moving north. At the last minute, however, Brusilov decided to add the railway junction at Kovel as a secondary target for Eighth Army and sent two cavalry divisions to strengthen its right wing for that purpose.[2]

The Russian guns opened up at 4:00 AM along the entire front as ordered, but the display was far from impressive. After three hours of steady, concentrated, but not overwhelming shelling, the Russian guns fell quiet again. The Habsburg forces rushed to man their forward lines, anticipating the attacks their intelligence had been predicting. The Russians, however, remained in their trenches while observers checked the damage done to the Austro-Hungarian positions. Only a few weak reconnaissance patrols emerged to challenge the Habsburg forces; after an hour or so, the shelling resumed—slow, steady, and deadly accurate.[3]

Colonel Rudolf Kundmann was in the Austro-Hungarian Army's headquarters at 10:30 that morning, celebrating what seemed to be a favorable turn of events. Not only did the date mark the sixtieth birthday of Field Marshal Conrad, but there was also news of panic in both Rome and St. Petersburg. Rumors flew about serious negotiations for a separate peace between the Russians and the Germans that were well underway—and, incidentally, the Russians had opened a bombardment along the Austro-Hungarian Front. Kundmann was sure it was nothing to worry about.[4] In the headquarters of the German Army Supreme Command (OHL), Quartermaster General Erich Ludendorff dismissed the attacks as insignificant—"demonstrations," as he wrote later—upon hearing the initial reports.[5] Likewise Erich von Falkenhayn, the German commander in chief, believed that the Russians were mounting local attacks both to relieve the Italians and to reconnoiter the ground for a July offensive that would be launched in conjunction with British and French efforts on the Western Front.[6]

Reports from the northern half of the Austro-Hungarian Front certainly supported these conclusions, and the commanders of the Central Powers' armies were confident in their defenses against the usual, plodding efforts of the Russians. The concentration of fire against the 2nd Infantry Division and the 70th Honved (Hungarian Reserve) Infantry Division of the Austrian Fourth Army made it clear that the Russians intended to attack toward the railway junction at Kovel, exactly as expected. The Austrian Fourth Army command immediately dispatched the 10th Cavalry Division to reinforce the strong point of Lutsk in accordance with its own planning.[7] An aerial force was dispatched to bomb the headquarters of the Russian Eighth Army at Olyka; to calm the nerves of the Habsburg commanders and nip rumors of a shell shortage in the bud, the Austro-Hungarian High Command (AOK) sent additional supplies of shell to its armies. At the same time, the Habsburg army commanders were cautioned to use their ammunition sparingly.[8]

Colonel General Alexander von Linsingen, the de facto front commander for the northern sectors, also sent messages warning his generals to husband their reserves for a concentrated counterattack once the Russian infantry had shattered against the Austro-Hungarian positions. He fully expected to halt the "weak attack undertaken by the Russians to counter [the Habsburg] success in the south Tirol" without having to deploy significant reserves.[9] Even if the Russian attack managed to break the Austro-Hungarian lines, Linsingen believed the Central Powers already had in place adequate forces to contain and eventually repel the invader.

The Central Powers' Order of Battle on the Russian Southwestern Front, 4 June 1916

Headquarters: Teschen
Commander in Chief: *Feldmarschall* Franz Conrad von Hötzendorf
Chief of Staff:
Quartermaster: *Feldzugmeister* Franz Kranik

Army Group Linsingen*
Headquarters: Kovel
Commander: *General Oberst* Alexander von Linsingen
Group Gronau (82nd ID, 5th KD, Guards KD, 81st ID, 65th ID) *General der Kavallerie* von Gronau
Cavalry Corps Hauer; *General der Kavallerie* Hauer
Polish Legion (11th HID, 9th KD) *Generalmajor* von Puchalski
Corps Fath (26th ID, 53rd ID) *General der Infanterie* Fath

Fourth Army*
Headquarters: Lutsk
Commander: *General Oberst* Archduke Josef Ferdinand
X Corps (37th HID, 2nd ID) *General der Infanterie* Martiny
Corps Szurmay (70th ID, 7th ID) *General der Infanterie* Szurmay
II Corps (4th ID, 41st HID) *Feldmarschalleutnant* Kaiser

First Army**
Headquarters: Ziechov
Commander: *General der Infanterie* Paul Puhallo von Brlog
XVIII Corps (7th KD, 46th ID, 25th ID) *Feldmarschalleutnant* Czibulka
Group Marwitz (7th (German) ID, 22nd ID, 107th ID, 48th (German) ID) *General der Kavallerie* von der Marwitz

Second Army**
Headquarters: Brody
Commander: *General Oberst* Eduard *Freiherr* Böhm-Ermolli
Group Kosak (17th ID, 4th KD, 29th ID) *Feldmarschalleutnant* Kosak
V Corps (31st ID) *Feldmarschalleutnant* von Goglia
IV Corps (14th ID, 33rd ID) *General der Infanterie* Schmidt von Georgenegg

Südarmee
Headquarters: Brzesany
Commander: *General der Infanterie* Count Felix von Bothmer
IX Corps (19th ID, 32nd ID) *Feldmarschalleutnant* Kralicek
Corps Hofman (54th ID, 55th ID) *Feldmarschalleutnant* Hofmann
48th Reserve Infantry Division (German)

* The Austrian Fourth Army was technically under the command of Army Group Linsingen.
** The Austrian First Army and Second Army formed Army Group Böhm-Ermolli.

Seventh Army
Headquarters: Kolomea
Commander: *General der Kavallerie* Karl von Pflanzer-Baltin
   VI Corps (39th and 12th IDs) *General der Infanterie* Arz von Straussenberg
   XIII Corps (36th ID, 2nd KD, 15th ID) *General der Infanterie* Rhemen
   Group Hadfy (6th KD, 21st ID) *General der Infanterie* Hadfy
   Group Benigni (51st ID, 5th KD, 8th KD, 42nd ID, 30th ID, 3rd KD) *Feldzugmeister* von Benigni
   XI Corps (24th ID, 40th ID, 5th ID, Brigade Papp, Hauptmann Grund) *General der Kavallerie* von Korda

His own army group, consisting of (north to south) the German Group commanded by General Gronau (3rdInfantry Division and 2nd Cavalry Division), Cavalry Corps Hauer (3rd Cavalry Division and the 7th Brigade of the Polish Legion), Corps Fath, II Corps, and Fourth Army (X Corps and Corps Szurmay) under Archduke Josef Ferdinand, held the northern end of the Habsburg line. It faced the Russian Eighth Army under the command of General Aleksei M. Kaledin (XXXIX Corps, VIII Corps, XL Corps, XLV Corps, and the 3rd Cavalry Division) and parts of the Russian Eleventh Army (XXXII Corps and XVII Corps) under the command of General Sakharov. Because Brusilov had assigned the Eighth the key role in the offensive, all of the Russians' mobile reserves (4th Finnish Infantry Division, 12th Cavalry Division, and the 24th Heavy Artillery Division) were placed under Kaledin's command as well, giving the Russians a numerical advantage of some 50,000 men. Eighth Army also commanded more than half of Brusilov's artillery. On his crucial 48-kilometer front, Kaledin placed 206 field guns, 44 field howitzers, 44 heavy howitzers, 22 heavy cannon, and 4 medium howitzers.[10]

The center of the Austro-Hungarian line was held by Army Group Böhm-Ermolli. On its left wing stood the Austrian First Army under General Puhallo (XVIIII Corps supplemented to the north by the 7th and 81st infantry divisions as well as by Cavalry Corps Ostermuth), which covered Linsingen's southern flank opposite the remainder of the Russian Eleventh (VI Corps, V Siberian, and XLV Corps). To Puhallo's right were Second Army (Group Kosak [5th Infantry Division and 1st Cavalry Division], V Corps, and IV Corps) under the direct command of General Eduard Freiherr von Böhm-Ermolli and then Südarmee under the Bavarian General Count Felix von Bothmer, which included the German 48th Reserve Infantry Division and Corps Hoffmann along with the Austrian IX Corps. Against them was arrayed half of General Dmitri G. Scherbatschev's Sev-

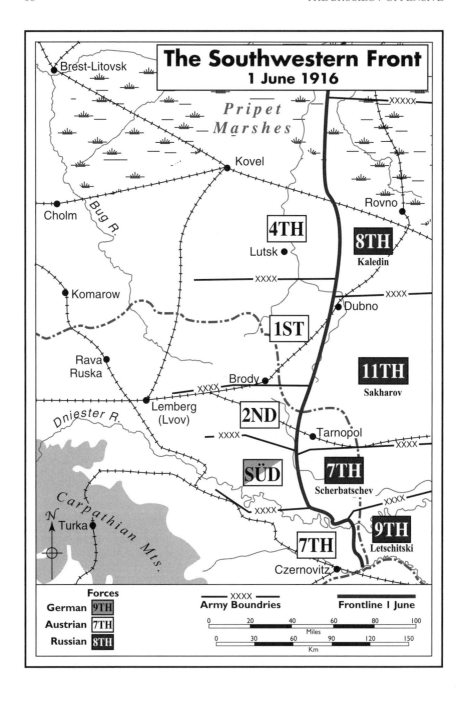

The Southwestern Front
1 June 1916

Brest-Litovsk

Pripet Marshes

Kovel

Cholm

Bug R.

Rovno

4TH

Lutsk

8TH
Kaledin

Komarow

XXXX

XXXX

Dubno

1ST

Rava Ruska

Brody

11TH
Sakharov

Dniester R.

Lemberg (Lvov)

XXXX

2ND

Tarnopol

XXXX

SÜD

7TH
Scherbatschev

Carpathian Mts.

N

Turka

XXXX

9TH
Letschitski

XXXX

7TH

Czernovitz

Forces

German **9TH**

Austrian **7TH**

Russian **8TH**

XXXX
Army Boundries

Frontline 1 June

| 0 | 20 | 40 | 60 | 80 | 100 |

Miles

| 0 | 30 | 60 | 90 | 120 | 150 |

Km

enth Army (XXXIII Corps, III Caucasian, and VII Siberian, along with II Cavalry and a combined cavalry division). On the southern end of the front the Austrian Seventh Army under General Karl von Pflanzer-Baltin (north to south: VI Corps [12th Infantry Division and 5th Cavalry Division], XIII Corps, Group Hadfy, Army Group Benigni, and XI Corps) faced the remaining units of the Russian Seventh (north to south: XXII Corps, XLI Corps, and XVI Corps) and the Russian Ninth Army under General Letschitski (XXVI Corps, II Corps, XXXVI Corps, XXIV Corps, and V Cavalry Corps).

While the Russians held a small advantage in numbers and guns on almost every sector of the front, only the Russian Eighth possessed anything near overwhelming superiority. Overall, the Russians deployed some 650,000 men (including more than 50,000 cavalry) on their Southwestern Front, while the opposing Austro-Hungarian forces numbered almost 500,000 men, including 30,000 German troops and 22,000 cavalry.[11] Linsingen, like the Habsburg commanders, firmly believed that any shortfall in the numbers of men and artillery was more than compensated for by well-prepared, tried-and-true defensive positions and by the quality of their officer corps. For nearly a month, the Austro-Hungarian forces had been preparing for attacks against Okna in the south, Tarnopol in the center, and Kovel in the north, with the main weight of Russian forces expected to advance against the last objective.[12]

The Russian artillery lifted around noon, and the Austrian artillery, expecting an infantry attack, began raining fire on the open ground in front of its defensive positions. But the Russian infantry again remained in the trenches, with the exception of reconnaissance forces and a few weak probing units. As the afternoon wore on a hail of grenades and mortars fell intermittently on the Habsburg lines, sending the troops scurrying back to their dugouts. Not until almost 6 PM on 4 June did the first strong Russian infantry battalions emerge from their trenches and push across no-man's land to attack the Austrian positions. When darkness fell, the Russian thrust had been repulsed everywhere along his sector of the front. Linsingen's predictions had been borne out, as few Habsburg reserves were called upon in the effort. Despite the heavy and prolonged Russian artillery fire, the Austrian Fourth Army stationed near Lutsk, for example, reported few wounded and little damage to its defenses. Corps Szurmay reported sixty-two dead and 177 wounded. The mixed Austro-German Südarmee under General Bothmer held the southern end of the northern half of the front with little effort.[13]

The Austrian Second Army around Sapanov had not been so fortunate. While the Russian artillery barrage had created few casualties, it had achieved Brusilov's objectives. Long stretches of Second Army's defensive obstacles had been shredded, and entire stretches of trenches collapsed. The Austrians' communications between front and rear had been thoroughly disrupted. Confused by the pauses between barrages, the troops were increasingly hesitant to man the front lines. When thirteen armored vehicles of General Sakharov's Eleventh Army appeared out of the smoke and dust along the Tarnopol-Lemberg railway line, the Habsburg forces were thrown into disarray. This allowed the Russian 3rd Infantry Division to push into the second position occupied by Second Army's Krakow 16th Light Infantry Regiment close to where the Austrian First and Second armies' fronts met.

At roughly the same time, a Russian infantry thrust collapsed the Austrian First Army's forward position on the east bank of the Ikvanie River and threatened the seam from the opposite direction. A counterattack by a Viennese *Landsturm* brigade stationed on the southern wing of the Austrian Second Army then forced the Russians back across the Ikvanie River. To strengthen the connection between the Austrian First and Second armies, however, the Austrian High Command shifted the Austrian 25th Infantry Division (Fourth Army) from its position near Lutsk to Sapanov. It was a small move that would have important consequences.[14]

Even as the Austrian 25th Infantry Division was en route to Sapanov, First Army's 84th Infantry Regiment launched a night counterattack to regain the bridgehead First Army had held previously with disastrous results. The bridgehead position had been unfavorable to begin with, surrounded on three sides by Russian artillery and cut off from the main Austro-Hungarian forces by the river; First Army command maintained that it was important for "prestige purposes." Shortly after the attack began at 9:45 PM, however, the troops of the 84th Infantry Regiment found they were surrounded; forty-nine officers and almost two thousand men were lost before the remainder of the regiment made it back across the river to safety.[15]

The Breakthrough at Okna

Things were going even worse for the Austrians on the southern half of the Russian Front, where the High Command believed it held strong positions on either side of the Dniester River. On the far right wing, abutting the Romanian border and protecting the important junction at Czernovitz, was the Austrian XI Corps (Seventh Army) commanded by General Korda. In the center of the line (moving north) were Army Group Benigni and Army Group Hadfy, consisting of two corps each. On the northern end of the front, in contact with Bothmer's Südarmee and covering the road to Lemberg, were XIII Corps (Lieutenant General Rhemen) and VI Corps (Lieutenant General Arz). The Austrian Seventh Army withstood the initial, predawn Russian artillery barrage on 4 June—which included gas shells—with few casualties and little trouble. Though the Russian Ninth continued to shell the Austrians for nearly two days, it had little direct effect on the troops. Reports indicate the Austrians suffered only two dead and twelve "deafened" in those sectors.[16]

The commander of the Austrian Seventh Army, General Pflanzer-Baltin, had been expecting the attack for weeks and prepared his positions taking the direction of the most intensive Russian sapping into account. With eleven infantry divisions and four cavalry divisions facing only ten Russian infantry divisions and four Russian cavalry divisions, Pflanzer-Baltin had good reason to be confident in his defenses. Despite the reputation of the Russian XI and XII Corps (Ninth Army) as crack troops, Benigni and Korda had held firm during the winter battles of 1915–16 and inflicted severe casualties upon the enemy. Four of the battle-hardened Austro-Hungarian units that had defended that sector (the 3rd, 10th, 34th, and 43rd IDs), however, were now in Italy, and most of Seventh Army's heavy artillery had since been diverted to the Tirolean offensive as well. Pflanzer-Baltin nonetheless had sixteen battalions in reserve, and his remaining Hungarian and Croatian troops had a reputation for unwavering loyalty. As with the Austrian First and Fourth armies, however, the Austrian Seventh would crack because of small and apparently meaningless oversights.

Just a few days before Brusilov launched his offensive, Pflanzer-Baltin took the 79th Honved Infantry Brigade from the 30th Infantry Division, which was intended as the army reserve, and put it in the front line of the army group commanded by General Benigni. While he had no particular reason to doubt the mettle of the Hungarians, Pflanzer-Baltin knew that the 79th was untested in battle. Like many of the troops sent to replace units diverted to Tyrol, the 79th had spent most of the winter shoveling snow and drilling, not training. Nonetheless, he placed it not only directly in the path of the anticipated Russian attack, but also directly opposite the Russian 3rd Transamur Infantry Division—and Central Asian troops had a reputation for giving no quarter to Hungarians, who thus feared them more than other Russian units. The most glaring error in Pflanzer-Baltin's calculations, however, was that the 79th Honved Infantry Brigade contained more than twice as many men as the unit it replaced in the line. This meant that the defensive lines, though well built, provided inadequate shelter for the men of the 79th Honved Infantry Brigade. Those who could took shelter during the initial shelling from two hundred Russian guns, but a pause of fifteen minutes drew them out of the claustrophobic shelters. The renewed Russian artillery barrage, more precisely directed in the light of day, took a fearsome toll both physically and mentally.[17]

When the well-prepared Russian attack on the southern end of the front unfolded around noon on 5 June, it met little resistance. Letschitski had chosen to attack in a narrow sector perhaps 4,000 yards wide and crisscrossed with ravines that limited the range and effectiveness of the Austro-Hungarian artillery. His own staff had managed to procure twenty-three heavy guns from the Black Sea fortress of Ochakov that, with a range of up to 9,000 yards and firing high explosive shells, afforded the Russians a singular advantage. Nineteen of those guns were brought to bear on the front Letschitski had chosen for the attack. Having sapped within one hundred paces and then removed their own obstacles during the artillery barrage, three Russian infantry divisions—the 11th, the 32nd, and the 3rd Trans-amur—were upon the Habsburg forces before they had time to organize their defenses.[18] The 79th Honved Infantry Brigade simply gave way; 4,600 of the brigade's 5,200 men became casualties or prisoners of the Russians. Four Habsburg batteries were captured as well. Shocked and, by his own account, ill, Pflanzer-Baltin rushed fifteen battalions of reserves forward piecemeal to stem the tide. By 3:00 PM the initial advance thus had been halted, but in keeping with Brusilov's prescribed tactics Letschitski broadened the attack by sending additional divisions forward to roll up enemy lines. Russian forces took more than 4,000 Austro-Hungarian prisoners.

This renewed thrust took the right wing of the Russian Ninth primarily in a southwesterly direction, toward the Austro-Hungarian position at Okna, though the Croatian 42nd Infantry Division was driven from its front line to the north as well. By 6:00 PM, the Russian Ninth Army had overrun the Austrian position at Czarny Potok and taken another 7,000 Habsburg troops prisoner. Only the continual influx of Austrian reserves along with nightfall and sheer exhaustion on the part of the advancing Russians brought a halt to the battle that evening. Benigni's remaining troops were forced to entrench in open fields more than five kilometers behind their original lines, having lost almost one-third of their artillery.[19]

The Russian Order of Battle on the Southwestern Front, 4 June 1916

Headquarters of the Southwestern Front: Berdichev
Commander in Chief: *General der Kavallrie* Aleksei A. Brusilov
Chief of Staff: *General Lieutenant* Klembovski
Quartermaster: *General Lieutenant* Dukhonin

Eighth Army
Headquarters: Rovno
Commander: *General der Kavallrie* Aleksei M. Kaledin
V Cavalry Corps (Orenburg Cossack KD, 11th KD); *General Lieutenant* Veliarshev
XXX Corps (71st, 80th, and 100th IDs); *General Lieutenant* Zaionchkovski
XXXIX Corps (125th and 102nd IDs); *General Lieutenant* Stelnitski
XL Corps (2nd and 4th Rifle Divisions); *General Lieutenant* Kastalinski
VIII Corps (14th and 15th IDs); *General Lieutenant* Vladimir Dragomirov
XXXII Corps (101st and 105th IDs); *General Lieutenant* Federov
7th and 12th KDs

Eleventh Army
Headquarters: Volochisk
Commander: *General der Kavallrie* Vladimir V. Sakharov
XVII Corps (3rd and 35th IDs); *General Lieutenant* Yakovlev
Transamur KD
VII Corps (10th and 34th IDs); *General Lieutenant* Ekk
VI Corps (16th and 4th IDs); *General Lieutenant* Gutor
XVIII Corps (37th and 23rd IDs); *General Lieutenant* Kruzenstern

Seventh Army
Headquarters: Guzyatin
Commander: *General der Infantrie* Dmitrii G. Scherbatschev
XXII Corps (1st and 3rd Finland IDs); *General Lieutenant* von der Brincken
XVI Corps (47th and 41st IDs); *General Lieutenant* Savich
II Corps (26th and 43rd IDs); *General Lieutenant* Pflug
3rd Turkestan ID
II Cavalry Corps (Composite Cossack KD, 2nd Don Cossack Cavalry Brigade, Composite, Cossack Cavalry Brigade, 9th KD)
1st Independent Cavalry Brigade
V Caucasian Corps
2nd Finland ID Front Reserve
4th Finland ID

Ninth Army
Headquarters: Kamenets-Podolsk
Commander: *General der Infantrie* Platon A. Letschitski
XXXIII Corps (1st and 2nd Transamur IDs); *General Lieutenant* Krilov
XLI Corps (74th and 3rd Transamur IDs); *General Lieutenant* Belkovich
XI Corps (11th and 32nd IDs); *General Lieutenant* Barantsev
XII Corps (19th and 12th IDs); *General Lieutenant* Kaznakov
Composite Corps (82nd and 103rd IDs)
III Cavalry Corps (1st Don Cossack KD, Terek Cossack KD, 10th KD); *General Lieutenant* Count Keller

Letschitski, however, did not press the Austrians as hard as he might have. Not until noon the following day, following a renewed but unfocused artillery barrage, did he send XII Corps forward in an attempt to retake the heights of Czarny Potok they had abandoned to the Austrians overnight. The Russians found, however, that without the precise artillery preparation and the element of surprise their attacks declined in effectiveness. The reorganized Habsburg artillery shredded the deep waves of advancing Russian infantry, firing on them even when they had reached the forward Austrian positions. Though the positions changed hands four times in the course of the day and casualties mounted steadily on both sides, Pflanzer-Baltin's troops still held the line when darkness fell on 5 June. The Austrian reserves, however, were being consumed at an alarming rate. The 16th Infantry Regiment, for example, lost 2,300 men (of 3,200) during the course of the day, forcing Pflanzer-Baltin to send units from the 51st Honved Infantry Division and the 8th Cavalry Division to plug the gap in the line. He therefore decided to pull back under cover of darkness, crossing the Dniester River to establish a shorter, more defensible line on the south bank. When this position held against renewed Russian attacks on 6 June, it appeared that disaster had been averted.[20]

It had not; misfortune merely struck the Austrian Seventh Army on the northern flank the following day instead. While Letschitski's Ninth Army licked its wounds in the south, Scherbatschev's Seventh Army launched an assault against the left wing of Pflanzer-Baltin's overstretched forces. With only twenty-three heavy guns, Scherbatschev chose to deploy II Corps (26th, 34th, and the 3rd Turkestan Guards infantry divisions) along a narrow, seven-kilometer front opposite the town of Jazlovice, where the Russian positions overlooked a small salient in the Habsburg line east of the Strypa River. He believed the defenses to be particularly vulnerable at that point because some 80 percent of the Habsburg troops of the 36th Infantry Division holding the line there were ethnic Slavs. For the first two days of the offensive, Scherbatschev restricted his attacks, using his heavy artillery against the Jazlovice positions and gas grenades on other sectors of the front. British Major General Alfred Knox, a liaison to the Russian forces, reported that:

> The guns opened fire at 4 a.m. on June 4th. The enemy replied by firing at the Russian observation posts and batteries, but soon ceased, as it afterwards transpired, because all his telephone wires had been cut.
>   Fire was continued all day methodically with careful observation of each

shot. After dark the volume of fire slackened and was chiefly directed upon the passages cut through the enemy's wire during the day to prevent all possibility of repair.

From 12.30 midnight to 2.30 a.m. on the 5th, fire was lifted to enable scouts to examine results. After dawn, fire was once more directed on the enemy's front lines.

The results "exceeded all expectations." The first line was entirely destroyed; the second and third lines were destroyed with the exception of some of the shelters.[21]

Not until 4:00 on the morning of 6 June though, following a short but intense artillery bombardment, did the Russian infantry move against the Habsburg lines. They met with limited success, pushing elements of the Austro-Hungarian 15th Infantry Division back almost two kilometers from the first line and briefly establishing a foothold in the second line before the Austrians deployed reserves to retake it. By nightfall, the Habsburg artillery had pinned the Russians down all along the five-kilometer breakthrough, forcing them to dig in.

Both sides had lost about 6,000 men in the day's engagement, but while the Russians had ample reserves, the Austrians could ill-afford the casualties. At 10:00 PM on 6 June the commander of the Austrian 15th Infantry Division, Major General Rhemen, reported from the field that his unit was no longer capable of defense. Pflanzer-Baltin had already sent four battalions from VI Corps south to assist in the defense of Jazlovice and two regiments of dragoons were en route from Hadfy's forces as well, yet he had no reinforcements available to give the 15th Infantry Division. Those he had not sent forward on 6 June he had sent south to Benigni in the previous days. Thus when Scherbatschev sent elements of the II Cavalry Corps forward at noon on 7 June after bombarding the Jazlovice positions all morning, the Austrian 15th Infantry Division collapsed. Some 7,000 troops simply surrendered on the spot, while others fled heedlessly to the third position behind the Strypa River. Rhemen, gathering together what forces he could the next day, told Pflanzer-Baltin that in his opinion the battle for the Strypa was lost; XIII Corps was in shock, demoralized, and incapable of further resistance.

As the Habsburg commander pondered this news around noon on 8 June, panicked reports came in that the 36th Infantry Division, on the left flank of XIII Corps, was in retreat as well. The reports were false; though the Russians had temporarily seized the unit's second line, the Austrians recovered it even as news of the "retreat" reached Pflanzer-Baltin. When he heard of the purported retreat though, General Arz, in command of VI Corps adjoining the 36th Infantry Division to the north, declared that he was pulling back to the northwest in order to protect his southern flank. Pflanzer-Baltin, already convinced that the Russians would drive northwest toward Lemberg (Lvov), began to plan for a broad strategic retreat that would take the center of Seventh Army back behind the Dniester and Pruth rivers—some 80 kilometers to the rear. He ordered Arz to withdraw to the south and west. While Pflanzer-Baltin recognized that this would separate Seventh Army from the Südarmee and create a gap of some 100 kilometers in the Central Powers' line, he believed it was more important to keep his forces together. If he could manage that, he argued, Seventh Army would be positioned to strike at the exposed Russian flank when Scherbatschev moved against Lemberg. Arz appealed to Conrad, as did Bothmer, the commander of Südarmee, who asked that VI Corps be placed under his command to prevent such drastic action. The Habsburg commander in chief declined Bothmer's request, but ordered Pflanzer-Baltin to maintain contact with Südarmee at all costs.

While this drama played out from 8 to 9 June, the Russian Seventh was moving slowly forward. Scherbatschev's cavalry units forced the Habsburg 2nd Cavalry Division out of its position in the middle of XIII Corps's line in the afternoon of 9 June, which now truly forced the 36th Infantry Division to its north to withdraw to the third position as well. VI Corps had no choice but to bend its south wing back as well the following day in order to cover its flank and maintain contact to XIII Corps. By the afternoon of 10 June, XIII Corps had managed to entrench itself behind the Koropiec River, some 30 kilometers east of the Strypa. VI Corps, which Conrad now placed under Bothmer's command, stretched just far enough to remain in contact with Seventh Army. The Austro-Hungarians had been driven back along almost 30 kilometers of front, and the Russians had captured nearly 16,000 men, but it looked as if the line would hold.

Even as Pflanzer-Baltin's northern wing stabilized, however, the Russians were again collapsing the southern end of the front. The Russian Ninth Army, with two fresh divisions—the 74th (XLI Corps) and 1st Trans-amur (XXXIII Corps)—now poised on its right wing, renewed the artillery bombardment against Benigni's lines at dawn. Around 10:00 AM, after nearly three hours of shelling, Letschitski sent three infantry divisions (the 3rd, 74th, and 17th) forward. Lieutenant Alphons Bernhard, who had been assigned to command a squadron of the 42nd Infantry Division, described the confusion of that day: "The units in the trenches had no munitions, the reserves lay fully uncovered, the regimental command had allowed a squadron to be taken to another sector in return for another, at the moment unserviceable unit."[22]

The Austrian lines, manned largely by reserves and dismounted cavalry units, managed to deflect the initial attacks. The effort absorbed Benigni's final five battalions of reserves. With no additional forces to draw on and only fifty-four battalions in the line, the Austrians were unable to hold any longer against the overwhelming Russian numbers (122 battalions). The Habsburg 42nd Infantry Division, in the center of Benigni's line, crumbled in the face of the second Russian wave at 10:30 AM; Bernhard was unable to even rally his troops into formation for a counterattack once they had sighted the sixteen-deep Russian column advancing. Most of the Austrian 8th Cavalry Division, which had been sent to reinforce his sector, was captured. Taking hundreds of prisoners, the Russian infantry quickly secured the break, allowing the third wave to penetrate deep into the Austrian rear and expand the attack to the north. By noon Benigni's entire northern wing was in retreat, and Pflanzer-Baltin felt compelled to order the withdrawal of the southern half of the front back behind the Pruth at 1:00 PM. "Benigni is not capable of resistance," wrote the commander of the Austrian Seventh Army. "There is at present absolutely no possibility of holding against an enemy attack. The decision to attempt it would lead to the total destruction of Group Benigni."[23]

Once again though, Conrad countermanded the order. Where Pflanzer-Baltin had decided to retreat southwest in order to cover the Carpathian passes, Conrad demanded he retreat northwest to maintain contact with Südarmee and cover the rail junction at Stanislau. Benigni's troops proved incapable of an orderly retreat in any direction, however. Most were taken captive at the front; the remainder had already begun to move south when the order came to move northwest. As the demoralized Habsburg troops attempted to reverse course, a gap appeared in the line between Benigni's shattered force and XI Corps to the south. Pflanzer-Baltin ordered the 3rd and 8th Cavalry Divisions into the area to screen the retreat; the 800 men remaining in the 8th Cavalry Division, however, proved insufficient to hold the Russians along a 14-kilometer front. General Korda's XI Corps now had to retreat to the west as well to cover its flank. Unprepared to move, XI Corps abandoned huge stores of supplies and munitions in its haste. As one soldier wrote later: "It was a pitiful parade. Endless columns of horse-drawn vehicles (*Führwerke*) in one row after another with artillery placed in between. The battle trains of the divisions streamed back on all sides, pressing together on Valava. The troops came from all sides, tired and harassed."[24] Letschitski's Cossack cavalry units exacted a fearful toll on the scattered and confused Austrians as they struggled west in a landscape where most transit routes ran north-south. Korda's 24th Infantry Division lost 7,000 men—half its strength—between 10 and 11 June. The Russian XI Corps alone reported capturing over 24,000 Austro-Hungarian soldiers, including 564 officers, during the surge.

The Austrian Seventh Army, incapable of defending in the open ground, continued to retreat. Letschitski sent his troops forward in pursuit, led by the Cossack cavalry units. By day, the weary Habsburg troops attempted to fend off the persistent Russian attacks; by night, they marched west. The gaps in the line continued to grow; by 12 June, Hadfy's and Benigni's forces were separated by nearly 30 kilometers. By the morning of 14 June, the Austrian Seventh Army was so spread out that Letschitski had to divide his forces in order to maintain effective pursuit. Three Russian divisions—the 3rd Infantry Division and the 1st and 2nd Transamur infantry divisions—continued to push Benigni and Hadfy to the west while seven more (north to south: the 74th, 17th, 19th, 5th, 12th, 32nd, and 82nd) moved south against Korda. Desperate and believing that reserves were on the way, Pflanzer-Baltin decided to make a stand on the ground between the Pruth and the Dniester. Anchoring his weakened forces behind the Pruth in the south, where Korda's main position on the south bank overlooked both the northern approaches and the Habsburg beachhead on the opposite bank, Pflanzer-Baltin set up a thin line of outposts along the front. He then withdrew his main force to a central position in the rear, where it would act as a reserve to be deployed against the main Russian attacks.

Even as he did so, however, the situation worsened on the northern end of the front, where it had appeared Pflanzer-Baltin had managed to steady his northern wing. The "Russian steamroller" had begun moving implacably forward again almost immediately. Pflanzer-Baltin's forces fought well enough, but neither VI Corps nor XIII Corps proved entirely capable of stopping Scherbatschev's Seventh Army. Each time the Austrians held a position, Scherbatschev shifted his focus to the opposite wing and managed to breach the line. On 10 June, the Russians broke the center of the line, pushing the Austrian 12th Infantry Division across to the west bank of the Strypa River. On 11 June, while the 12th Infantry Division fought gallantly in the center of the Strypa River Line, the Russian XVI and XXII Corps broke the Austrian 39th Infantry Division to the north. General Bothmer dramatically ordered the Austrian VI Corps to take "not a step backward" on 12 June; they fought the Russians to a standstill that day, but a report that the 39th Infantry Division had been destroyed triggered a panicked retreat at 3:00 PM the following day.

Having suffered great losses themselves during the battles on the Strypa, the Russians were in no hurry to pursue the fleeing Austro-Hungarian troops. Scherbatschev sent out only reconnaissance parties on 14 June, and he was on the verge of breaking off the attack on 15 June when the random charge of a Cossack patrol inexplicably sent the Austrians into chaotic retreat once again. Only the arrival of the German 105th Infantry Division on the south wing of Südarmee and Scherbatschev's reluctance to pursue the Habsburg forces vigorously prevented a complete collapse.

To make the situation worse, Pflanzer-Baltin received word at 2:30 PM on 15 June that no reserves would be coming to the Austrian Seventh. The 24th and 30th infantry divisions each had only 3,500 men; the 42nd Infantry Division, which had absorbed the remnants of the 5th and 51st infantry divisions, still had only 5,200 men. Nonetheless, the Austrian Seventh Army was expected to hold—at least nominally. As German General Hans von Seeckt, newly installed as chief of staff for the Austrian Seventh Army, noted in a report to Conrad on 16 June: "The position of the Seventh Army is, for the task set it, a difficult one. Whether it still has the internal disposition to hold against a strong, well-prepared, overall attack is doubtful. I fear that in the task of the army to cover the area between the Pruth and the Dniester with its main forces and to secure the Bukovina with the other group, the army will be broken apart in the middle."[25]

Seeckt's assessment was all too accurate. Strong Russian attacks on Korda's position near Czernovitz, on the northern bank of the Pruth, in the afternoon of 17 June proved too much for the Austro-Hungarian XI Corps. After hours of desperate fighting, the Russians seized the beachhead around 4:00 PM; they forded the swollen river in three places under the cover of darkness. Only a single Russian soldier was even wounded in the effort. Disheartened, Korda ordered his troops to fall back yet again, this time taking up a line behind the Sereth River further south. Letschitski's forces were relentless, however, forcing the Austrian XI Corps out of its defenses on the Sereth on 17 June, breaking the line in several places and pursuing the Austro-Hungarians east and south over the next six days. XI Corps was shattered; isolated groups attempted to slow the Russian advance through the valleys of the Bukovina, but without success. By 24 June, Letschitski's forces had occupied most of the Bukovina. The Russian Ninth Army stood on a line that ran from Kolomea in the north through Kuty and down to the Romanian border, threatening both the mountain passes into Hungary and the rear of Hadfy's beleaguered forces. The Austro-Hungarian High Command issued a proclamation to the troops: "Every man in the army must be aware that he is fighting here to decide the campaign, and to decide the fate of the Fatherland."[26]

Dramatic as it was, the proclamation fell somewhat short of the truth. Though the Austrian Seventh had suffered severe losses—some 133,000 men, by Pflanzer-Baltin's estimate, with 40,000 of those taken prisoner— the Russians were also at the limits of their strength.[27] Having advanced past the westernmost point of the northern Romanian border salient near Czernovitz, the Russians now faced the task of pursuing the Habsburg forces across a much broader network of valleys in order to reach the Carpathians. Letschitski managed to take Kolomea on 29 June, inflicting another 40,000 casualties on the Austro-Hungarians, but that was the final bolt in his quiver. He possessed neither the men nor the munitions either to force the Carpathian passes or to take advantage of the virtually undefended space between Benigni's and Hadfy's forces. There remained the hope that the Romanians would enter the war and effectively reinforce the Russian right wing, but negotiations were dragging. In keeping with his original plan therefore, Brusilov had shifted forces from the southern end of the front to Galicia. It was there that the fate of two empires was truly being decided.[28]

The Battle for Lutsk

After limiting his attack to shelling the Austrian positions on the first day of the offensive, Kaledin had finally unleashed the Russian Eighth Army at Olyka on 5 June. The artillery barrage, which had persisted throughout the night of 4–5 June, increased in intensity around 8:30 AM until by 9:00 AM "a firestorm of unprecedented intensity crackled along all lines of the position, stirring up thick yellow sand and dust clouds that then hung over the field."[29] The Russian infantry, which had sapped to within forty-five paces of the Austrian lines during the barrage, then rose from its trenches and moved forward, materializing out of the swirling dust before the Habsburg units had a chance to react. The Austrian 82nd (2nd Infantry Division, X Corps) and 40th infantry regiments (70th Honved Infantry Division, Corps Szurmay) were still in their protective shelters when the enemy broke into their forward lines; entire units surrendered without resistance.[30] As one soldier remembered it:

> [I]n the dugouts of the first trench of the 82nd IR, because one still had the echo of the drumming fire in his ear, it was already five seconds after [the artillery] was no longer directed at the first trench. In the sixth second perhaps a spirited defender cried: to the trenches! In the seventh second he ran into someone in the stairwell, and under a low-hanging balcony that was splintered and torn to pieces a hand grenade skidded after him. And in the eighth second a voice from above called down to the men in the cellar that they should give themselves up. All resistance was useless. Machineguns already stood in front of every entrance to the caves. The trenches had been taken.[31]

The Russian XL Corps quickly rolled up the forward lines of the Austrian 2nd Infantry Division (X Corps, Fourth Army) while VIII Corps overran those of the Habsburg 70th Honved Infantry Division, where the largest percentage of defenders had been taken in their foxholes. The 70th Honved Infantry Division lost almost 7,000 men (from an initial strength of 12,200)—4,730 from the 40th Infantry Regiment alone (of 5,000). X Corps lost 80 percent of its strength, including 4,682 men from the 82nd Infantry Regiment (of 5,330)—most of them captured. Officers reportedly deserted their men and fled to the rear, taking the units' artillery with them. The Austrian 2nd Infantry Division nonetheless managed to lose thirty-seven field guns to the advancing Russians.

In desperation the Austro-Hungarian division commanders, without either seeking or gaining approval from headquarters, threw what local reserves they had into the fray. This enabled the Habsburg defenders to retake the first trench briefly, but as Russian infantry continued to move forward, they were pressed back once again. Communications with the rear had been disrupted so badly that some reserve units could not be located in time, and there was no forward command to speak of. By the time Linsingen decided to release units from the army reserve at 1:30 PM the Russians were pressing into the Austro-Hungarians' second and even third trenches. Linsingen had ordered them to use the reserves with care, deploying them only for a concentrated counterstroke at the appropriate moment, but his commanders threw them in piecemeal, essentially squandering two infantry divisions (11th and 13th). At 4:20 PM General Martigny, the commander of X Corps, reported that the Russians had taken the Austrian 2nd Infantry Division's second trench, clearing out the 1st and 24th regiments of the elite Vienna Guards, and he asked Linsingen for permission to retreat to the third position.[32]

With all local reserves expended and the 25th Infantry Division—which had been part of Fourth Army reserve—now engaged in the futile battle for the forward salient near Sapanov, the Austrian commanders once again petitioned headquarters to allow them to withdraw. The order finally came at 7:00 PM: "If further resistance forward is useless, then the troops are to be taken to the third position."[33] In fact, both wings of the Fourth Army still held their positions in the first line; only the center had been breached to the depth of the second line. The commanders of X Corps and Corps Szurmay, however, decided that the weakened state of their units endangered the entire position. At 10:00 PM, just as a heavy rain began to fall on the field of battle, the retreat began.[34]

Kaledin made no serious efforts to pursue the retreating Austro-Hungarian forces during the night of 5–6 June, yet the withdrawal was conducted hastily and without any attempt to regroup. Not until the center of Fourth Army reached the eastern bank of the Styr River near Lutsk—some 75 kilometers west-southwest of their original position—did the retreat halt. At least one unit, the 314th Honved Infantry Regiment, continued to fall back even further, though its commander (who had spent two years in the area) later claimed that this was merely a navigational error. Clearly, as Kundmann put it, "the front was cracking."[35] Conrad telegraphed Falkenhayn asking for German reinforcements to be sent south once again. Contemptuous of his ally's efforts and abilities, the German commander replied that aid would be forthcoming only under the terms previously agreed: if Russia were to shift troops south from the German Front. Falkenhayn recommended instead that the German units from Südarmee be brought to reinforce the Austrian Fourth Army. Through a back-channel, Falkenhayn also let Conrad know that Austria-Hungary would have to recall its own units from the Tirolean Offensive—which he had, after all, counseled against—before Germany would send troops south.[36]

Faced with this situation, Linsingen decided to transfer five German infantry battalions from Group Gronau on his left wing to Lutsk, where they were to join two regiments of the 45th Guards Division (II Corps, Fourth Army) and the 89th Guards Division for a counteroffensive. Before these troops could arrive, however, Kaledin's Eighth Army renewed the attack and quickly overwhelmed the Austrian Fourth Army once again. Though the archduke had prepared the third position on the Styr line with belts of wire and concrete fortifications, the Russian artillery had occupied the heights of Krupy to the south during the night and began shelling the Austrians before they could settle in. Several Habsburg units broke immediately, fleeing across the Styr on pontoon bridges. When the Russian XXXII Corps, supported by the 2nd Finnish Guard Division and the 12th Cavalry Division, moved forward at 8:00 AM on 6 June though, it appeared as if the Austrian artillery would repel the attack. They quickly ran out of shells, however, and without this defense, several more Habsburg units turned and ran. Many Galician regiments simply surrendered. By 9:00 AM the Russians had occupied the Austrian positions, captured another thirty-eight guns, and created a hole between X Corps and Corps Szurmay that left the road to Lutsk open. Archduke Josef Ferdinand immediately cast his last reserves into the breach, if only to cover the retreat of the supply trains over the Styr. At the same time, he sent a message to Linsingen informing him that Fourth Army might have to pull back.[37]

Linsingen instructed X Corps to maintain contact with Corps Szurmay, but Fourth Army's position continued to deteriorate. The 70th Honved Infantry Division, which had suffered severely in the previous day's fighting, had been under attack since dawn on 6 June; at 10:00 AM that day its commander again ordered a retreat. This forced the rest of Corps Szurmay to follow suit in order to avoid exposing its flanks and reopened the gap to X Corps, which now grew to almost six kilometers. Reports that Kaledin's forces were advancing into the breach then convinced Martigny, the commander of X Corps, that he had to retreat as well in order to cover his flanks. He initiated this maneuver at 11:15 AM, though he informed Linsingen only at 11:20. Linsingen replied twenty-five minutes later, demanding that X Corps hold the position it had abandoned half an hour earlier until the counterattack being prepared could be initiated.

It was too late; X Corps was already in full retreat, which closed the gap to Corps Szurmay but also created a new hole to the north between X Corps and II Corps more than 20 kilometers wide. Though II Corps had hardly been engaged at all, it was now forced to abandon its positions as well or risk being flanked. Corps Szurmay settled into a new, rearward position only fifteen minutes after receiving Linsingen's order to hold its original line. The 70th Honved Infantry Division, however, was so completely shattered as to be incapable of defense. Under pressure from Kaledin's advancing cavalry units the 70th Honved Infantry Division, which had by now been reduced to some 700 men, broke again at 3:00 PM, setting the chain reaction of withdrawals in motion once again. The entire Austrian Fourth Army was now in full retreat.[38]

Furious, Linsingen demanded that both Martigny (X Corps) and Archduke Josef Ferdinand (Fourth Army) be relieved of command and that the 29th Infantry Division be transferred from the reserve of Second Army in Galicia (Böhm-Ermolli) to Fourth Army. Reluctant to abandon the Tirol Offensive and anxious to placate his German ally, Conrad agreed to both measures. First Army (Puhallo) not only extended its northern wing, but also sent the 25th Infantry Division and the 46th Guards Division to augment Fourth Army. Linsingen's plan, again, was to mount a strong counteroffensive under the command of Feldmarschalleutnant Smekal to seize the initiative. It was entirely unrealistic. Fourth Army, even after reserves had been brought forward, numbered only 27,000 men; the 11th Infantry Division and 70th Honved Infantry Division had been shattered beyond repair, and the Habsburg troops in general were demoralized. Linsingen, however, was encouraged by the Russians' apparent hesitation. Rather stunned by the success of the offensive, Kaledin had not pursued the Austrian Fourth on the night of 6–7 June. Delayed by the need to bring reserves forward and reestablish order in their own lines—XXXII Corps had broken off pursuit to search the Habsburg positions for alcohol, for instance—the Russians had, in fact, lost contact with the retreating Austrians.[39]

Spurred on by Brusilov's order to broaden the attack, however, Kaledin renewed the offensive early on 7 June, sending five corps forward against the Habsburg positions defending Lutsk and Kolki. The Habsburgs' Corps Fath repelled the early attacks of the Russian XLIV and XXX Corps in the northern sectors using strong field artillery to sweep the flanks of the Russian infantry. Puhallo's First Army also held against the attacks of the Russian XLV Corps in the southern sector. In the center of the line, however, the weary and depleted Austrian Fourth was again reeling under attacks by the Russian XL and VIII Corps. Once again it was the Habsburg X Corps that proved to be the weak link in the defense.

The retreat of 6–7 June left the Austrian X Corps defending a prepared bridgehead on the eastern bank of the Styr in front of Lutsk, with Corps Szurmay just to the south. The position had been built up since the autumn of 1915 to protect nine bridges that crossed the Styr—at that point only some 25 meters wide but quite deep—and contained two distinct defensive lines, each with its own system of obstacles, bunkers, and batteries. The apparent strength of the outpost was now countered, however, by Russian positions on the heights overlooking the bridgehead from the south and the east. Kaledin's VIII Corps struck the bridgehead directly from the east, while XLV Corps drove against the hinge between Corps Szurmay and X Corps from the south.

The break came in the center of the line, where the Habsburg positions seemed strongest. The Austrian 13th Infantry Division, having barely had time to deploy before the Russian onslaught began at 7:30 AM, was unable to locate its artillery—which had been split between two other divisions during the confused retreat of 6–7 June—and one brigade fell back almost immediately. Archduke Josef Ferdinand, still in charge of Fourth Army pending the final word from the emperor, now decided that the bridgehead had to be held at all costs. He ordered Smekal's division in the southeast to relieve the pressure on the 37th Infantry Division, which held X Corps's northern wing, and then drew his headquarters further to the rear. Not only did Smekal's force fail to make headway, it soon found itself in full retreat across the Styr, taking the 37th Infantry Division with it. The Russian XLV Corps, in hot pursuit, captured numerous prisoners as well as the supply train of X Corps. Thus, even while the Austrian 13th Infantry Division had managed to stabilize its position in the bridgehead, Smekal's ill-fated stroke had exposed the northern flank of X Corps's line, and the afternoon had just begun.

Extraordinarily poor communications kept the commanders in X Corps and Corps Szurmay in the dark about the true course of events and generally made the situation worse. Though X Corps still occupied the bridgehead, General Martigny had no confidence at all that they could hold it. His troops were exhausted, their artillery was on the western bank of the river, and communications with the rear were sporadic at best. Archduke Josef Ferdinand, himself in retreat and completely unaware of the debacle Smekal had fallen into, nonetheless demanded unconditionally that X Corps maintain its position when Martigny sought permission to withdraw. Adding insult to injury, he also informed Martigny that he had officially been relieved of command earlier that morning. In what turned out to be his final act though, Martigny had already ordered his troops to prepare to blow up the bridges across the Styr at 2:40 PM—twenty-five minutes before he was removed. Less than an hour later, news of Smekal's retreat arrived at Fourth Army headquarters, where the archduke had just learned of his own removal as army commander. Josef Ferdinand quickly left his post. Command of the entire front, including the bridgehead at Lutsk, now passed to Linsingen, while Feldmarschalleutnant Sellner, formerly commander of the army reserve (2nd Infantry Division), temporarily took command of X Corps despite having reported himself ill only half an hour before. Sellner immediately ordered the 37th Infantry Division to halt its retreat, even as the Russian attacks on the bridgehead intensified.[40]

By 7:00 PM, it was clear to everyone in the Habsburg high command that the outpost on the east bank of the Styr would be lost and that any attempt to hold even the west bank would be fruitless. "It's a complete debacle," the chief of staff for the 11th Infantry Division reported. "Our troops aren't worth anything any more."[41] Sellner ordered the train tracks at Lutsk destroyed, and the provisions burned. An eyewitness reported that:

> In Luck [Lutsk] it began to threaten, to shake, to thunder, and to crack. Towering columns of smoke shot up to the heavens. The pressure raised the roofs of houses when the munitions warehouses exploded. The shutters split and rattled and fell in splinters on the streets. Flames shot up from the row of munitions dumps built from several hundred ancient, giant Volhynien trees. The rich scent of the earth bubbled up, glowed, swelled, and dispersed. All of the wonderful white flour, the hay, the straw, the bread, the meat, and whatever else lay in these rooms, more than enough to feed thousands and to let thousands forget their wants. All of the fruits of uncounted days of labor by innumerable hands, assembled with care and effort, were destroyed.[42]

Russian artillery had already destroyed two bridges over the Styr and was decimating the Austro-Hungarian units that remained trapped in the bridgehead position, but no Habsburg commander was willing to take responsibility for ordering a withdrawal. Finally, at 7:50 PM, Linsingen agreed to pull Fourth Army back behind the Styr. The panicked troops of X Corps and Corps Szurmay proved incapable of even this, however, and blew most of the remaining bridges over the river before the evacuation was complete. Many of the soldiers of the 11th Infantry Division got caught up in their own obstacles or drowned trying to swim across the Styr. Faced with pouring rain and heavy Russian artillery, the 7th Infantry Division (Corps Szurmay) was broken by a single Russian regiment during the retreat, and many units simply surrendered on the spot. Others threw their rifles into the river and swam across under enemy fire. The unit lost some 11,000 men during the withdrawal. Horror-stricken, the unit commanders beseeched Linsingen for permission to withdraw even further, to previously prepared positions on a line running between Kovel and Sokal. By the time Linsingen agreed at 10:00 PM, some units of Corps Szurmay had already arrived near Sokal.[43]

The Russian Eighth Army crossed the Styr River on the night of 7–8

June 1916 without encountering resistance from the Austro-Hungarian forces, which were scrambling backward in confusion. According to Böhm-Ermolli, X Corps simply refused to heed orders to mount a counterattack and continued to retreat.[44] This time Kaledin pressed the attack, sending the 4th Finnish Guards Division to occupy Lutsk and maintaining contact with the retreating Austrians. The Russian XL Corps engaged the Austrian X Corps again in the early afternoon of 8 June, and pushed the Habsburg forces back an additional five kilometers. Another engagement on the morning of 9 June sent X Corps reeling once again and forced Corps Szurmay to draw back as well to maintain the integrity of the line. Böhm-Ermolli, commanding the Austrian Second Army, cabled headquarters asking permission to release some of his forces for the relief of Corps Szurmay. Second Army had not as yet faced concentrated attacks, and Böhm-Ermolli was confident his reserve would not be required. The reply, which came two hours later, insisted that Second Army extend aid only to the 7th Infantry Division, as the 70th and 11th infantry divisions were to remain the concern of Fourth Army. Shortly after that message was received, Corps Szurmay lost contact with the Austrian Second Army and relief was out of the question.

Early on the morning of 10 June, Kaledin sent the fresh XXXII Corps against the depleted forces of Corps Szurmay, with predictable results. What defensive fire the Austrians could muster was overwhelmed by the first wave of Russian infantry. The second wave drove into the lines of the Austrian 7th Infantry Division on the southern flank, wiping out a brigade and opening a gap between the Austrian Fourth and First armies. To forestall Russian interdiction of communications, the Habsburg 4th and 7th cavalry divisions were remounted and sent out to patrol the gap. By noon the Austrians' situation had deteriorated so much that Puhallo believed he had to pull First Army back, even though this broadened the gap between his forces and Fourth Army to almost 45 kilometers.

Meanwhile, the Russian XXXIX Corps, by deploying armored vehicles once again, had managed to break the Austro-Hungarian lines on the northern side of the salient as well, forcing the Austrian II Corps to retreat behind the Stochod River. With Fourth Army thus isolated and retreating with no end in sight, it appeared the Habsburg line might collapse completely, but Kaledin had outrun his supply lines once again. His supply of shell was dangerously low, and Eighth Army had already suffered some 35,000 casualties. Kaledin had already dismounted much of his cavalry to make the push of 7 to 9 June, and now he had no reserves left to throw into the breach. The Russians broke off the attack on the night of 10–11 June, allowing the depleted Habsburg forces to recover slightly.

The battle had pushed the Central Powers' forward lines back 45 kilometers along some 80 kilometers of front over four days, creating a deep salient that reached almost to Vladimir-Volynsk in the center and netted over 44,000 Austro-Hungarian prisoners of war. The Habsburgs' X Corps had been reduced to about 3,000 men when its new commander, Feldmarschalleutnant Csanady, arrived on 10 June; II Corps was even weaker, having perhaps only 2,000 men after the prolonged fighting. Between these two depleted forces were six kilometers of undefended territory. On the southern edge of the front, Puhallo's First Army had been forced to stretch northward, with only a single cavalry corps maintaining tenuous contact with Fourth Army across a gap of at nearly 50 kilometers. The Austrian 7th Infantry Division, once part of Corps Szurmay, had become so detached from that unit that it was now incorporated into First Army for command purposes. The road southwest to Lemberg (Lvov) lay open in front of the advancing Russians, but so too did the road to Kovel, an important railway junction to the northwest. The offensive had reached a critical juncture.[45]

Klembovski, chief of staff for the Southwestern Front, urged his commander to press directly west with Eighth Army. Most military analysts, including Brusilov himself, agreed after the war that had the Russian Eighth been able to press its advantage at this point, the Habsburg Empire might well have been forced to sue for peace or even have collapsed entirely.[46] In his memoirs, Böhm-Ermolli noted that surrendering so many long-held and well-prepared positions—in many cases without firing a shot—not only weakened the Habsburg defensive line, but damaged the collective morale of the troops. He feared that much more than Lemberg could be lost.[47] As Kundmann more correctly surmised though, even if the Central Powers proved unable to continue on the Italian Front while simultaneously defending the Eastern Front, the Russians also lacked the forces, if not the will, to exploit the situation.[48]

Scherbatschev and Letschitski's forces were just now fully engaging the Central Powers on the southern half of the front, and their success precluded the rapid transfer of any forces north at this point. Evert had not yet taken action against the Germans on the Western Front, moreover, and Kuropatkin's forces remained motionless in the north as well. Evert, in fact, had formally requested and received a change in objective that would delay the start of the northern offensive until 14 June. Brusilov was worried that this would allow Falkenhayn to send a strike force into the flank of the Russian Eighth Army—as he had in September 1915—if the drive extended too far. In response to Brusilov's request for assistance in guarding against this possibility, Alekseev dispatched V Siberian Corps from Evert's front along with two corps (XXIII and the Grenadiers) from Kuropatkin's and the 1st Turkestan Infantry Division as reinforcements. Brusilov complained bitterly about the failure to launch offensives in the north, but Alekseev was unable (or unwilling) to convince Evert and Kuropatkin to attack in support of the Southwestern Front. Brusilov therefore took a more cautious approach, putting the southern wing of Eighth Army on the defensive while shifting forces northward in preparation for a concentrated drive on Kovel. The question was which side would be able to regroup and reinforce first.[49]

CHAPTER FOUR

STALEMATE AND RENEWAL

By mid-June 1916, it appeared as if the Brusilov Offensive might provide the dramatic breakthrough to decide the war that generals on both sides and both fronts had been seeking for nearly two years. On the northern end of the front, the Russians appeared poised to overwhelm the combined forces of the Central Powers. Kaledin's Eighth Army could drive southwest and take Lemberg (Lvov) or strike northwest toward Brest-Litovsk. In either case, a Russian success would imperil the entire Eastern Front. The Russian Seventh and Ninth armies, meanwhile, had broken the Habsburg line decisively in the south; Brusilov's forces were moving forward in the Bukovina and threatening to carry the war into Hungary. Conrad's offensive in the Tirol was grinding to a halt, and the Austro-Hungarians were scrambling for reserves. If Evert and Kuropatkin could prevent the Germans from sending reinforcements south while Kaledin regrouped, the Austro-German alliance might be shattered. If, moreover, the Russians could finally convince Romania to enter the war and provide reinforcements for their southern forces, the Habsburgs might be forced to sue for peace. "If Romania comes in now [. . .] that is the end of the war, and to our disadvantage no less," Conrad told his adjutant.[1] For a few days, the entire war seemed to hang in the balance.

Both Conrad and Falkenhayn recognized the gravity of the situation and, despite personal reluctance on both sides, acted quickly to save the Central Powers' position. Falkenhayn derided the abilities and performance of the Habsburg troops, but he recognized that simply abandoning Austria-Hungary to its fate would lead to the "speedy exhaustion" of Germany as well.[2] The simultaneous collapse of the Habsburg Fourth and Seventh armies had brought Conrad to his senses as well; "the boss [Conrad] holds this to be the greatest crisis of the campaign," Kundmann noted.[3] Though Conrad still believed that "Italy is our destiny," he realized that he had to make concessions if he expected German assistance. "In the end," the Habsburg commander wrote, "the numbers of men and munitions alone decide the power."[4] Thus when Falkenhayn sent word on 7 June that he was sending four German divisions (the 108th Infantry Division, along with the 19th and 20th infantry divisions from Germany's X Corps, and Division Rusche) to aid in the defense of Kovel, Conrad reluctantly agreed to meet the next day in Berlin to discuss moving troops from Tirol to Galicia. To his own commanders, Conrad had already conceded that the Austrian 9th and 61st infantry divisions would have to return to Galicia, but he feared that any concession to Falkenhayn would only be followed by further demands. Just going to Berlin was hard enough for Conrad; "It is the hardest punishment of all if one sends me to Falkenhayn," he wrote.[5]

Falkenhayn's first goal was to stage a counteroffensive that would reestablish the lines of 1915. In the long run, however, the German commander was determined to take control over the entire Eastern Front. In addition to the four divisions already promised for 14 June, the German commander indicated that a fifth, the 11th Bavarian Infantry Division, would be shifted to Hindenburg's Eastern Command from the Western Front. In return, he expected Conrad to send no less than two and a half divisions from Tirol to Galicia. The plan was to form an attack group of seven and a half divisions (the four German divisions plus the Habsburg II Corps, the Austrian 29th Infantry Division, and the 89th Light Infantry Brigade) to halt the Russian initiative via a counterstroke. Two days later, Falkenhayn sent a telegram demanding that Linsingen be placed in command not only of the attack group, but also of the Austrian First and Fourth armies, in order to control the operation.[6] The German commander also stipulated that full reports on the condition of the Habsburg units under Linsingen's command be made available to the German general staff in order to facilitate accurate decisions. In the same communication, Falkenhayn opened the question of Pflanzer-Baltin's competence, suggesting that it might be better if a German general were in command of the Austrian Seventh Army. On grounds that the Austro-Hungarian High Command had already proven unable to maintain the southern half of the front, Falkenhayn further proposed on

12 June that Mackensen, the hero of 1915, now be placed in charge of the Eastern Front between the Pripet and Dniester rivers. "It would have been presumptuous," Falkenhayn noted with some sarcasm in his memoirs, "to rely on a failure of the Russian leadership similar to that of the autumn of 1914."[7]

Conrad naturally refused this emasculating proposal, but he did agree to accept German Major General Hans von Seeckt as chief of staff for the Austrian Seventh Army as a stabilizing measure. He also conceded the necessity of closer coordination with the Germans and promised that Austria-Hungary would undertake no further operations without consulting its ally.[8] Conrad had already surrendered his dream—at least temporarily—on 10 June and ordered a full stop to operations on the Tirolean Front. The Austrian 48th Infantry Division was ordered to join the 61st in heading to Galicia, along with many of the reserves intended for the operation against Italy. Humiliated and despondent, Conrad now mainly sought to avoid coming under complete German control, but saw few alternatives. "I showed them a finger," he told Kundmann dejectedly, "and now they want the entire hand."[9] Conrad suggested to Falkenhayn that he might accept Mackensen as the commander of an army group comprising the Südarmee and the Austrian Seventh if more German troops were sent to that sector. The solution to the problem, he hinted, was not German generals but German divisions. Falkenhayn declined. He had done enough to stabilize the front, in his estimation, and if he could not have control of the entire Eastern Front, he was looking forward to a decision in the west.[10]

Falkenhayn's lack of presumption notwithstanding, the response of the Russian command to the situation was sluggish at best. Brusilov continued to demand that Alekseev spur Evert and Kuropatkin into action so that his own forces might regroup. On 14 June, however, the very day when he was due to launch the main attack on the Northern Front, Evert telegraphed Alekseev to request a delay of four days on grounds of bad weather. The Pinsk marshes, Evert claimed, were not dry enough to allow an infantry advance. Brusilov was understandably furious and telephoned Alekseev on 17 June in an attempt to get the tsar to order Evert to attack immediately. When the chief of staff declined, Brusilov wrote to Nicholas II directly to plead his case. The tsar did not commit himself one way or the other, as was his habit, but Brusilov's requests for additional munitions were approved, and the 1st and 2nd Turkestan infantry divisions were dispatched to the Southwestern Front as reinforcements.[11] He also assured Brusilov that operations in the north would commence on 18 June. On that day, however, Evert again contacted Alekseev, this time with a report that the Germans had shifted large numbers of forces, including a significant number of heavy guns, to the precise sector of the front where he had intended to strike. This time, he asked only that he be allowed to shift the location of the attack—though this would again entail a delay to cover the movement of forces. News of the tsar's approval this time carried assurances that Evert would attack by 3 July, but Brusilov recognized that the poor condition of the Russian railways and Evert's general inertia (which was readily matched by Kuropatkin on the Northwestern Front) might easily delay the operation by six weeks or more.[12]

Brusilov's arguments made no impact. As Nicholas II wrote to Alexandra on 18 June, the decision already had been made to shift the focus of operations to the Southwestern Front. Instead of conducting the main strike, Evert and Kuropatkin were now tasked with carrying out "demonstrations" in support of Brusilov's offensive. Kuropatkin was ordered to send I and XXIII Corps to support the Russian Ninth Army, and the 113th Infantry Division would be created to support Seventh Army. Third Army became (on 24 June) a permanent part of Brusilov's force, and a new Guards Army (often referred to as the Special Army) would be formed to supply fresh units as the offensive continued, but otherwise nothing had changed. "Brusilov," Nicholas told the empress, "is firm and calm."[13]

Brusilov was, in fact, anything but calm, for he saw his chances slipping away while Kuropatkin and Evert sat idle with some ninety divisions—nearly 750,000 more men than the German forces opposing them—and two-thirds of the Russian Army's artillery. Given little choice, Brusilov postponed his own offensive again and again, first because Evert refused to move, and then because of the need to coordinate with the Allies' planned summer offensive, which was scheduled for early July. He warned Alekseev, however, that continued inaction in the north could cost Russia more than a battle, complaining that he never would have offered to attack had he known there would be no support; members of Brusilov's command spoke of Evert as a traitor.[14] In his memoirs, Brusilov made it clear where he felt responsibility lay:

> I was well aware that the Tsar himself bore no guilt, because he was a mere amateur in military affairs. Alekseev grasped very well though, how the situation had developed and how criminally Evert and Kuropatkin conducted themselves.

[. . .] Had another military man stood at the head of the Russian Army as supreme commander, Evert would have been dismissed without delay from his post for his indecisiveness, and Kuropatkin never would have found a place in the active army.[15]

The Defense of Kovel

On 11 June, Kaledin's cavalry had still been enough to drive the unorganized Austrian Fourth from its ill-prepared defensive positions with only minimal support from the infantry. In stopping the offensive for three days to refill their ranks and stores, however, the Russians had given the Austro-Hungarian forces, now commanded by General Karl von Tersztyanszky, who had a reputation as an inspiring, old-school disciplinarian, sufficient time to dig in and reorganize themselves. The four German divisions arrived in Galicia on 12 June, and they were immediately dispatched on a forced march to the front lines as Group Marwitz, which was intended to form the core of Linsingen's attack group. This allowed the Austrian Fourth Army to shorten its front and strengthen its defensive positions even further. Thus when Brusilov renewed the offensive on 14 June, he found that the moment had passed.

Using the Russian Third Army, which had been placed temporarily under his command, Brusilov orchestrated a feint toward Pinsk on the northern end of the front. In the center, he sent Kaledin's Eighth Army, reinforced now by I Corps from the Northern Front and by XXIII Corps (originally intended for Ninth Army), directly against Kovel, where the north-south railway crossed two east-west lines. The Russian Eleventh Army was to make a pinning attack against the Austrian First, using XXXII and XVII Corps to press the Habsburg forces back behind the Plazevka and Ikva rivers to the southwest. The Ninth and Seventh armies were to renew their pursuit of the Austro-Hungarian forces in the Bukovina in order to ensure that the Central Powers could not shift additional troops northward. The aim was to roll up the Germans' southern flank and separate them from their Habsburg allies.

The brunt of the Russian attacks struck the new Army Group Linsingen (north to south: Group Gronau, Cavalry Corps Hauer, Corps Fath, Group Bernhardi, Group Marwitz, Fourth Army, and First Army) in the center of its front, yet the most significant developments came on the wings. The Russian Third Army, commanded by General Lesch and holding a five-to-one numerical advantage over the German forces opposite, met with total disaster in the north. The German defenders under General Woyrsch lost only 150 men while inflicting over 7,000 casualties on the poorly led Russians, who had not adopted Brusilov's tactics. This further convinced Alekseev, among others, of the futility of attacking the Germans, especially when things were going so well against the Austro-Hungarians. Sakharov's Eleventh Army struck the Austrian First head-on in the south, for instance, and made significant gains. In the center, where Brusilov hoped to break through once again, Kaledin launched a surprise strike to the west, aiming at Vladimir-Volynsk instead of Kovel and using XLVI Corps and the IV cavalry to pin Bernhardi on his right wing while XXX Corps advanced westward. With their resolve stiffened by Tersztyanszky and German reinforcements at their back, the Habsburg forces battled the Russians to a standstill in the center of the line on 14 June, but at heavy cost.

The Austrian First Army fought gallantly through the next morning when the Russians renewed their attack, but showed signs of buckling as the afternoon wore on. Sakharov's XXXII Corps (Eleventh Army) eventually smashed through the front lines of the Austrian 25th and 46th infantry divisions (XVIII Corps), opening a small gap between the Austrian First and Second armies. General Puhallo, fearing another breakthrough could lead to disaster, sought permission to draw the forces on his right wing back to Radzivilov. Linsingen replied immediately in the affirmative and sent three cavalry divisions under General Kosak, along with several battalions from Marwitz's attack group, to plug the 12-kilometer gap between First and Second armies created by the maneuver. This not only forced Linsingen to postpone his counterattack to 16 June, but also thinned the center of the Austro-German position. The Austro-Hungarian XVIII Corps, on the right (southern) wing of First Army, had been pulled back to a more favorable position in the evening of 15 June, and Böhm-Ermolli (Second Army) had thus been compelled to pull Kosak's forces back as well in order to maintain contact.

This had presented the Russians with a chance to catch both Austrian armies in flux, but Kaledin was unable to take advantage. Brusilov, concerned at Eighth Army's tremendous losses, had ordered Kaledin to retain four divisions as a reserve. Thus while the Russians drove into the front lines of the Austrian Fourth Army at several points in the course of the day, they lacked the weight to force a break in the line. While Brusilov angrily blamed Evert for his failure to attack in the north and draw off German forces, the Austrians retreated in orderly fashion to more secure positions during the night.[16]

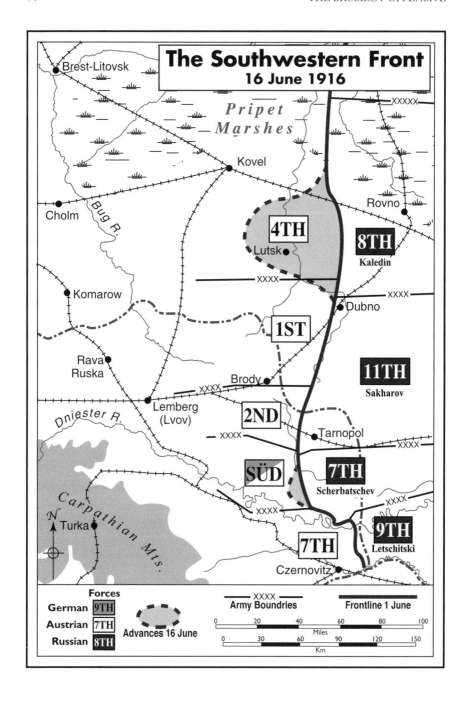

The Southwestern Front
16 June 1916

Brest-Litovsk

Pripet Marshes

Kovel

Rovno

Cholm

4TH

Lutsk

8TH
Kaledin

Komarow

Dubno

1ST

Rava Ruska

Brody

11TH
Sakharov

Lemberg (Lvov)

Dniester R.

2ND

Tarnopol

SÜD

7TH
Scherbatschev

Carpathian Mts.

Turka

7TH

9TH
Letschitski

Czernovitz

Forces

German	9TH
Austrian	7TH
Russian	8TH

Advances 16 June

XXXX
Army Boundries

Frontline 1 June

0   20   40   60   80   100
Miles

0   30   60   90   120   150
Km

Figure 1. A foxhole and observation stand between the Rowno and Duno highways. Courtesy of the Austrian State Archive, War Archive (ÖKA, *Nachlass Otto Berndt, Ritter von*; B2-3-3, *Beilage* VI).

Figure 2. The entrance to a foxhole, with a machine-gun stand under construction at the same location. Courtesy of the Austrian State Archive, War Archive (ÖKA, *Nachlass Otto Berndt, Ritter von*; B2-3-3, *Beilage* VI).

Figure 3. A tunnel ("*Untertritte*") near Teremno. Courtesy of the Austrian State Archive, War Archive (ÖKA, *Nachlass Otto Berndt, Ritter von*; B2-3-3, *Beilage* VI).

The Habsburg position, however, remained vulnerable. The Austrian Fourth Army, for instance, had only 28,000 men left, while two days of fighting had left the 4th Infantry Division (Second Army) with only 6,300 men to occupy more than 60 kilometers of front. Strong Russian attacks early on the morning of 16 June soon overwhelmed the 4th Infantry Division's thinly held line along the Ikva River, threatening Brody. By 9:00 AM, however, Linsingen had launched his counterattack, sending six divisions (the German 19th, 20th, 29th, and 108th, the Austrian 61st, and Division Rusche) forward against the center of the Russian salient and drawing off many of the Russian reserves.

While Linsingen thus blunted Kaledin's offensive, his own made only slow progress. Though the attack group consisted of just over twelve divisions (including four German divisions), many of the Austrian formations were depleted, and some of the new troops had been deployed as reserves in the previous days' fighting. Brusilov's opposing forces consisted of twelve divisions (each containing four more battalions than an Austrian division and seven more than a German division) in the front line, centered on XXIII Corps (the 20th and 53rd infantry divisions) and holding a fresh reserve. The Habsburg 61st Infantry Division, working in conjunction with the 7th Infantry Division on the left wing of the Austrian First Army, thus advanced about six kilometers at terrible cost but proved unable to hold its ground against the overwhelming Russian defense. Marwitz's German troops, who had completed a 60-kilometer forced march to the line on 15 June only to be thrown immediately into the fray, advanced slowly in the center of the line as well. Early on, progress was limited by the need to secure the bridgeheads on the Styr, but to the surprise of the Germans, the Russian forces also fought much harder, and much better, than they had in 1915. "Just to show the *Pickelhaube* [the distinctive spike atop the Germany infantry helmet] over the top of the trenches," Jerabek writes, "was no longer enough to strike fear and horror into the Russians."[17] At the end of the day, the center of the Austro-German line had moved only seven or eight kilometers to the east, hardly what Linsingen had hoped for. On the northern end of the salient, Bernhardi was fortunate just to have held his position.[18]

Linsingen's offensive found no greater success over the next two days despite repeated strikes. Marwitz's attack group made little or no headway. German intercepts of Sakharov's radio communications allowed the Austrian armies to successfully defend against Russian attacks on the morning of 17 June, but the depleted Habsburg forces cracked in the afternoon. The Russians forced the Austrian 46th Guards Infantry Division (First Army) back on the town of Redkov, and fearing that his flank might collapse, Puhallo drew back the entire northern wing of the army. This left the First and Fourth armies with only a tenuous connection, as the Fourth suffered defeat as well, but this time on its right flank. As the battle loomed, the army's officers panicked, with many simply reporting sick rather than lead the attacks. Left to their own devices, many of the troops simply surrendered. "The conduct of Fourth Army," Kundmann wrote, "was a scandal; it was a defeat, politically and morally very uncomfortable."[19] Even when they fought, the Habsburg forces proved incapable. The 4th Infantry Division proved unable to hold its position in the swampy woodlands west of Lockazy and was forced to withdraw. The German commanders requested reinforcements to solidify the line, but were told that none were available. Desperate, Linsingen telegraphed headquarters, only to have it confirmed that no additional troops were available. Frustrated, the German commander ordered his troops to go on the defensive and secure their positions.[20]

Linsingen still believed, however, that the counteroffensive could succeed. He was wrong. Each time he ordered new attacks, initial success—usually small—was soon followed by defeat, and often by a loss of additional territory. On 18 June Linsingen, alerted by intelligence reports that the opposing Russian formations on the south flank of Fourth Army were weak, sent the Austrian 70th Infantry Division forward along with Corps Szurmay and X Corps. His forces took the town of Kozlov that morning, but were driven out again in the afternoon. The next morning Linsingen again ordered attacks, this time on Fourth Army's north flank. Three German divisions, the 19th, the 29th, and the 108th, advanced along the Stochod River that morning; in the afternoon, Brusilov sent XXXIX Corps and the 71st Infantry Division to restore the Russian positions, which they did. On 20 June, Linsingen tried a new approach. He created a second attack group from units of the Austrian First and Fourth armies and threw it into the fray, attempting to create a concentric attack on Lutsk by sending Marwitz (in the center) and Bernhardi (from the northwest) forward at the same time. Reinforced by the newly arrived V Siberian Corps, the Russians held their ground across the entire front and inflicted heavy casualties on the Austro-German attackers.

With German reinforcements trickling in, Linsingen nonetheless pressed ahead with attack after fruitless attack in typical fashion. Reinforced by the 11th Bavarian Infantry Division in the north and with a new attack group comprising the 43rd Reserve Infantry Division and 48th Infantry Division under Major General Falkenhayn (brother of the German commander) in the center, Linsingen hoped to push the Russians back over the Styr River. He sent his troops forward again on 21 June, only to discover that Kaledin's troops had abandoned their positions overnight and retreated to a better-fortified line. Falkenhayn's attack group advanced a few kilometers the next day, but then heavy counterattacks by the Russian 15th Infantry Division and 4th Finnish Infantry Division brought the drive to a standstill.

Reinforced again by Hindenburg, who sent the German 107th Infantry Division and the 5th Reserve Infantry Division south, Linsingen determined to push forward. Despite his "stimulating order, in Napoleonic style, to attack" on 24 June, the Habsburg Fourth simply was not up to the task. An officer from Fourth Army reported that "[t]he detachments don't march like Imperial troops, but like a herd poorly supervised by the shepherd! Stretched out, spread all across the street, followed by countless stragglers, these columns offer a model of how not to march."[21] Not even two days' rest restored their fighting capacity. When ordered to counterattack on 26 June, Tersztyanszky could only reply that he had neither sufficient shell nor an effective force at his disposal.

Linsingen plunged ahead regardless, ordering new attacks for 29 June. Marwitz's attack group (north to south, the Austrian 61st Infantry Division, the German 43rd Reserve Infantry Division, the Austrian 7th Cavalry Division, the German 22nd and 108th infantry divisions, the Austrian 7th and 48th infantry divisions) immediately sent two columns forward, moving only under cover of darkness. Falkenhayn, with two infantry divisions and one cavalry division, was to take Pustomyty in the north while Marwitz's four remaining divisions swept forward over Gubin. The Austrian Fourth Army, moving through the woods to the south to conceal their movement, would strike northeast toward Zaturcy. When they arrived in the front lines on 29 June, however, Linsingen's forces found fresh Russian troops awaiting them. Brusilov had dispatched VIII Corps to cover the seam between Eighth Army and Eleventh Army in the north, and placed two additional divisions (1st Combined Cossacks and 1st Transamur Cavalry) at Sakharov's disposal as a reserve. Undeterred, Linsingen ordered his troops forward in a "general attack along the entire front of the Army Group, which must be carried out with full force."[22]

Attacking in the rain on 30 June, Marwitz's forces met with limited success despite an intense preparation barrage using heavy artillery. Only the 43rd Reserve Infantry Division, on the left wing, managed to take even the first enemy trench before strong Russian counterattacks drove them back. The Austrian 7th Infantry Division, which attempted to surmount the Russian position on the heights overlooking Lipa, suffered particularly heavy losses. The Austrian Fourth fared even worse. Otto von Berndt, a member of Fourth Army's general staff, reported that "[o]nly the 89th Infantry Regiment pushed into the enemy's first positions; the rest of the regiments could not be brought to the attack, [but] remained on the field the entire day and suffered very severe losses under the Russian artillery."[23]

In fact, only the 37th Honved Infantry Division refused to attack, on grounds that the weather did not allow it; the Austrian 11th Infantry Division initially asked for rest as well, but went forward when Tersztyanszky demanded. They spent the day caught in the crossfire of Russian artillery, suffering miserably. Linsingen still hoped to seize Lutsk before the Russians unleashed their new offensive, but the division and regimental commanders of Fourth Army warned him that their units were incapable of further action. Tersztyanszky managed to stir the Fourth Army into action on 1 July, but it gained no ground. Thus, though Marwitz's group pushed nearly 10 kilometers to the east along a front of some 20 kilometers over the next two days, Fourth Army's inability to keep up forced Linsingen to break off the counteroffensive on 3 July. While Marwitz reorganized his forces to strengthen the left wing for another attack, Linsingen ordered the Austrian Fourth and German X Corps to establish "permanent" positions along the Styr-Stochod line.[24]

But if Linsingen and the Central Powers found only limited success, so too had Brusilov's efforts been frustrated. The Russian Eighth Army continued to take prisoners—over 200,000 Austro-Hungarians had been captured since the offensive opened—but failed to make any significant breakthroughs. Each Russian attack was quickly countered, and precious reserves were expended regaining ground lost to Linsingen each morning. Sakharov's position had only worsened since the offensive was renewed on 14 June, and Kaledin's XL Corps, in the center of his line, had actually been driven back by Marwitz's forces before XXIII Corps had come to their aid and restored the original position. Beginning on 19 June, therefore, Brusilov issued orders that those units not advancing on the northern sectors of the Southwestern Front should dig in and make preparations for a renewed offensive in early July.[25]

New Armies

It had been clear in fact to the commanders on both sides for some time that neither the Russian offensive nor the Austro-German counterstrike would succeed without large numbers of additional reserves. The question was what to do about it. Brusilov decided, much earlier than Linsingen, to wait for additional reinforcements; he had little choice. The Russian Seventh was advancing with unexpected ease and speed in the Bukovina, and Russian diplomats were working in concert with Italy to bring Romania into the war. The British and French were committed to launching an offensive along the Somme River on 1 July, which would preclude any further movement of German troops to the Eastern Front. If all went well—though Brusilov doubted it would—Evert and Kuropatkin soon would begin supporting operations in the north. Alekseev, having finally grown frustrated with Evert and Kuropatkin, sent four corps (I, XXIII, V Siberian, and the two Turkestan infantry divisions) and additional heavy artillery and shells to reinforce Brusilov's armies by 24 June, in addition to placing Third Army permanently under his command. The Special Army, moreover, was scheduled to be ready soon, which would add two prize corps to Brusilov's forces.

The Imperial Guards (I and II Guards) had been created by Peter the Great. With each of the 65,000 handpicked and well-trained men standing over six feet tall, it represented Russia's elite force. Knox referred to them as "the finest human animals in Europe."[26] Most Russian rulers had used them sparingly, much as Napoleon Bonaparte deployed his own Imperial Guards, but Nicholas II sent them into the front lines early in the war. Like every Russian ruler since Peter the Great, Nicholas II held the honorary rank of colonel in the Guards' most elite unit, the *Preobrazhenski* Regiment, and the Guards Army was designated as his personal reserve. After it suffered heavy losses in the Great Retreat of 1915, however, the Guards Army had been held out of combat while the ranks were refilled and the men trained.

Their commanders, by all accounts, were somewhat less splendid; Stone notes that none of them had any real experience or idea of modern warfare.[27] The president of the Russian Duma, Mikhail Rodzianko, wrote to Brusilov after inspecting the Guards Army that while the troops appeared splendid and well equipped, their leaders appeared incapable. Brusilov's own judgment was even harsher:

The commander of the Special Army, the General Adjutant Bezobrazov, was an honorable and upstanding man, though of limited understanding and unbelievably stubborn. His chief of staff, Count Ignatiev, knew absolutely nothing about serving on a staff and had no idea of staff work, regardless of the fact that he had graduated from the General Staff Academy with honors. The chief of artillery, the Duke of Mecklenburg-Schwerin, was a good man at heart but had only a very vague concept of the role of artillery, though the use of artillery had grown vastly in importance and there could be no more success without the meaningful support of the artillery. [. . .]

The commander of the I Guards Corp, Crown Prince Pavel Aleksandrovitch—overall a very sensible and doubtless personally courageous man—understood absolutely nothing of military affairs. The commander of the II Guards Corps, Rauch—a clever and well-versed man—had a difficult weakness for a soldier: his nerves gave out as soon as shots were fired, and in danger he lost his spirit of resistance and it was no longer possible for him to lead.[28]

General Aleksandr Bezobrazov had been relieved of several prior commands for incompetence and insubordination, and had a reputation in military circles for poor judgment. Nicholas II had selected him largely because of his noble birth, and considered him "honest and well-bred"; Knox, however, judged him "a difficult old man."[29] According to Rodzianko, moreover, the Grand Duke Pavel Aleksandrovich also had at least one failing in addition to those cited by Brusilov: "[he] does not even carry out even the orders of his superiors."[30] Brusilov wrote to Alekseev in an attempt to replace the Guards' commanders, but only the tsar could appoint or relieve the leaders of his personal guard, and Alekseev was unwilling to even pose the request. Brusilov would have to go ahead with what resources he had, and be glad for them.[31]

His plan now differed little from that of early June. Evert had pledged to move on 3 July, by which time the Somme Offensive would already be underway on the Western Front, and Brusilov therefore ordered his armies to prepare their attacks for that day as well. On his right wing, Lesch's Third Army, reinforced with the XLVI Corps and IV Cavalry Corps taken from Kaledin's Eighth as well as the 78th Infantry Division from First Army, would once again strike at Pinsk, since unhinging the fronts was the key to Brusilov's plan. Eighth Army, augmented to the north by the Special Army, would drive west against Kovel. The Seventh and Ninth armies would continue their advance as far as possible in the south, with the former aiming at the railway junctions of Halicz and Stanislau while the latter hoped to seize the Carpathian passes. Sakharov's Eleventh Army—the weakest of

Brusilov's forces—was charged with pinning the Austrian Second and the South Army and, if possible, pushing west to prevent the movement of Austro-German troops from north to south.

Kaledin immediately protested, fearing a German attack on his exposed flank, as had happened in 1915. In his view, Eighth Army should have been retreating and consolidating its position, not deepening an already dangerous salient. If ordered to advance, moreover, he preferred to move directly west, in the direction of Vladimir-Volynsk, rather than against the new German forces defending Kovel.[32] Angered and disappointed, Brusilov worked to overcome Kaledin's doubts: "I finally had to repeat [my] directives and went to him twice personally, in order to arrange for him to defend to the west and direct all his attention and all his forces to the northwest for the conquest of Kovel."[33]

By most accounts, this was a miscalculation on Brusilov's part. Both Stone and Lincoln criticize Brusilov for abandoning his innovative tactics and returning to more orthodox methods in July 1916. According to Stone, Brusilov should have realized by this time that Evert was simply unreliable; even if he did attack, the chances of success were small, and the assistance rendered would be minimal. Further, Stone argues, the terrain around Pinsk was simply unsuitable for an advance, with a limited number of paths available through the marshes.[34] As Lincoln points out, Brusilov no longer had the trained and battle-hardened troops to carry out such an operation successfully.[35] Since opening the offensive on 4 June, Russian forces had lost some 285,000 men killed and at least that many wounded or taken prisoner, and the reserves on the Southwestern Front were increasingly raw recruits.[36]

Such criticism, however, seems wide of the mark. Brusilov was certainly aware of the shortcomings of the Russian armies. He did not expect much from Evert, and in fact seemed to be counting on him for nothing more than a pinning operation, an attack that would prevent the Germans from sending additional forces south, and even then he had sent Third Army on much the same mission. In his memoirs, Brusilov argues that he was fully prepared to defend against a strike against Kaledin's northern flank:

> The fact that the Germans and Austrians, while they held against us in the direction of Kovel and Vladimir-Volynsk, were creating a strong force in the area around the Manievicze railroad station in order to strike Kaledin's right flank had great significance for us. By attacking in this direction with both of the aforementioned armies [Third and Eighth], I anticipated the intention of

the enemy and negated [*durchkreutzte*] not only the tactical significance of the Kovel-Manievicze flanking maneuver, but also finally secured my own position in Wolhynia.[37]

This may well be a case of perfect hindsight, but the fact remains that the focal point of the operation had to be Kovel if there was to be any strategic significance for Russia and the Allies. The greatest flaw in the plan, which was not entirely within Brusilov's control, was that he had to rely on two commanders in whom he had little faith—Kaledin and Bezobrazov—to attain that goal. Most important, however, is the fact that Brusilov's plan was, by Stone's own admission, well prepared and successful—at least where it was carried out according to orders.[38] For Russia and the Allies— the Somme Offensive on the Western Front notwithstanding—Brusilov's operations still represented the best chance for a decisive stroke in the war. If he succeeded in breaking through yet again, it seemed likely that Romania would join the Allied Powers, and Austria-Hungary would be driven from the war. To achieve that goal meant taking a risk.

The Central Powers' response to this threat was divided. In Falkenhayn's view, Germany had already done enough to stabilize the front on the line of the Styr and Stochod rivers, and that was sufficient. He still believed that the decision would come on the Western Front, at Verdun, and viewed the Eastern Front as a holding action. Falkenhayn's main concern, therefore, was ensuring the survival of the Austro-Hungarian armies with as little cost as possible. In addition to the four new German divisions already in Galicia, the 43rd Reserve Division and the Bavarian 11th Infantry Division (drawn from the Western Front) were en route to the theater. This, he believed (correctly), would allow Linsingen to continue his attacks, this time with the more modest aim of draining the Russian reserves that were arriving in Brusilov's command. In his opinion the worsening situation in the south—the Russians took Czernovitz, the regional capital of the Bukovina, on 18 June—took priority, and Falkenhayn accordingly ordered the German 105th Infantry Division (stationed at the time in Macedonia) to join the Austrian 48th Infantry Division (en route from Tirol) in reinforcing the South Army.

Conrad was furious, believing Falkenhayn was reneging on his promise to send additional German troops south to match any Russian north-south troop shifts. While he doubted Linsingen would achieve any great success, Conrad was still convinced that eliminating the salient between Kovel and Brody was vital and that the key to defending the area was more

German troops.[39] "Doubtless the current superiority of the Russians is in their rich replacements that they brutally throw into battle," he wrote to von Seeckt on 18 June. The Austrian Fourth, Conrad pointed out, had lost more than 100,000 men (57 percent of its men) since 4 June, and morale was plummeting. "If the Germans don't help soon," he concluded, "the whole thing will go bad."[40] For the Austro-Hungarian Empire, combating Brusilov's offensive was a matter of life and death, not a sideshow.

Conrad therefore did what he could to force Falkenhayn's hand. On 19 June, he informed the German commander that he had redirected the Austrian 48th Infantry Division—which had just arrived at South Army headquarters—to join the Austrian First Army in the defense of Lemberg (Lvov). The two additional divisions—the 44th Honved Infantry Division and the newly formed 59th Infantry Division, comprising the 6th and 18th mountain brigades plus the 10th Fortress Artillery (*Festungsartillerie*) Brigade—coming from Tirol, he told Falkenhayn moreover, had encountered difficulties and could not be expected to arrive in Galicia before 25 June.[41] "Overwhelming Russian pressure in the direction of Lemberg could make the entire East Galician Front untenable," Conrad warned.[42]

Falkenhayn responded by asking Conrad what forces he planned to make available to defend the city. He also noted that while the Russians would no doubt focus on the Galician Front, since their gains there had been "easily won," in his opinion the forces already in place could hold the line "if only every man at his post does his duty." Nonetheless, because Hindenburg had received reliable reports that the Russians would concentrate their attacks in the south and was now prepared to send his reserves to aid Linsingen, Falkenhayn agreed to send the German 107th Infantry Division and the 5th Reserve Infantry Division south. In return, however, he once again demanded that the Italian "adventure" be curtailed and that the Habsburg troops diverted there be returned speedily to the Galician theater with their artillery. As a final jab, he recommended to Conrad that the Austrians put more officers like Mackensen in place to ensure that the troops did, indeed, fulfill their duties.[43]

Conrad's response, sent on 21 June, was to raise again the specter of a Romanian entry into the war—which would of course require additional German troops to combat. Intelligence indicated that negotiations were already underway in St. Petersburg to bind Romania to the Allies, he reported. To preclude a Romanian declaration, Conrad proposed that Falkenhayn support an offensive to clear the Bukovina "with strong German forces." He himself, Conrad reiterated, was in no position to offer any troops before early July, when the retreat in the Tirol would free up three additional Austro-Hungarian divisions. Even then, if Falkenhayn was unwilling to provide German support, they could only be deployed in tenuous defensive positions. "I am thus unfortunately not in a position to unleash simultaneous attacks on both sides of the Dniester, deflect the pressing attack of the Russians toward Hungary, and keep the Italian Front steady as it presently is," the Habsburg commander wrote.[44]

Exasperated, Falkenhayn summoned Conrad to Berlin again, where the latter immediately began to expound upon his plan to "destroy the Russian Front" through the attacks on the Dniester. The German commander did not reject Conrad's plan directly. Instead he pointed out that the Germans, despite facing superior numbers on the Western Front, had already contributed ten divisions (Division Rusche from the central sector of the Eastern Front; the 107th and 108th Infantry Division from the northern sector, along with the 5th Reserve Infantry Division; the 105th Infantry Division from Macedonia; and the 7th, 19th, 20th, 43rd, and 11th Bavarian infantry divisions from the Western Front) to the Habsburg Front while the Austro-Hungarians had brought only two (the 48th and 61st infantry divisions) from Italy and declared two more (the 44th and 59th infantry divisions) ready to return. According to Ludendorff, this had already reduced the German reserves on the northern half of the front to "battalions of recruits."[45] Conrad, without revealing that the Archduke Eugen had promised to send the Habsburg I Corps (the 10th and 34th infantry divisions, along with the 43rd Honved Infantry Division) to Galicia once the retreat was completed, insisted that he needed more German troops. "You are obliged," he pleaded, "it is a matter of existence or destruction."[46]

Falkenhayn, who had decided to make one final and hopefully decisive strike at Verdun before the Allies launched their own summer offensive, simply replied that there were no troops available.[47] The Austrian 44th and 59th infantry divisions would go to support the Austrian Seventh in the Bukovina, and if Hindenburg and Ludendorff could spare any troops they would support the South Army in a limited offensive. Linsingen would continue to try and recapture Lutsk, but his main goal would be the defense of Kovel, for the overall defense of Lemberg (Lvov) remained paramount. Conrad, naturally, was disappointed, for he saw—correctly—in Falkenhayn's offer another attempt to extend German influence over the Habsburg war effort. "There was nothing to be had," he wrote upon his return to Teschen, "nothing more out of the west; only what Hindenburg can surrender will come down here."[48] As usual, Conrad was wrong. Not only did Hindenburg send the German 22nd Infantry Division, but in return for Austrian heavy artillery sent to Linsingen from the 48th Infantry Division—and over heavy objections from the German general staff—on 27 June Falkenhayn sent the German 119th Infantry Division and the 1st Reserve Infantry Division to the Austrian Seventh and the South Army, respectively.[49]

The German commander was keenly aware that an Austro-Hungarian collapse on the Eastern Front would mean not only the end of his plans for the Western Front, but possibly an unfavorable end to the war. He agreed, furthermore, with Conrad's argument that the best way to forestall a Romanian entry into the war—and thus to alleviate the threat to Hungary—was to launch a counteroffensive along the Dniester River. The issue, as always between the two commanders, was control. Falkenhayn had favored using the South Army, as it was under his control, while Conrad had wanted German troops to support the Austrian Seventh Army.

The egalitarian dispatch of a German division to each army was thus the first stroke in Falkenhayn's political campaign to gain control over the southern half of the Eastern Front. The second came in the form of a proposal to create a Twelfth Army from those units, along with the Austro-Hungarian divisions coming from Italy, to carry out the attacks on the Dniester. To ensure Habsburg acceptance of the proposal while also gaining some control over the operation, Falkenhayn shrewdly proposed the Habsburg Archduke Karl Franz Josef, heir to the throne, as the army's commander, with German officers filling out his staff. Seeckt would shift from the Austrian Seventh Army to serve as the archduke's chief of staff. Falkenhayn was aware that the Habsburgs had been seeking a post for the archduke for some time; placing him in charge of the now-vital southeastern defenses—at least nominally—Falkenhayn believed, guaranteed an all-out commitment from Austria-Hungary.

Conrad, of course, viewed the proposal in the exact opposite light. Having a commander with the "substance" of the archduke, he believed, might finally enable the Habsburg command to override its Teutonic partner in dictating the course of the war. The fact that the archduke's staff would be composed of German officers, moreover, would force Falkenhayn to support the operations of Twelfth Army unconditionally. Conrad did ask, however, that at least one of the senior staff officers be Austrian. After some slight negotiation, Falkenhayn agreed that both the new quartermaster of Twelfth Army and von Seeckt's replacement as chief of staff of the Austrian Seventh would be appointed by the Austro-Hungarians. Falkenhayn also proposed now that Twelfth Army be not just an attack group but an army group, with command over the Austrian Seventh and the Austro-German South Army as well—the so-called Army Group Dniester.

Delighted, Conrad took the proposal to Emperor Franz Josef in person on 30 June, telling him that it was "critical to give the Archduke this command."[50] The end result, however, was exactly what Falkenhayn had intended: implicit German control over the front. German units and German officers were now intermingled with Habsburg units across the entire front, supporting them, in the eyes of the Germans, like stays in a corset (*Korsettstangen*). From Army Group Linsingen in the north to the South Army under Bothmer, Germans commanded the front. Twelfth Army was, in a sop to Habsburg pride, the last Austro-Hungarian command, at least nominally. In addition to von Seeckt, three of the four other general staff officers of Twelfth Army were Germans. There was at least one German officer in every department of Twelfth Army command, and German officers held virtually all of the key posts at lower levels. Within the general staff of the Austrian Seventh Army, a "Prussian party" declared its loyalty to Seeckt by wearing the German Iron Cross as their only field decoration. The Habsburg army commanders would issue the orders, but only after consultation with their German counterparts, and all reports from Twelfth Army went to both commands simultaneously. Even Conrad's proposal to name the new formation after the archduke was defeated, as Falkenhayn insisted that a unit containing substantial German forces had to have a "neutral" name. Thus, on 5 July the Archduke Karl Franz Josef assumed command of "Army Group Dniester"; Conrad had his attack force, but the cost was high.[51]

The Second Phase

It was the Russians, however, who struck first. Surprisingly, and somewhat unfortunately, Evert launched his attack on 2 July. On his northern wing, the Russian Tenth Army (General Radekievitsch) faced the German Tenth Army (General von Eichhorn) in the area around Smorgon. His remaining forces were concentrated around Baranovichi, where Evert had spread over one thousand guns, ranging from 15 to 28cm in caliber and each provided with a store of over one thousand shells, across the front. The main attack would come on a 7-kilometer front along the Servecz River some 20 kilometers north of Baranovichi. There the bulk of the Russian Fourth Army

(north to south: XXV Corps, IX Corps, X Corps, and the Imperial Grenadiers Division; with XXXV Corps, III Siberian, and II and III Caucasian
Corps as a reserve) under General Ragosa was to concentrate against the
established positions of the Austrian XII Corps (16th and 35th infantry
divisions). His commanders, having only recently shifted their aim from
Vilnius to Baranovichi as Evert waffled, had had less than two weeks to
prepare for the battle. Their maps were poor, the guns were mostly unreg-
istered, and with few aerial observers to adjust the artillery fire, the opening
barrage was largely wasted. The Russian 5th and 42nd infantry divisions
(IX Corps) had sapped trenches forward in the middle of the line against
the Austrian 16th Infantry Division, according to one Austrian officer.

> The Russian trenches opposite this sector of our old positions, whose lines we
> had so trusted that we could have drawn them with our eyes closed, had altered
> themselves strongly in the weeks since our observation had been withdrawn.
> Countless saps, well defended with zig-zags and good, flanking shoulder arms,
> had been pushed forward from the front lines against our trenches using every
> fold in the wavy landscape; the saps were connected by cross-trenches, and thus
> the entire trench system had been extended against our lines.[52]

Since they were the only units to properly sap, however, the Austrians
were prepared for the assault. Taking their lessons from Brusilov's initial
attack and also the German defense at Stolovicze (13–14 June), the Austrians placed most of the their troops in the second line, and rushed them
forward immediately when the Russian artillery attempted to destroy their
guns. Having begun the shelling of the Habsburg positions at 4:00 AM,
Ragosa finally sent the infantry forward at 4:00 PM. They were met with
concentrated artillery fire and driven back.

After a short artillery barrage, Ragosa renewed the attack at 2:00 AM
on 3 July. Following Evert's dictum that the infantry would decide the
battle, Ragosa dedicated five divisions (IX Corps, XXXV Corps, and the
46th Infantry Division from XXV Corps) to the assault. Communications
were so poor that it took nearly four hours for the Russian commanders
to learn that the initial infantry attack had penetrated the southern wing
of the Austrian 16th Infantry Division, though the Austrian commander,
General Henriquez, was informed within the hour. The Central Powers
were therefore able to rush reserves into the line before the Russians could
fully exploit their gains. The Austrian 35th Infantry Division shifted its
weight northward to cover the gap, and General Woyrsch sent the German 37th Light Infantry Regiment to aid in the effort. The battle raged

between the first and second trenches of the Austrian position throughout the afternoon. In the evening, however, waves of Russian reserves—who had been trapped behind the cavalry in the rear—finally came forward and secured the first trench. Faced with a possible disaster, Prince Leopold of Bavaria, commanding the neighboring German Ninth Army, sent his 5th Reserve Infantry Division and two heavy artillery batteries from the XXV Reserve Corps, while Hindenburg dispatched three hastily assembled battalions of recruits and three additional artillery batteries from his own army group. Everything, Henriquez told his troops, depended on the Austrian XII holding the line that night.

His assessment turned out to be fairly accurate. With the German reserves and additional artillery at their disposal, the Austrian 16th and 35th infantry divisions succeeded in fending off renewed Russian assaults through the whole of 4 July. Ragosa sent the III Siberian forward in the afternoon, and they managed to widen the battlefront but were unable to penetrate any further. Undaunted, Evert renewed the attack on 5 July, only to see his troops mowed down once again without being able to break the enemy. He informed Stavka that evening that he intended to pause and regroup before resuming the offensive the following day. On 6 July, however, Evert took no action, while the Central Powers added two more regiments to the line and strengthened their positions; nor did he move the following day. Not until 2:00 AM on 8 July did Ragosa renew the battle, sending the III Siberian forward along with the 3rd Grenadiers (XXV Corps) in ranks ten or twelve men deep. The assault wave broke in the face of concentrated defensive fire and was not renewed. Evert decided to wait for the reinforcements promised by Stavka (IV Siberian) rather than pursue the enemy.[53] Six Russian divisions had failed to defeat a single Austrian corps plus one German reserve division. "Many of our commanding generals are silly idiots who, even after two years of warfare, cannot learn the first and simplest lessons in warfare," the tsar complained when informed of the result.[54]

While in tactical terms the battle was probably a standoff, from a strategic point of view it could only be seen as a heavy defeat for the Russians. In only seven days, Evert had expended more shells than all of Brusilov's armies had in June, and the Russian armies had lost 80,000 men while inflicting only 16,000 casualties on the Central Powers.[55] To make matters worse, Evert's attack had neither drawn forces away from the Southwestern Front nor prevented the Germans from transferring additional forces there. Kuropatkin, who was supposed to strike south and west from the bridgeheads at Riga, made only one brief, unsuccessful foray against the German Eighth Army on 5 July before lapsing into immobility once again.

This lack of support was regrettable, as Brusilov's main force swung into action just as Evert and Kuropatkin ceased to be active. Kaledin's Eighth Army and Lesch's Third initiated their artillery barrages on 4 July at 4:00 AM, and almost immediately opened some gaps in the Austro-German lines. After knocking out the enemy's artillery with carefully directed fire, the pounding of the Russian guns stirred the dust of the dry marshes, blinding the defenders in many areas and allowing the infantry to approach virtually unmolested. On the northern edge of the Lutsk salient, units from the Russian XXX Corps and Turkestan Guards division penetrated the front lines of Corps Fath by 8:00 AM, and soon proceeded to roll the front up to the northwest. By noon, the Russians had taken the town of Kopyli, and threatened to cave in the entire sector. Fath deployed the corps's cavalry, which slowed the Russians briefly, but when an attempted counterattack failed around 3:00 PM, Fath was forced to withdraw his entire force to the west in order to find a defensible position. He had but three Hungarian reserve (Honved) battalions and a cavalry squadron remaining in his reserve. Further north, the Russian 100th Reserve Infantry Division (XLVI Corps) had forged a 1.5-kilometer gap in the line of General Hauer's Cavalry Corps, driving between the Habsburg Polish Legion and the Austrian 53rd Infantry Division. The Polish Legion managed to make a stand on a hilltop commanding their sector of the front, but the initial gap and the retreat of Corps Fath meant that Hauer had to pull back the south wing of his corps. Fortunately for the Austrians, Lesch did not pursue his opponents aggressively, choosing instead to establish a line on the western bank of the Stochod.

The Russian Third attacked in force again on 5 July, with XLVI Corps and Corps Bulatov striking repeatedly at the interior wings connecting Fath's forces to Hauer's. Both the Honved units and the Polish Legion managed to hold their positions on Hauer's southern wing for most of the day, but near evening the superior weight of the Russian forces began to make itself felt. The Poles were driven west with heavy losses, and this time Lesch pursued them closely. Fath tried to rally his forces along the highway leading to Gradnie the following day, but lacked the strength to hold the Russians off. A Bavarian *Landsturm* battalion that had been sent to reinforce the Polish Legion on 5 July, for instance, had already been reduced to fewer than 1,300 men in less than one day's fighting. Lesch's forces tore easily through the weakened interior wings of the two Austrian corps, once again threatening to roll up the remainder of the Styr Front. Fath hurriedly drew his left wing back once again, hoping to shorten the line and thus maintain the connection to Hauer's right wing, which was retreating with equal haste. The Austrian II Corps under General Kaiser, which was supposed to shift northward and support Fath, failed to engage. Kaiser claimed that the 11th Bavarian Infantry Division, intended as the core of the counterattack group, had suffered too severely from the summer heat during the forced march north. Engaging the Russian XXX Corps in its established positions around Kolki under such conditions, he argued, would be suicide. Unfortunately for Fath, neither Falkenhayn nor Conrad could supply additional reserves.

Lesch's close pursuit led to the destruction of the Austrian Styr line the next day. The Russians broke the Polish Legion, which they had kept under fire throughout the night, repeatedly on the morning of 7 July, forcing them to retreat to the northwest while the Austrian 43rd was chased westward. This created a gap of nearly four kilometers between the two forces, into which the Russians continued to pour. The seemingly endless waves of Russian infantry had collapsed both of Fath's wings by that afternoon, leaving the center of the corps trapped in a salient with the Russians threatening to cut it off completely. Fearing the worst, Linsingen ordered the withdrawal of the entire northern sector—nearly 100 kilometers in length and comprising, north to south: Army Group Gronau, Cavalry Corps Hauer, Corps Fath, and the Austrian II Corps—behind the Stochod River.

Hauer's forces, already in retreat, never received the order. The Polish Legion thus found itself facing an entire Russian division and part of the Russian IV Cavalry Corps with only the Honved units alongside that afternoon, and it was decimated before it could disengage and retreat. Only about 1,000 of the Hungarians survived. Overall, Corps Hauer lost more than 3,000 men. Fath was equally hard pressed; he had to divide his forces in the center and abandon three batteries, which he exploded, in order to escape the Russian noose. By nightfall though, both Fath and Hauer had managed to separate from the Russians and reach the new defensive lines; it took Lesch a full day to reestablish contact, so far had they retreated.

Elated, Brusilov ordered Kaledin and Lesch to press forward and destroy the Stochod line before it could be fully fortified. The Austrians, however, had already managed to blow the bridges over the Stochod River and reinforce the line before the Russians could engage. Linsingen had sent the German 108th Infantry Division from Marwitz's front, Hindenburg directed a division (commanded by General Clausius) south to aid in the defense, and Falkenhayn rushed the 121st Infantry Division to the line. Before they even arrived, however, Fath managed to stage a small counterstrike on 8 July; using only nine battalions, he inflicted heavy casualties on Lesch's forces, threw them back from the banks of the Stochod, and blew the bridges they had repaired. A Russian assault on the remaining Honved units on the southern end of Hauer's new front on 9 July was likewise turned away with relative ease, as was an attack against his north wing on the following day. Even a concerted attack against Bernhardi's right wing with two full corps (I and XXXIX) failed to breach the Stochod line. Both Alekseev and Brusilov now were convinced that it would take another concerted attack to force the Stochod positions, and since Kaledin's westward drive—advancing much more slowly over swampy ground and into the heart of Linsingen's new defenses—had already been halted on 8 July, they decided to regroup. In that first week of July 1916, Brusilov's armies had taken an additional 40,000 prisoners of war, but they had also suffered casualties of nearly half a million men, including 5,000 officers (60,000 killed; 370,000 wounded; and 60,000 "missing," over and above the officers).[56]

Any ideas Alekseev might have cherished about driving the Germans back in the north had long since been abandoned. Stavka therefore shifted all available forces to the Southwestern Front and issued directives to the commanders on the Western and Northwestern fronts to support Brusilov's offensive. Kuropatkin in particular received explicit instructions from Alekseev to attack, even if he could send significant forces against only a single sector of the front. The point, the Russian commander emphasized, was not to break through the German lines but to pin down their units. Surely, with more than a two-to-one advantage in manpower (420,000 Russians faced 192,000 Germans on the Northwestern Front), he could manage that? Kuropatkin agreed to prepare an attack on Bausk for 16 July, by which time Brusilov hoped to be on the attack once again on the Southwestern Front.[57]

Rather than continuing to drive on Kovel directly with Eighth Army, however, Alekseev and Brusilov orchestrated a flanking strike from the northwest. To facilitate this, Ragosa's Fourth Army was dissolved and its components distributed between the Russian Tenth and Second armies. The Guards Army, combined with some former reserve units from the Russian Tenth and now known officially as Fourth Army, was put under Brusilov's command and inserted into the line between Lesch's Third Army

and Kaledin's Eighth. In addition, Alekseev ordered Evert to send two corps
(III Corps and IV Siberian) to Lesch as reinforcements. This gave the Russians an overwhelming numerical advantage of 247,000 men facing only
114,000 Austro-German troops defending the northwestern approaches to
Kovel. In the south, Alekseev had sent the Russian 108th Reserve Infantry
Division and the Ussuri Cossack Division from Second Army (Evert) to
Letschitski's Ninth in the Bukovina already on 1 July. Letschitski, however,
was unwilling to wait a week for reinforcements, so Scherbatschev sent
the 47th Infantry Division from his own XVI Corps south, and the 108th
Infantry Division was redirected to Seventh Army. This gave Seventh Army
a total of 157,000 troops to face 87,000 Austro-German troops, while Ninth
Army had 144,000 men on its sector of the front, opposing only 89,000. In
the center of the line Sakharov's Eleventh, though recently reinforced by
V Corps, held only a slight numerical advantage in comparison (163,000
against 131,000); overall Brusilov now had some 711,000 troops against only
421,000 for the Central Powers. As Stavka solemnly informed him on 9
July, Brusilov was being entrusted with "the battle of decision."[58]

CHAPTER FIVE

A TALE OF NORTH AND SOUTH

On 9 July 1916, the army commanders of the Central Powers believed that the Brusilov Offensive had to be regarded as a failure. Though they had faced "seemingly [. . .] the greatest crisis of the world war" less than a month earlier, they were now convinced that the Russians' moment had passed.[1] North of the Pripet Marshes, Evert and Kuropatkin were no longer seen as a threat to the German positions. Indeed, while they possessed more than a two-to-one numerical superiority, the Russian commanders—including Alekseev—were thoroughly convinced that the German troops were simply superior. All future Russian operations in the north would be intended as either pinning or diversionary. The advance on Kovel had been halted and the front secured; neither Lemberg (Lvov) nor Brest-Litovsk seemed in the slightest danger of being overrun. Kaledin and Lesch had pushed the Central Powers out of their positions on the Styr River, it was true, but new and seemingly stronger positions had been established on the Stochod River. Brusilov still possessed vast resources, including the elite Guards Army, but the Germans in particular were confident in their defenses. "In Galicia," Falkenhayn wrote later, "the most dangerous moment of the Russian Offensive had been passed before the first shot on the Somme was fired."[2]

The only remaining threat seemed to be in the Bukovina. The Hungarian leadership and population were war-weary, and reportedly lacked the will to continue—at least under Habsburg command. Pflanzer-Baltin's Seventh Army, charged with holding the Carpathian passes, had lost nearly 60 percent of its original strength. The 24th Infantry Division alone, which had begun with 16,000 men, had suffered more than 13,000 casualties.[3] It still appeared likely, moreover, that Romania would enter the war on the side of Russia and thus possibly tip the balance decisively in favor of the Allies.[4] If that were to happen, and the Habsburg Empire either collapsed or made a separate peace with the Russians, Germany's military outlook would be bleak indeed. Though Falkenhayn found it utterly distasteful, German troops would have to support the Habsburgs.

Because of the continuing crisis in the north around Kovel, however, neither the Germans nor the Austro-Hungarians had been able to take measures sufficient to check the southern Russian advance that had begun in early June. The Austro-German armies had blown two key crossing points on the Czeremosz River, five bridges over the Dniester, and six roads spanning the Pruth without slowing the Russian advance significantly.[5] Even Brusilov's inattention to the southern sectors and the timely arrival of the German 119th Infantry Division on 30 June had simply prolonged the emergency. The Russian Ninth eventually had broken even the German units, which, ironically, had to be driven back into the lines at saber-point by Austrian officers. Letschitski's supply difficulties, however, prevented him from driving to the Carpathians.[6]

Pflanzer-Baltin's Seventh Army nevertheless remained in a state of perpetual crisis. His forces were divided, with one-third of his army, the Austrian XI Corps, pinned behind the Moldova River nearly 20 kilometers to the south. XI Corps was hardly a significant fighting force; it consisted of (north to south) the 24th Infantry Division, the 40th Honved Light Infantry Division, the 5th Infantry Division, three battalions of guards infantry known as Group Kaltenborn, and Brigade Papp, which was an irregular formation of *Landsturm* units, local gendarmes, and the Bukovina Volunteer Regiment. The remaining two-thirds of his force (north to south: Group Hadfy, VIII Corps [formerly Group Benigni], and Cavalry Corps Brudermann) stood on a line that ran from the Dniester River in the north down to the Czeremosz River. Their defenses were, in general, hastily constructed, badly cared for, and in tactically poor positions. The morale of the troops and their trust in their commanders was almost unbelievably low. The outlook was so dismal that the commander sent to relieve Benigni on 1 July, Feldzugmeister Scheuchenstuel, resigned almost immediately after arriving and reviewing the situation.[7] By the time Archduke Karl took command of Army Group Dniester (which included both the South Army under Bothmer and the Austrian Seventh under Pflanzer-Baltin), the Russians occupied most of the Bukovina, having taken Czernovitz (18 June) and Kolomea (29 June), and were threatening the important rail junctions at Stanislau and Halicz as well as the Carpathian passes leading to the Hungarian plain.[8] The archduke's first task, to which four divisions—the German 105th and 119th infantry divisions, as well as the Austrian 44th Guards Infantry Division and the 59th Infantry Division, both recently arrived from Tirol—had been dedicated, was to "break through the enemy's front in southeast Galicia in order to open the paths against the flanks and rear communications of the opponent where he has thrust through the Bukovina."[9] He never got the chance.

Karl Franz Josef, archduke of Austria-Hungary and heir to the throne, arrived in Chodrow at 11:00 AM on 5 July to assume command of Twelfth Army. That afternoon, the Russian XXI Corps (Ninth Army) struck Benigni's right wing, separating the Austrian 30th Infantry Division from the adjoining Austrian 42nd Infantry Division to the north. Pflanzer-Baltin responded by ordering Benigni to fall back, but by the time the orders reached the front, the Russians had overrun the Habsburgs' fall-back positions as well and were driving to the southwest. With Benigni now in full retreat, Pflanzer-Baltin hurled the last of his reserves—twelve battalions scrounged from four different divisions—into the fray. Heroic resistance by the 1st Carinthian Mountain Guards Regiment, the 2nd Upper Austrian Guards Regiment, and the 8th Cavalry Division halted a flanking movement by the Russian XII Corps the following day. Suddenly, however, the Russian XI Corps appeared in the gap created by the earlier strike, negating a planned counterattack and forcing Benigni's northern wing back to the Pruth River. The German divisions that had been sent to spearhead Twelfth's counterattack (the 105th and 119th) found themselves instead on the defensive, and the two Austrian divisions (the 44th and 59th) were sent to plug the gaps in the line.

The archduke, with his initial low estimates of both Pflanzer-Baltin and the troops of Seventh Army confirmed, informed Teschen that he required at least one additional division if he was to have any chance of holding. The 44th and 59th infantry divisions had already suffered irretrievable losses, according to his staff, and at least five other divisions under his command (the 5th, 24th, 30th, 42nd, and 51st, all from Seventh Army) possessed only the fighting strength of regiments. Conrad responded by ordering the Austrian 34th Infantry Division to shift from

Tirol to the Bukovina. Because it would not arrive at Seventh Army before 12 July, however, he also sent an urgent request to Falkenhayn for additional reinforcements. With the renewed Russian offensives in the north, unfortunately, neither Falkenhayn nor Hindenburg felt they could spare any troops. The Habsburg commanders, Falkenhayn told Conrad, would simply have to find a way to increase the fighting spirit (*Kampfgeist*) of the forces they had. "The time for operations is over," wrote Kundmann. "It is [now] a great battle that must be fought through."[10]

It was unlikely that any increase in "fighting spirit" could rescue Seventh Army, however. The Russian strikes had left only the Austrian 5th Infantry Division, already greatly weakened, holding a 20-kilometer front between VIII Corps and Brudermann's cavalry, which, with only 6,000 men, now faced the Russian 32nd and 82nd infantry divisions on its own. Without additional forces, Pflanzer-Baltin reported, he would have to abandon the Bukovina in order to defend the Carpathian passes. The archduke readily took up the proposal. The Austrian Seventh was divided in two on 9 July, with Pflanzer-Baltin reduced to command of the southern third of his former army and tasked solely with the defense of the Carpathians. The northern two-thirds, now renamed Third Army, were placed under the command of the Habsburg General Hermann Baron von Kövess von Kövesshaza, who had commanded the original Austrian Third in Serbia during 1914–15.

Once again though, it was not the actions of the Central Powers that halted the Russian drive in the Bukovina. Letschitski, who had threatened Delatyn on 8 July, was forced to pause on the following day; he had lost 70,000 men since the beginning of the month, and his supply of munitions was dangerously low. Between 4 and 7 July, moreover, the Russian Southwestern Front as a whole had seen losses of some 5,000 officers, 60,000 troops dead, more than 370,000 wounded, and a further 60,000 men missing in action.[11] And so in the south, as in the north, both sides regrouped on 10–11 July for what promised to be a tremendous, and possibly decisive, battle.[12]

The Fall of Brody

The Central Powers had hoped to launch a counteroffensive on 18 July, using the Austrian Second Army, still relatively intact, and the South Army to push back the Russian Eleventh Army in the center of the line. Though the Russians continued to shell the Austrian and German positions along the Stochod, intelligence reports were unable to discern any significant Russian troop movements on the northern half of the front between 11 and 15 July. Neither the Austrians nor the Germans believed that Brusilov had abandoned the offensive, but while the Austrians generally believed the Russian strike would come against Radzivilov and Brody—General Puhallo (First Army), in particular insisted the Russians would strike at Lemberg (Lvov)—the Germans were convinced that any Russian attack would center on Kovel.

In the short run, it was the Austrians who were correct. Brusilov had, of course, intended to strike at Kovel on 15 July. Because the Guards Army did not arrive at the front until that date though, the attack had been postponed to 20 July. In the interim, Brusilov's well-developed intelligence networks had uncovered the Central Powers' plan for a strike in the center of the line. Brusilov therefore ordered Sakharov's Eleventh Army to preempt the Austro-German strike. He had, he claimed later, neither the hope nor the intention of breaking the Central Powers' line.[13] "I measured the significance of Eleventh Army's actions only insofar as the enemy had to fear making arrangements for going over to the offensive. He could not remove troops from this sector of the front. In and of itself, the Eleventh Army was not strong enough for any other operations."[14]

Sakharov accordingly renewed his artillery barrage on the night of 15–16 July, targeting a narrow sector of the front opposite the V Siberian Corps in the center of the Austrian First Army's front instead of focusing, as the Austrians anticipated, on the area where First and Second armies joined. The relatively narrow front of the Austrian Second (north to south: Corps Kosak, V Corps, and IV Corps) followed the 1914 border between Russia and the Habsburg Empire from Brody south to the Sereth River and had remained largely stable since mid-June. The collapse of Puhallo's First Army during the initial stages of the offensive in June had forced Böhm-Ermolli to draw his left wing back behind Radzivilov, but the retreat had been orderly and under little pressure from the Russians. Though Second Army's strength had dropped from over 85,000 men on 1 June to only 75,000 on 1 July, most of the "losses" were actually due to units having been sent northward to assist First Army during the days of crisis.[15] Like Bothmer's South Army, Böhm-Ermolli's Second was considered a stable and reliable force, while Sakharov considered the Austrian First vulnerable.

The initial infantry attack of the Russian Eleventh, which supported pinning artillery barrages against the north wing of the Austrian Fourth, met with almost immediate success. The Russian 50th Infantry Division (V Siberian Corps) overran the lines of the Habsburg 61st Infantry Division in the center of the sector just after dawn. A Hungarian *Landsturm* regiment simply panicked and fled without resisting, forcing the neighboring units to withdraw along with it to a depth of nearly eight kilometers. Just to the south, moreover, the Russian 10th Infantry Division (V Corps) had outflanked the Austrian 11th Mountain Brigade at 6:00 AM and opened a five-kilometer gap between the Habsburg 61st and 7th infantry divisions. Though the 7th's division reserve came forward to prevent the Russians from expanding the hole by noon, the Habsburg forces had been significantly weakened in the battle.

Fearing the line would collapse if nothing was done, Linsingen diverted the German 108th Infantry Division and three regiments from the reserve of Corps Szurmay to reinforce the line north of Berestecko and requested additional German forces from Falkenhayn. The Austro-Hungarian units, he asserted, were simply incapable of resisting the Russians on their own. A successful defense, Linsingen believed, could be accomplished only if German troops and German officers were thoroughly mixed in with the Habsburg units. Though Falkenhayn agreed, he refused to send additional troops south, telling Linsingen that the German forces already under his command should suffice. Szurmay, believing the Russians were about to launch a gas attack against his forces, disobeyed Linsingen's orders and held back his reserve. The Russian 50th Infantry Division was thus able to push the Habsburg forces back behind the Lipa River by evening, though it lacked the strength for close pursuit across that boundary.[16]

It took Sakharov three days to re-order his forces for a river crossing, which allowed the Austrian First to strengthen its fortifications on the western banks of the Lipa and Styr rivers. Though both Linsingen and the Habsburg High Command expressed doubts that Puhallo's forces could hold against overwhelming numbers—in one sector, six Russian infantry divisions and two Russian cavalry divisions faced two Austro-Hungarian divisions—Puhallo remained confident. As usual, such confidence was misplaced.

Aided by bright moonlight that revealed the Russian preparations, the Austrians were able to deflect the initial attempt of the Russian 10th Infantry Division to cross the Styr at 3:00 AM on 20 July. Sakharov persisted, however, bombarding the Habsburg positions throughout the morning, and when the Russian infantry went forward again at 2:00 PM it was able to force a crossing of both the Styr and the Lipa in several locations. The most significant break, however, came just after midnight on 21 July when the Russian 7th Infantry Division stormed the central sector of the Austrian First Army's lines between the two rivers near Berestecko. The Russian attack broke the interior wings of the Austrian 7th and 46th infantry divisions and opened a gap in the line that threatened to roll up Puhallo's right wing. By 7:00 AM, the southern wing of First Army was in full retreat, with no reserves immediately available, and the Russians were driving to the southwest. Sakharov now directed forces from the 10th Infantry Division and Eleventh Army's reserve cavalry to move south in an attempt to turn the flank completely, and sent his 101st Reserve Infantry Division forward into the line there as well. Instead of driving through the Habsburg line though, the Russian forces became entangled, and the enemy managed to retreat without suffering further damage. Rather than pursuing the Austrian First, moreover, Sakharov decided that evening to shift the weight of his attack south, against the relatively undisturbed front of the Austrian Second Army defending Brody.

It took a further three days for the Russian Eleventh to complete preparations for this new attack, and during that time the Central Powers discovered Sakharov's intentions through radio intercepts and aerial intelligence. This allowed Böhm-Ermolli to recall the 33rd Infantry Division, which had been sent to assist First Army on 21 July; Conrad also sent the 106th *Landsturm* Infantry Division to reinforce Second Army's northern wing. The Habsburg commander expected the addition of the 106th Infantry Division to be more than sufficient for Böhm-Ermolli to hold his position against the Russians, so much so that he ordered Second Army to release the 33rd Infantry Division again once the new unit had taken its position. According to the estimate of Austrian headquarters, the four corps of Second Army (north to south: XVIII, Corps Kosak, V, and IV) were facing only three Russian corps, reinforced by a few infantry and cavalry divisions plus a portion of V Siberian Corps held in reserve. It was a serious miscalculation.

By 25 July, Sakharov in fact had positioned four corps (north to south: V Siberian, XXXII, XLV, and XVII), two additional infantry divisions, and two cavalry divisions against the northern front of the Austrian Second Army held by XVIII Corps and Corps Kosak to create an overwhelming numerical advantage. On the 30-kilometer stretch of front occupied by Kosak's 30,000 men (including the 106th *Landsturm* Division), for instance, the Russians had nearly 80,000 troops. To the north, the Austrian XVIII Corps—reduced to some 10,000 men during the battles of June and early July 1916—faced almost 20,000 Russians. And with the Russian VI and XVIII Corps facing the Austrian V and IV Corps on the 100 kilometers of the southern half of the front, Böhm-Ermolli could hardly expect to shift forces to plug any gaps that appeared.

The Russians drove holes into the Austrian lines almost immediately upon launching their attack. In the early morning fog of 25 July, the Russian 105th and 126th reserve infantry divisions were able to approach the trenches of the Habsburg 25th Infantry Division (V Corps) south of Brody almost undetected and quickly forced the Austrians to abandon their positions. The Viennese division, led by the steadfast defense of the 84th Infantry Regiment, managed to stabilize its position in the afternoon, but renewed waves of Russian infantry broke the line decisively just before dark. With no reserves at hand, the commander of the 25th Infantry Division decided to retreat; this maneuver, however, exposed the units on either flank.

Corps Kosak, to the north, was already retreating in any case. Following Brusilov's methods, the Russian XVII Corps had focused its artillery on a well-established sector of the front opposite Radzivilov, just north of Brody, and pounded away for the entire morning. At 3:00 PM, the infantry rose from its saps and quickly penetrated the Austrian line, throwing the defenders back to their second position. A second wave of attackers deepened the hole briefly, allowing the third wave to move in and spread out behind, rolling up the Austrian trenches to the north and south. With his entire left wing retreating, Böhm-Ermolli telegraphed headquarters with a desperate plea for additional reserves. Unless the South Army could provide IV Corps with some support, he stated, the entire Second Army would have to retreat.

Spurred by Linsingen who, having already surrendered the 33rd Infantry Division, believed he could spare only two weak battalions from the Austrian 46th Guards Infantry Division, Falkenhayn responded by sending the 10th German *Landsturm* Division, which had originally been directed to Linsingen's command, to the assistance of Second Army. The German 22nd Infantry Division, moreover, would be sent to Linsingen's front to make good the loss of manpower, and in order to consolidate the front against the threatened flank attack, the Austrian First Army command was dissolved and First Army integrated fully into Linsingen's front. Böhm-Ermolli, for his part, attempted to rally his commanders and their troops with an impassioned dispatch: "Should the enemy, against expectations, be able to break into the front, then it becomes the holy duty of the infantry in each area to destroy the enemy with their fire and their bayonets in tough, unshakeable perseverance, with unbending will and deadly industry, no matter which side he comes from. The idea that an enemy break in the front leads to retreat must be driven off entirely."[17]

Böhm-Ermolli's troops responded, holding out against heavy Russian infantry and artillery attacks for the next two days. The overwhelming numerical superiority of the Russians took its toll before the German reinforcements could arrive though. Just after 4:00 PM on 27 July Sakharov's forces, having shelled and probed the Habsburg lines repeatedly, finally broke through Corps Kosak's defenses along the highway between Radzivilov and Brody. Corps Kosak, its reserves long ago expended, fought desperately. At 5:30 PM, the Austrians managed to regain control of the highway, but by 6:30 PM they had lost it again. Finally, at 8:00 PM, Kosak felt he had to abandon the position, and he drew his troops out of Brody. Still, he was not entirely ready to retreat; after communicating his situation to Böhm-Ermolli, Kosak agreed to try to close the front around Brody the following day. If he failed, then he would retreat.

He failed almost immediately. The Russian XVII Corps entered Brody at 4:30 in the morning, having halted briefly to recover from its own rather severe losses, and immediately resumed the attack, sending two and a half divisions forward against Kosak's weakened line. The German 10th *Landsturm* division still had not arrived, and Kosak, judging the situation untenable, asked for permission to retreat. By 5:30 AM, not only had Kosak abandoned Brody, the entire Austrian Second Army was in retreat. Sakharov's forces had captured more than 13,000 prisoners and seized three large ammunition depots stocked for the putative counteroffensive. The Habsburg commanders had finally lost all faith in the ability of their troops to hold the line, and therefore had ordered the center and southern wings of Second Army—still relatively undisturbed—to withdraw to prepared positions 20 kilometers to the rear as well. Böhm-Ermolli even gave the order to prepare for the evacuation of Lemberg, now only 30 kilometers behind the front, though it quickly was countermanded.[18] "I don't understand how it is that we just cannot hold anymore," Kundmann wrote. "Have the Russians become so good?"[19]

A Change in Command

Fortunately for the Habsburgs, the answer to Kundmann's question was "no." According to the account of the commanders of the Russian Eleventh Army, their own forces deserved only limited credit; the shortcomings of the Habsburg troops were the main reason Brody fell. "The third phase of general operations for the Eleventh Army ended with the taking of Brody. Completing this operation required three bloody days of fighting on both sides. Despite the outstanding work of the artillery and the unceasing forward pressure of the troops, the enemy never provided persistent opposition, which was recognized by many brave, combat-proven participants of this battle."[20]

Unfortunately, the other half of the answer was that the Austro-Hungarian troops, and the Austrian commanders in particular, had become so bad. "If the Austrian artillery doesn't inflict losses on us then we have an easy time of it," a Russian prisoner stated. "[. . . W]e think little of the Austrian infantry."[21] There had been sharp criticism of the Habsburg military leadership in both Germany and Austria-Hungary even before the Brusilov Offensive, and it naturally increased as the defeats mounted. The representative of the Habsburg Foreign Ministry to Conrad's headquarters at Teschen, Friedrich von Wiesner, had filed a particularly damaging report in late June 1916. He accused Conrad of being out of touch and irresponsible, and argued that only a thorough mixing of Habsburg and German troops would restore the fighting spirit on the Russian Front.[22] In early July, a representative in the Hungarian parliament claimed that "[t]he present evils have, with few exceptions, their origins in the leaders."[23] The Habsburg foreign minister, Count Burian, asked on 20 July if it was possible "that the morale of our troops is so low that our units on the Russian front can no longer hold in the way expected earlier?"[24] Many Austro-Hungarian and German observers thought Conrad would be relieved of command, and the Hungarian political leadership especially favored the creation of a unified command under German leadership.

The Habsburg troops' continued inability to counter the advance of the Russian Seventh and Ninth armies along the Dniester River and into Bukovina had, in mid-July, forced Falkenhayn to send the German 2nd *Jäger* Brigade as part of a special German "Carpathian Corps" to reinforce the Austrian Twelfth Army. A second German division would later be sent to augment Kövess's Third Army as well, and the German 9th *Landsturm*

Brigade was detailed to the South Army as part of the *Korsettstangen* strategy.[25] Already there were eighteen German divisions operating south of the Pripet, and German officers directed most of the front, either directly or obliquely. Pflanzer-Baltin had already been sidelined in favor of Seeckt and "the Prussian clique" on the southern end of the front, and with Puhallo's command gone, Linsingen controlled the northern half of the front.

Now, in the aftermath of Second Army's retreat, the Austrian High Command concluded that "[t]he positions, fighting ability, and condition of the troops are, according to all reports, good and confident. It is only the steadfastness and the energy of the leaders that leave something to be desired."[26] Even Conrad's long-time aide and faithful assistant Kundmann now agreed, noting that the Habsburg generals and their staffs remained too far from the front and thus out of touch with their field commanders and their troops. The only answer, he admitted, was what Linsingen and Wiesner had suggested earlier: to mix German and Habsburg troops within units, since German troops generally performed better in the field and so did Austro-Hungarian troops under German command.[27]

Such widespread ineptitude and admissions of failure naturally opened the door for what Falkenhayn had long desired: a single, unified command of the Eastern Front under German—preferably his—control. He had proposed, again, in early July, as almost an afterthought to the arrangements made for the Austrian Twelfth Army, that Hindenburg be given command over the entire Eastern Front. For reasons of their own, both Wilhelm II and Conrad had vetoed the project.[28] Falkenhayn's proposed "compromise"—that Hindenburg be given command over all German troops on the Eastern Front or at least over Army Group Linsingen—was also rejected. Conrad noted sourly that the German commanders had already sacrificed the Austrian Seventh Army to protect the flank of the (mostly German) South Army, and he did not wish the scene to be repeated in the north.

Unfavorable developments on several fronts led to a change of heart on the German side, however. The failure of Falkenhayn's Verdun strategy, along with the Allied offensive on the Somme, the apparent readiness of Romania to enter the war, and increasing reports of war-weariness in Hungary, had severely lowered the German commander's stock. Burian reported that both emperors now approved of the proposal to place Hindenburg in sole command of the Eastern Front. Behind the scenes, Burian and the officials of the Habsburg Foreign Ministry not only were working to remove Conrad, they were also conniving with many of the leading German politicians to replace Falkenhayn with Hindenburg. The German emperor was reluctant to elevate Hindenburg, but his ministers convinced him at least that a unified Eastern command was now a necessity. On 18 July therefore, at a conference with Conrad in Berlin, Falkenhayn broached the subject again, this time at the urging of Wilhelm II. Conrad, having naively asked Burian to intervene in order to obtain more German troops for the southern sectors of the front, now found himself in a quandry: he could have the German troops, but at the cost of his command.

Conrad deftly replied that it was a question of troops, not generals. Besides, he argued, the name "Hindenburg" might have a negative effect on the Slavic troops of the Habsburg armies, since the German field marshal was associated with German nationalism. With Hindenburg looming increasingly as not just a rival but a replacement, Falkenhayn was only too glad to play along for once. He presented Conrad's arguments as irrefutable to the German ministers who supported Hindenburg, and pointed to his own gains. In return for promises to shorten the Italian Front (which had already been done in essence) and the exchange of two Habsburg divisions for two German ones, he had offered Conrad only four battalions. Ironically this tied his fortunes directly to those of Conrad, whom he by and large despised; only by supporting Conrad was he able to fend off Hindenburg. In hopes of solving both problems at once, Falkenhayn devised a clever new proposal that he presented on 23 July: Hindenburg would take command of the front between the Pripet and the Dniester, while the Habsburg Archduke Friedrich—or another Habsburg commander—would be given a command on the northern half of the front. Conrad relayed the idea to Franz Josef, who approved it the next day, but events had already outpaced the scheme.

The near-collapse of the Austrian First Army had drawn attention once again to the ineptitude of the Habsburg commanders, and leading politicians in both Austria-Hungary and Germany continued to work for the removal of Conrad and Falkenhayn. The Hungarians, moreover, had now openly thrown their support behind Hindenburg; Count Julius Andrassy, one of the leading opposition politicians in Hungary, had approached the German embassy in Vienna on 22 July to ask for Hindenburg's appointment as commander of the entire Eastern Front. Burian had therefore proposed that Hindenburg be given command of the entire Eastern Front with the Archduke Friedrich serving as the Austrian command's representative to Hindenburg. Conrad would be retained as the archduke's adviser. One day after he approved Falkenhayn's proposal, Franz Josef also gave his assent for Burian's plan to the archduke. The German emperor, in light of the worsening situation in the southeast, also lent his support to Burian's proposal and called for a conference to mediate between the alternatives, which was duly arranged for 27 July.

In light of the imperial attitudes, both Conrad and Falkenhayn buck-led. During a private meeting on 26 July, Falkenhayn abandoned his own plan and once again proposed that Hindenburg be given command of the entire Eastern Front. He also mooted the possibility of an Austro-Hungarian treaty with Italy, in order to free up troops for the defense of the Bukovina. Conrad angrily refused both propositions initially, but then relented on the question of a united front. Franz Josef's approval of Hindenburg as sole commander, he believed, overrode his personal beliefs; the conference need only settle the details.

Falkenhayn, having made his opposition to the ascension of Ludendorff and Hindenburg clear and lost in a private conference earlier, excused himself from the meeting that evening on grounds of illness. Conrad, struck by the news that Brody had been abandoned that day, agreed to give Hindenburg control over the Austrian Second Army as well as Army Group Linsingen. Only in this fashion, he now believed, could he procure the German reinforcements necessary to hold Lemberg. It was further decided that while the Archduke Karl would command the front held by the Austrian Third and the Austrian Twelfth, which included both the South Army and the Austrian Seventh, it was the German High Command that would issue orders for the entire Eastern Front. Orders affecting the southern sectors, of course, would be agreed upon in advance with the archduke and the Austro-Hungarian command. To save face for the Habsburgs, Archduke Friedrich would be given a command north of the Pripet, and the Austro-German Twelfth Army was renamed (on 2 August) Army Group Archduke Karl. "The Austrians could not yet make up their minds to go the whole way," Ludendorff wrote later, "but still the new arrangement offered such considerable advantages that I regarded it as a great step in the right direction."[29]

In many ways though the change, which both emperors approved on 29 July, was insignificant. Linsingen had even before this essentially taken his orders from the German High Command, as had Bothmer (Südarmee), and von Seeckt had been the real power in the Austrian Twelfth since it was created. The threat of German troops, and the fact that the shift in command was coordinated with the Bulgarians and the Turks, may well have deterred the Romanians from entering the war, but their government was in any case still divided. "Thank God they are such cowards that they cannot make a decision," Kundmann had commented at one point.[30] On the Habsburg side, only the Austrian Second Army was directly affected. Though Böhm-Ermolli remained in place as commander, Hindenburg quickly installed his own man, General von Morgen, as army group commander for the reorganized Second and South armies. This punctuated a clear victory for Hindenburg and his camp in the campaign against Falkenhayn, however, as the latter was now virtually powerless to influence events on the Eastern Front. And, in that sense, the change in command only furthered the legend of Hindenburg and Ludendorff as "saviors," since the final destruction of the Brusilov Offensive now accrued to them.[31]

The Guards Army

The shift in the Central Powers' command structure coincided almost perfectly with the onset of another massive Russian assault. A continuous downpour had prevented Letschitski and Scherbatschev from launching their attacks as planned on 20 July, and the Guards Army's artillery still was not fully supplied by 22 July. Then on 24 July Bezobrazov requested a delay because the disposition of German troops opposite the Guards Army—Hindenburg had sent the 121st Infantry Division to augment Linsingen's forces—had altered his plan of attack. To counter the German move, Alekseev sent I Siberian Corps (from Second Army) to augment the Guards' strength, which was already at four infantry corps (north to south: I and II Guards plus I and XXX) and three cavalry divisions under the command of the general khan of Nakhichevan. Facing this 134,000-man force were (north to south) the Austrian Division Rusche, the Habsburg 29th Infantry Division from northern Bohemia, the German 121st Infantry Division, the Habsburg II Corps (formerly Group Bernhardi) and Lüttwitz's (German) X Corps (formerly commanded by Marwitz). To the north, Lesch's Third (north to south: IV Siberian, III Corps, IV Cavalry Corps, and XLVI Corps, with I Turkmen as a reserve) squared off against (north to south) the German Group Gronau, Cavalry Corps Hauer, and Corps Fath. On the southern wing, Kaledin's Eighth Army (north to south: XXIII, V Siberian, XXXIX, XL, and VIII Corps, augmented by the V Cavalry Corps) faced the severely weakened Austrian Fourth Army (X Corps and Corps Szurmay) and the remainder of the Austrian First Army (Cavalry Corps Ostermuth and the 61st and 7th infantry divisions). These three armies, in conjunction with the Russian Ninth and Seventh armies in the south, renewed the offensive on 28 July, just as Sakharov's strike in the center of the line was winding down.[32]

Brusilov's guns opened a barrage along the entire front at 4:00 AM that day, using gas shells in several sectors. In the south, Scherbatschev sent the six infantry divisions of II and XVI Corps forward against the right flank of the South Army after only half an hour's shelling. By dawn, the Russians had broken into the line of the 36th Infantry Division (XIII Corps) and established positions on the western bank of the Koropiec River. Despite a renewed barrage and several waves of attacks in the afternoon, however, Scherbatschev's forces were unable to either roll up the German flank or crack the center of South Army's line. The attack did, however, succeed in keeping the German forces of Bothmer's army fixed in place, which greatly aided Letshitski's attack against the newly constituted Austrian Third just to the south.

The Russian Ninth Army had indulged in a much longer artillery preparation, targeting some of the Habsburg batteries with gas shells and holding the infantry until nearly 11:00 AM. The first wave of attackers, coming from saps often no more than 50 meters distant, penetrated the Habsburg line with relative ease. Troops from Letschitski's XII Corps quickly engaged the 6th Guards Infantry Regiment on the northern wing of Group Hadfy and destroyed the unit. The Austrian commander immediately dispatched five battalions—his entire reserve—to plug the gap, but even as he did so the Russians punched a second hole in the center of his line, decimating the 21st Guards Infantry Regiment. Letschitski's forces flooded through and soon were swarming the flanks of the German 119th and 105th Infantry Divisions, which had held firm (like the *Korsettstangen* they were intended to be) to that point. Threatened with encirclement, the Germans beat a hasty retreat, abandoning several pieces of artillery. Letschitski's forces took more than 8,000 prisoners and captured thirty-five guns. With the stability of the entire front endangered, not only did Third Army have to pull back some five kilometers to a prepared position in front of Stanislau, but the South Army was also forced to withdraw its right wing in order to maintain contact with the embattled Habsburg units.[33]

As gloomy as the outlook was for the Austrian Third Army, the situation in the north was worse. The Habsburgs' Fourth Army broke almost immediately under the Russian offensive. By 5:00 AM, the Russian 14th Infantry Division had smashed a hole in the line of the Austrian 70th Infantry Division and captured five batteries. The attackers moved so quickly that they overran Szurmay's second position before he could withdraw both divisions safely, and by 6:00 AM the 3rd Orenburg Cossacks were fanning out behind the Habsburg lines and creating havoc. The 70th Infantry Division was in full retreat, with the 208th Infantry Brigade completely destroyed. The neighboring 13th Infantry Division had managed to hold its sector, but now found itself forced backward in disarray because of the 70th Infantry Division's retreat. The Austrian 11th Infantry Division was likewise flanked and routed, with the 312th Honved Infantry Regiment taken prisoner en masse. From his headquarters command post, Szurmay called for two regiments of Hussars to deploy and combat the Russian cavalry; he was told that they had already been chased from the battlefield.

With Corps Szurmay in panicked retreat, the neighboring Habsburg X Corps was an easy target. Kaledin's XXX Corps ripped into the exposed right wing, overwhelming the 37th Infantry Division and taking many of the Habsburg soldiers prisoner. The attackers wiped out the 208th Honved Infantry Regiment and then proceeding to roll up the line of the 2nd Infantry Division before reserves could even make it into position. The 13th Guards Infantry Division, in the middle of X Corps's line, managed to hold long enough to withdraw in reasonable order, but General Csanady ordered the entire corps to retreat rather than risk the remainder of his troops. The entire front of Fourth Army was pushed back between three and five kilometers by the initial Russian surge, and its connection to the German units on the left flank was endangered. Only a swift, desperate counterattack by the 10th Cavalry Division, supported by German units from the north, managed to deflect the Russians and maintain a continuous line.

Both Linsingen and Tersztyanszky were furious and rather ashamed. The 11th Infantry Division, Fourth Army's commander wrote in a confidential report, was the "problem child" [*Schmerzkind*] of the army, which was itself an embarrassment.[34] "This is the first defeat I have suffered," Tersztyanszky declared. "Until today, I was an undefeated field commander."[35] In a single day's battle, the Austrian Fourth Army had lost 15,000 men—some 60 percent of its force—ninety machine guns, and forty-five artillery pieces.[36] In the official Austrian history of the conflict the loss of so many guns is ascribed, probably correctly, to the bravery of the Austrian artillery crews, who this time stayed by their guns to support the infantry. In at least one case, all the members of a battery were cut down by Russian sabers as they attempted to defend their position. The official version also, however, claims that the failure of several Ruthenian units to mount even a token resistance led to the collapse of the line.[37]

In truth, it was quite simply a general lack of fighting spirit on the part of the Habsburg troops and their leaders that had caused the catastrophe. Units of all ethnicities had panicked and abandoned their trenches; nearly two-thirds of Fourth Army's losses—10,000 men—had been taken prisoner, often with minimal fighting. According to its own regimental history, for instance, the Habsburgs' 25th Light Infantry Regiment—drawn from the Austrian town of Krems in Styria—was captured intact.[38] And Kaledin had not sent overwhelming numbers forward against the Austrian Fourth Army, which held a front of only some 20 kilometers. At 8:05 AM, in fact, Linsingen had reported to the Central Powers' commanders that the Russians appeared to be staging a diversion on that sector of the front, as they had sent just three and a half infantry divisions and two cavalry divisions to face five (admittedly under-strength) Habsburg infantry divisions supported by the 10th Cavalry Division.[39]

That analysis was in fact correct; the strike at Vladimir-Volynsky was intended to merely pin down Linsingen's forces there while Brusilov's main attack force, comprising Third Army and the Guards Army, was to drive against Kovel directly from the east. A British liason officer to the Russian Imperial Army judged this to be a mistake: "Brusilov thinks he can rush these German positions by surprise, as he has done Austrian ones, but he is simply destroying the morale of the best troops in the army. The Stockhod is made for passive defence, and Kowel should be taken via Vladimir-Volinsk."[40] The heavy rains of late July had indeed made the Stochod River a formidable barrier, and it was not the only obstacle Brusilov's forces had to overcome.

The Guards Army in particular faced a difficult task, as the wooded, marshy terrain east-southeast of Kovel offered only three corridors along which the Russians might conceivably advance—if they even managed to breach the Central Powers' line on the Stochod River. A further impediment was the fact that the Russian maps of the area had not been updated since 1897, and Brusilov's aerial squadrons were unable to assist in plotting the terrain because the Germans had deployed superior air strength—more than twenty aircraft—in that quadrant. Because the single rail line from Archangelsk was overburdened, Stavka had been unable to shift the several aircraft available there to Brusilov's troops, and the Guards Army was thus unable to direct its artillery effectively.

In the initial assault, however, it appeared as if the terrain might favor the Russians. The Habsburg 41st Infantry Division, defending the Stochod salient in the center of II Corps's front, had been unable to dig adequate trenches in the wet, sandy ground and was thus exceptionally vulnerable to flanking artillery. Following a sustained barrage on the morning of 28 July, the Russian 71st Infantry Division (XXX Corps) forced the 20th Honved Infantry Regiment out of its trenches and back to its second line. Bezobrazov's forces now found themselves occupying the sandy, low-lying ground along the Stochod, however, while the defeated Habsburg units had managed to retreat to a strong position at the edge of the forest. Aided by units and flanking artillery fire provided by the German 107th Infantry Division, the 41st Infantry Division managed to hold its position for the remainder of the day despite repeated Russian assaults.

This experience was repeated along almost the entire front of the Guards Army. The initial assault of II Guards Corps, carried out with marked zeal, broke the center of Lüttwitz's line early in the afternoon of 28 July and captured several German batteries. Massive Russian infantry assaults also created gaps in the line of the Austrian 29th Infantry Division and Division Rusche in the early afternoon, and I Guards Corps managed to flank the German 19th Infantry Division and roll up the front of the neighboring Austrian units. In each case though, the Central Powers simply retreated behind the Stochod, and the Russians were unable to follow up their success. Wave after wave of Russian infantry, in columns twenty men deep and urged on by saber-wielding officers, was stopped cold by well-directed artillery fire from behind the rain-swollen Stochod. "The wounded sank slowly into the marsh, and it was impossible to send them help," Knox wrote after seeing I Guards Corps in action that day.[41] German fliers directed artillery and machine guns against the Russians, who were essentially trapped in the swampy no-man's land east of the river.[42] Falkenhayn wrote later:

> From all accounts, the Russian losses must have been nothing short of colossal. The poor shooting of their artillery, compared with their achievements in the early days of the war, was unable to give sufficient preparation for the attacks, and the infantry, driven forward in unwieldy mass formations, were usually unable to cross the zone of our machine gun fire. The objectives gained were, therefore, of little importance compared with the strength expended.[43]

Encouraged nonetheless by their early success on 28 July, Brusilov's commanders pressed the attack against Kovel using the full weight of their three armies. Continued infantry assaults against the interior wings of Corps Fath and II Corps southeast of Kovel slowly pushed back Bernhardi's northern wing during the afternoon of 29 July. Despite "suicidal attacks," the Russians were unable to force a break along the east-west railway line that marked the frontal boundary between II Corps and Corps Fath, largely because Fath was able to commit his entire reserve (the 53rd Infantry Division, three newly arrived German *Landwehr* battalions, and the 18th Guards Infantry Regiment) to the defense there. The Russians, Ludendorff noted, "fed their line regardless of losses," and the Central Powers were thus forced to throw all available troops into the battle just to be able to hold.[44] But hold they did.

The situation in the center of the Austrian II Corps's front nonetheless looked desperate, as the Guards Army threatened to overwhelm the Central Powers' defense in the Stochod salient. Bezobrazov's XXX Corps hammered the Austrian defenders from both sides with heavy artillery throughout the morning of 29 July, then launched massive infantry attacks just after noon. The 20th Honved Infantry Regiment gave way almost immediately, making it impossible for the rest of the 41st Honved Infantry Division to hold its position. "In the open field, they cannot withstand our rush," Nicholas II wrote to his wife on learning of the news.[45] Bezobrazov poured troops into the gap, sending waves of infantry forward to roll up the Habsburg line. Progress toward Kovel was slow and costly, however; the Central Powers were as committed to holding Kovel as the Russians were to taking it. As XXX Corps threatened to puncture the line, the Habsburg commander in that sector frantically rushed his reserves forward to plug the gap. He had only two battalions at his disposal, and by 3:00 PM they had been consumed in the battle for the salient, but the Russian advance had been slowed.

Bernhardi now sent additional reserves—two Polish brigades and a few battalions from the German 107th Infantry Division—north in an attempt to maintain the line. They managed to slow the Russian advance further, but attrition eventually took its toll. As darkness began to settle on the region, II Corps's right wing, which angled back following a westward bend in the river, appeared ready to collapse. Rather than risk being flanked, Bernhardi drew the entire corps back to the third position. The defenses there had not been well prepared, however, and the pursuing Russians managed to punch a hole in the line even before the defenders were fully settled. Bernhardi quickly ordered another retreat, and this time the Russians permitted II Corps to withdraw under cover of darkness. Bezobrazov did not attack on 30 July either, and mounted only weak assaults over the next five days, having consumed some 200 officers, nearly 30,000 men, and a good portion of his munitions in just a week's battle.[46]

While understandable in the face of heavy losses and uncertain terrain, the inability of Brusilov's commanders to coordinate their attacks and follow up their successes decisively was, as it had been in mid-June, costly. Kaledin, having smashed the Austrian Fourth Army on 28 July, launched only symbolic attacks the following day, which allowed Linsingen time not just to send reserves forward, but to implement a new defensive plan. Rather than simply putting German units in between the weaker Habsburg units to serve as "the stays in the corset," Linsingen—with Hindenburg's support—now mixed units. The commander of the German XXXX Corps (General Litzmann) was detailed to the Austrian Fourth Army, given command of Corps Szurmay, and tasked with organizing a counterattack. The men from several German regiments were dispersed into the Habsburg divisions, German officers were placed in command of Austro-Hungarian units, and all of the units of Fourth Army—including reserves—were now subjected to the same (German) combat training and preparation regimens. While the Habsburg commanders were rather put off by the Germans' "tactless" assumption of command, the moves had the desired effect on the troops. "What a feeling has come with the arrival of a few German troops in every command post," one field officer noted in his diary. "Everyone has the feeling that nothing more can happen to us."[47]

It was a close thing, but true enough in the end. When Kaledin renewed the attack against the Austrian Fourth on 30 July, the influx of German reserves proved to be the difference. A Russian infantry assault at 5:00 AM, undertaken after an hour's artillery preparation, cracked the interior wings of X Corps almost immediately, pressing both the 2nd Infantry Division and the 37th Honved Infantry Division backward. Three battalions from the regimental reserve commanded by German officers managed to clear the trenches by 8:00 AM, however, and while the Russians continued to send waves of infantry forward throughout the day, the line held. Kaledin then called off his attacks, sending only a few skirmish patrols forward over the course of the next two days.

Likewise Lesch, whose main task was to pin the Central Powers' forces around Pinsk and prevent the movement of reserves out of the area, failed to achieve his goal because he was unable to follow up his successes. The initial attack of the Russian Third Army, launched at dawn on 28 July, made some progress but then shattered in the face of strong natural defenses of the Stochod River. Using a covering aerial bombardment shrewdly, the 4th Finnish Guards Infantry Division, working in combination with forces from I Turkmen Corps, had forced the Habsburg 26th Heavy Infantry

Division to abandon its position on the east bank of the Stochod by noon. The only feasible means of crossing the engorged river, however, was a slender gangway that the Austrians had left in place during their hurried retreat. Now secure behind the fortifications on the west bank of the river, the Habsburg troops meticulously picked off the massed Russians as they struggled across the craters and ditches toward the crossing. The losses and withering artillery fire forced Lesch to withdraw far enough that the Austrians managed to recover and blow the crossing before nightfall.

Thereafter, the Russian Third made no serious attempt to force the position, as Lesch chose instead to engage in an artillery duel. The large cavalry force assigned to Third Army simply languished. This inactivity, like Kaledin's pause, allowed the Central Powers to deploy much-needed reserves elsewhere; had Lesch continued to engage, for instance, it seems likely Corps Fath might have been obliged to send some of its reserve north. As it was, Fath had just enough to hold in the southern sectors. Confident that the Central Powers' positions north of Pinsk were not threatened, moreover, Hindenburg repartitioned the front once it came under his command on 2 August. Army Group Prince Leopold von Bayern, which had been defending the sector immediately north of Pinsk, now extended its coverage south of the Pripet River, freeing Group Gronau to reinforce Group Fath and Bernhardi's II Corps in the defense of Kovel.[48] In both cases the movement of forces permitted by the Russians' inactivity, while relatively small in scale, was more than enough to thwart the drive on Kovel.

The failure to press home a marked advantage in the south produced similar results. The Austrian commanders south of Brody had been so disheartened by the events of 28 July that they retreated even further on 29 July, even though the Russians were no longer advancing. Böhm-Ermolli had reported that the troops presently under his command would not suffice to hold the line if the Russians did advance, particularly since he had sent reserves north in support of Linsingen. Conrad had unquestioningly agreed and approved Second Army's retreat behind the Sereth River. This maneuver, of course, exposed the flank of the South Army, and a furious Seeckt was forced to withdraw his northern wing (South Army) in order to maintain the line. Scherbatschev continued to attack, but he was completely unsupported by Ninth Army on his left and therefore was unable to break the line or turn South Army's flank.

There was little reason for the Russian Ninth Army not to move. Letschitski had at his disposal three full corps (north to south: XXXIII, XLI, and XII) with which to strike at the Austrian positions in the Bukovina. Kovess's Third Army consisting of only two corps (VI and XIII) was in tatters, and the Habsburg artillery was desperately short of artillery rounds after only one day of battle. Group Hadfy, bridging the broad front between Third Army and the much-reduced Austrian Seventh Army (XI Corps and the remnants of Group Benigni), did not even have a prepared defensive position. Yet Letschitski simply refused to advance. He disingenuously argued that the Austrian Third Army had occupied strong defensive positions that would require additional preparations to breach. Any successful drive on Stanislau, Letschitski reported, demanded additional resources and additional time. Frustrated, Brusilov telegraphed repeatedly to inform Letschitski that he was "misinterpreting orders" and should be attacking regardless of the enemy's position. Stavka also sent several messages asking Ninth Army to strike northward, but Letschitski did not move.

The Central Powers naturally took advantage of the respite. On hearing from Seeckt that the northern wing of the South Army had been endangered by Böhm-Ermolli's "unnecessary" retreat, Falkenhayn had directed the German 195th and 197th infantry divisions, along with the 34th *Landwehr* Infantry Battalion, to reinforce Second Army's right wing. Additional reinforcements, in the form of the German 34th *Landwehr* Battalion, would be sent on 3 August, after Hindenburg inspected the front and found it still wanting. In addition, the German 209th Infantry Battalion was sent to reinforce Third Army, which had withdrawn to a more defensible position and began to dig in once they were able to disengage from the Russians. On 30 July, moreover, Linsingen received news that Turkish troops, long promised, were now assembling in Belgrade; because neither he nor the Habsburg commanders believed the Turks to be suited to mountain fighting, the Turkish XV Corps would be sent to Galicia. Hindenburg would also dispatch the German 75th Reserve Infantry Division, on 2 August, to serve as part of the reserves defending Kovel. In return, Linsingen would send two divisions, including the German 1st Reserve Infantry Division that had just been removed from the front at Verdun, to assist Twelfth Army in the south. With the Carpathian Corps, commanded by General Korda, arriving in the Bukovina on 1 August, the Central Powers were confident they could not only hold the passes, but carry out a counterattack.[49]

CHAPTER SIX

THE OFFENSIVE SHATTERS

Like so many of the Central Powers' plans in the summer of 1916, the Carpathian Offensive turned out to be a chimera. The attack, set for 3 August, was to be carried out in three parts. In the center of the line Korda's Carpathian Corps would strike north and then east from Kuty along the Czeremosz River valley, while Pflanzer-Baltin's Seventh Army was to press northeast from its position behind the Moldova River in an attempt to reach the Sereth River. A third attack group, commanded by Feldmarschal-leutnant Rudolf Krauss would move east from its position behind Delatyn two days later with the aim of clearing the upper Pruth valley. If successful, the attack would shorten the Central Powers' line and reestablish its right wing on the Romanian border. All three forces were thus to converge on the city of Czernovitz.

Neither the terrain nor the weather favored the attackers. The Russians had positioned their forces, including the artillery, along the ridges overlooking the river valleys, and in early August 1916 the Carpathians were already cold and windy; fog and mist covered the mountains for much of the day. The Habsburg artillery nonetheless managed to zero in on the front lines of the Russian XII Corps defending the northern edge of the Czeremosz valley and pounded the enemy trenches throughout the morning. At noon, several German *Jäger* battalions launched an infantry assault that carried the Russian positions, capturing two guns and driving Letschitski's XII Corps back several kilometers to its second position. The terrain, however, prevented the Habsburgs from bringing their artillery forward rapidly enough to pursue the retreating Russians.

It proved difficult to build on the initial momentum of the attack on the southern edge of the valley as well. The Habsburg 40th Infantry Division, part of Korda's main attack force, scaled the eastern face of the mountains on the opening day of the offensive and, making its way through difficult wooded terrain, engaged the Russian 3rd Cossack Cavalry Division. Though the Austrians managed to drive the Russian horsemen back, they soon encountered the well-prepared main positions of the Russian XI Corps, which they were unable to overcome. Korda therefore broke off the attack for a day, in order to give his forces time to regroup and bring the artillery forward.

On 5 August the Carpathian Corps forced three positions, each over 1,000 meters in altitude, held by the Russian Ussuri Cossack Division and the 82nd Infantry Division. Once again, however, the terrain kept Korda's forces from carrying their momentum forward. The attack over the mountains had forced the German *Jäger* battalions to split from the Habsburg 68th Infantry Brigade that was supporting their southern wing, which had connected them to the supply lines. Both units had to halt their advance in order to regroup.

The Central Powers simply did not have the manpower to carry out the plan. Pflanzer-Baltin, using only the 67th Infantry Brigade and the 202nd Honved Infantry Brigade, managed to take the positions of the Russian XI Corps on the cliffs east of the Moldova on 5 August and continued to press forward along the mountain ridge the next day. The advance was measured in paces rather than kilometers though, and Pflanzer-Baltin lost some 1,000 men in the effort. On 8 August, after moving forward for three days, the Habsburg infantry encountered a well-prepared Russian position defended by three divisions (the Russian 11th, 32nd, and 79th) at Magura, and the attack ground to a halt. Pflanzer-Baltin requested support from the German 1st Reserve Infantry Division, which arrived in the area on 8 August, but the unit was still too scattered to use in the line. Not until 11 August could the attack resume, and by then it was too late.[1]

The Battle for the Center

Brusilov too had regrouped his forces during the first days of August, after meeting with both Kaledin and Bezobrazov to discuss the situation. He was under pressure from Alekseev, who was unhappy with the inability of the Southwestern Front to break the Central Powers' line decisively, to abandon the strategy of attacking along a broad front and concentrate his troops at one point. Although Brusilov disagreed with the idea in principle, Bezobrazov's cautious attitude about continuing forward forced him to concede some ground to Alekseev. While the attack would continue along the entire front from the Pripet to the Pruth, each army was now instructed to build "strong points" where they would have an overwhelming numerical superiority on a narrow front.

Accordingly, Brusilov sent the I Siberian Corps, which had arrived in Galicia on 31 July, to augment Lesch's Third Army on the northernmost sector and pulled back the IV Siberian Corps to serve as the army reserve. While Third Army would continue to be active around Pinsk, Lesch was directed to focus his efforts further south. Five infantry divisions were to attack along an eight-kilometer sector held by only sixteen Austro-Hungarian battalions, while a further three divisions of Russian cavalry would attempt to break through near Kamien-Kaszyrski and disrupt enemy communications. Three corps from Bezobrazov's Guards Army (I, XXX, and I Guards, with a total strength of some sixty-four battalions) would drive against the 15-kilometer-long Stochod salient held by twenty-eight battalions of mixed German and Habsburg troops. To cover the flanks of Bezobrazov's front, the three divisions of Guards Cavalry were dismounted and placed into the line, giving Guards Army a total strength of some ninety-six infantry battalions against only twenty-eight battalions for the defenders.

Brusilov's plan was that the two armies would punch separate holes in the Central Powers' line north and south of Kovel that would allow them to surround the Central Powers' forces and destroy them before uniting to take the rail junction. Kaledin's Eighth Army was to direct its forces solely against the Austrian Fourth Army defending Vladimir-Volynsk, thus limiting Linsingen's ability to shift troops northward. The Russian Eleventh Army would resume its offensive against Lemberg with the same intention, while Letschitski and Ninth Army were instructed to support Seventh Army's offensive against Stanislau.[2]

Letschitski objected immediately. The counteroffensive of the Carpathian Corps had begun one day before Brusilov's orders reached Ninth Army, and Letschitski argued that he would be unable both to defend against the strike on his southern wing and to assist Scherbatschev on his north with the forces currently available. Frustrated, Brusilov forwarded the report to Stavka on 5 August with the recommendation that Ninth Army be allowed to focus on the Carpathian sector of the front. Alarmed by the initial success of the Carpathian Corps and fearful that any loss of territory in the Bukovina would deter Romania from entering the war, Alekseev not only approved the proposal, but also instructed Brusilov to strengthen Ninth Army at the expense of the other fronts. The XVIII Corps (37th and 43rd infantry divisions), which was near Tarnopol on Scherbatschev's right wing, was therefore shifted to Ninth Army. In addition, Brusilov directed the 3rd Don Cossack Cavalry Division of Third Army and the 64th Infantry Division, which was forming in Odessa, to support Ninth Army in the Carpathians. The overall plan also changed, with the attack on Stanislau being delayed in favor of the drive for the Carpathian passes.[3]

While this squabbling and redistribution of forces delayed the renewal of the Brusilov Offensive on both the northern and the southern sections of the front, Sakharov's Eleventh Army had already resumed its drive toward Lemberg on 4 August. Böhm-Ermolli's hasty retreat of 29 July to prepared positions quickly proved that these were of little value. The V Siberian Corps, attacking on both sides of the Brody-Lemberg railway, smashed into lines of the Austrian XVIII Corps at 5:00 AM. At the same time, Sakharov's XII and VI Corps drove forward against the interior wings of the Habsburg V and IV Corps, which had taken up positions behind the Sereth River. On both ends of the front, a wild daylong battle ensued. The initial Russian infantry surge carried into the forward trenches of the Austrians, and it appeared by noon that Böhm-Ermolli's troops would be forced to withdraw again. By nightfall, however, the Habsburg forces had managed to reclaim their forward trenches and stabilized the sector. In the south, the 14th and 32nd infantry divisions, holding the connection between V Corps to the north and IV Corps on the southern end of the line, were hard-pressed throughout the day. After losing their front line of trenches in the morning, however, they too had battled back in the afternoon and actually pushed the Russians back across the Sereth by nightfall. Kundmann, back at the Austro-Hungarian headquarters, was nonetheless worried. "The army appears shaky [though] it has the best troops. It is inconceivable."[4]

His concerns were well placed. The Russian 13th Infantry Division, supported by elements of the 34th Infantry Division, renewed the attack against the Habsburg 32nd Infantry Division early the next morning, and quickly regained the initiative. By 10:00 AM, two Russian regiments had broken into the second line, where they were engaged and halted by the reserves of the Austrian 14th Infantry Division. The respite was temporary. At 1:00 PM, the Russian 34th Infantry Division stormed the heights west of the town of Zalocy, inflicting heavy casualties on the defenders and forcing them to withdraw by 4:00 PM. This left the southern wing of the Habsburg V Corps exposed, and the attack of the Russian 13th soon spread southward, pressing the Austrians back along the entire line. Desperate, the commander of the 14th Infantry Division now committed the last of his reserves; the Russians overwhelmed them within the hour. Just when it looked as if Sakharov's forces might achieve a decisive breakthrough, however, the first elements of the German reinforcements released by the lull in the fighting around Pinsk arrived in the theater. Böhm-Ermolli rushed the three battalions of the German 34th *Landsturm* unit into battle immediately, which halted the Russian advance and stabilized the line, at least temporarily.

Böhm-Ermolli worked furiously overnight shifting forces to meet the expected Russian thrust of the next morning. Units from the 14th, 31st, and 33rd infantry divisions were sent north to join the German 34th *Landsturm* unit and strengthen the connection to V Corps. Thus reinforced, the Austrian Second Army launched a counterstrike at 6:00 AM, attempting to reclaim the heights on the western banks of the Sereth River. It met a Russian infantry assault head-on, but managed to hold its own and even push forward in some sectors. The Russian 13th and 34th infantry divisions countered in the afternoon, sending waves up to thirty deep against the center of IV Corps's line and forcing it back once again with heavy losses. The Austrian 14th Infantry Division had lost half of its strength in only three days, including 1,000 men taken prisoner. Even the addition of the German units proved insufficient to stem the Russian tide, as an attack that evening succeeded in turning IV Corps's southern flank. "Thus, in the middle of August the collapse of the Austro-Hungarian Army seemed manifestly possible," Ludendorff wrote.[5]

Only the arrival of two batteries and two battalions diverted from the neighboring IX Corps (Südarmee), along with a battalion drawn from Corps Hoffmann in the center of South Army's line, helped prevent a complete collapse of Second Army's right wing. The German 195th and 197th infantry divisions, which had been released from the northern sectors when Lesch's strike at the end of July proved ineffective, were also now unloading behind Second Army's lines. The remainder of the Austrian 14th Infantry Division was amalgamated with this new German force under the command of General von Eben, and Böhm-Ermolli, under orders from headquarters to hold his positions at all costs, sent it forward into the line that evening.

The timing was fortuitous indeed, for Second Army had suffered severe losses in the battles of early August. In less than a week of fighting, Böhm-Ermolli's forces had suffered over 6,000 casualties, and a further 11,900 men had been captured by the Russians.[6] Fortunately for the Central Powers, Sakharov's forces too were very nearly spent. The Russian 13th Infantry Division, in fact, remained in position on 7 August, too exhausted to carry on despite the success of the previous day. Unsupported, the 34th Infantry Division once again attempted to separate the Austrian IV and V Corps, but the newly inserted German units helped fend off the attack in yet another day's hard fighting. By 8 August, Sakharov had been forced to curtail his attempts to cross the Sereth completely. Nor could he shift his attack northward to take advantage of the weakness of the Austrian Second Army, as both Brusilov and Alekseev had requested. Sakharov believed he would need at least two additional divisions to move west from Brody, but Scherbatschev refused to send reinforcements north as directed. The center of Brusilov's front thus once again went quiet just as the activity resumed on either end.[7]

To the Carpathians

The artillery of Letschitski's Ninth Army opened its barrage at 4:00 AM on 7 August, in keeping with Brusilov's usual timetable. Not until noon did the infantry go forward, but then the charge came in columns up to seventy men deep along the entire front of the Russian Ninth Army, using all four corps (north to south: XXXIII, XLI, XII, and XI). The left wing of the Austrian Third Army, anchored on a northern turn of the Dniester River by two German units (the 105th Reserve Infantry Division and 119th Infantry Division, known as Group Kräwel), collapsed almost immediately. With only two Austro-Hungarian infantry battalions in reserve, the German units were forced to make a fighting retreat to the northwest; this separated them from the Habsburg XIII Corps, allowing the Russian II Cavalry Corps to flood through the gap and wreak havoc with communications and supply lines. As the afternoon wore on, the right wing of Group Kräwel collapsed under the continued intense Russian pressure. The Russian III Cavalry Corps poured through the line, following close on the heels of the infantry, which was trying to widen the breach by moving north and south. With the Russian infantry already in the second line of trenches of Group Kräwel and little hope of regaining the position without massive reinforcements, Kövess opted for retreat.

According to his reports, the troops of Third Army had been shattered. Men from various units had been mixed during the panicked withdrawal, and it was impossible to separate the reserves; even if order could be restored, Kövess argued, the third position had never been completed and there was little chance of holding when the Russians renewed the attack. To cover the maneuver, which was carried out under cover of darkness, the Archduke Karl ordered the right wing of South Army to withdraw as well, though it had not been seriously engaged by Scherbatschev's forces, much less defeated. The strongholds east of Monasterzyska were abandoned, the bridges over the Dniester were mined, and new commanders were rushed in to take charge of the situation. Baron General Arthur Arz von Straussenberg, who had commanded the Austrian VI Corps north of Monasterzyska, was sent along with his chief of staff to take charge of the Austrian First Army that was being reformed as a last line of defense on the southern Hungarian border. He was replaced with the German Feldmarschalleutnant von Fabini, while the Prussian General Zanke took command of Third Army's reserves.

The attacks of 8 August confirmed Kövess's analysis. Letschitski's main attack force, XXXIII Corps, engaged the left wing of the Austrian Third south of the Dniester and again forced the German 119th Infantry Division out of its position almost immediately. Seeckt, reporting by telephone directly to Falkenhayn, noted that the situation "with Kräwel [was] uncertain. The infantry is badly shaken."[8] Embarrassingly, Group Kräwel found itself dependent upon the Austrian 2nd Light Infantry Regiment to steady its position and enable an orderly retreat. The unit fell back on the river, to the northwest, exposing the flank and rear of Group Hadfy (Seventh Army) and clearing the southern bank of the Dniester. Letschitski promptly sent his II Cavalry Corps forward against the right wing of South Army in an attempt to reach the north bank of the Dniester and establish an open corridor to the important rail junction of Stanislau. To counter the stroke, the Austrian 15th Infantry Division (XIII Corps) retreated due west, crossing over the Dniester toward Stanislau and blowing the bridges over the river along the way. The Habsburg 2nd Cavalry Division was left to defend the area north of the Dniester and to reconnect with Third Army. Hadfy was forced to rush the 6th Reserve Infantry Regiment—the only unit available—northward to close the gap, and drew his right wing back to the north and the west as well. Even as he did so, around 4:00 PM, the Russian XI Corps smashed through the line of the Austrian 42nd Infantry Division (VIII Corps) and forced the unit back to the west. With a salient in the center of its line, VIII Corps withdrew as a whole during the night.

The overnight retreat left the Austrian Third Army defending a line that ran southwest along the rail line to Kolomea for a short distance from the very gates of Stanislau and then south-southeast along another rail line down to the Pruth River near Delatyn. The Pruth itself provided the line for the remainder of Third Army. By shortening the line, Kövess had concentrated his forces and provided them with better-fortified positions. The Russian attacks on 9 August, carried out along the entire front of Third Army, were bloodily repulsed in every sector. Group Kräwel nevertheless retreated once again under the cover of darkness, in order to eliminate the salient just south of Stanislau. Reinforced with the German 6th *Jäger* Regiment and the Austro-Hungarian 346th Infantry Regiment, and with the Turkish XV Corps on its way to South Army's right flank after having been diverted from Galicia, Kräwel believed he could maintain the defense of Stanislau. He was wrong.

In straightening his own line for purposes of defense, Kövess had also allowed the Russians to concentrate their attacks. This brought the full force of Letschitski's XXXIII Corps against Group Kräwel on the morning of 10 August, while XLI Corps struck against Group Hadfy. On Third Army's south wing, VIII Corps now faced not only the Russian XI Corps, but also the newly arrived XVIII Corps (37th and 117th infantry divisions). By the afternoon, Letschitski's forces were pressing Third Army hard all along the line. On the southern wing, the Russian XI Corps pushed the Austrians out of their positions on the east bank of the Pruth and then pursued them into the forests west of the river. Group Hadfy (the 21st Light Infantry Division and the 6th Cavalry Division) managed to hold in the center of Third Army's line, but Group Kräwel once again gave way in the north.

Both German divisions, the 105th and the 119th, retreated in the face of the Russian infantry storm that was unleashed around noon. Kräwel managed to limit the damage by deploying the Habsburg 346th Infantry Regiment relatively early, but by evening the sheer weight of the Russian infantry was taking its toll again. The German 6th *Jäger* Regiment, which held the line between Group Kräwel and Group Hadfy, cracked under a Russian assault at 6:00 PM and was barely able to withdraw fast enough to avoid being flanked and encircled. With the units on either side in retreat, Group Hadfy now had to pull back as well, abandoning Stanislau. South Army, still relatively unscathed, had to draw back its right wing by some 30 kilometers in order to maintain the line with Third Army. Seeckt feared, in any case, that the Habsburg units holding the right wing of South Army would be unable to withstand much further fighting. On 12 August, he reported that "VI Corps has still not recovered from the heavy battles in June and July; its 39th *Landwehr* Division possesses some 5,000 rifles, is completely unreliable on the defensive and can at best be used only for the momentary re-establishment of a purely local break-in. The 12th Infantry Division is better, but also less reliable in attack then on the defensive."[9] Seeing little alternative, the Archduke Karl gave the order to broaden and deepen the retreat on the night of 10–11 August, hoping to find a stronger defensive line behind the Zlota Lipa and Bystryzyca rivers west of Stanislau.

With Letschitski's XI Corps having blunted the Carpathian Corps's offensive and driven Pflanzer-Baltin's forces south in the Bukovina, a broad corridor to the Pantyr pass into Hungary stood open to the Russians. Once again, however, Brusilov's southern armies lacked the resources to exploit the situation. Losses had been almost as heavy for the attackers as for the defenders, and the Russian success had more than doubled the length of their lines in the south. Letschitski pursued both the Habsburg Third Army and the mixed South Army as they retreated, but his troops were too exhausted to engage the enemy with any strength. The Russian XXXIII Corps was forced to remain in its position east of Stanislau for two days after the Central Powers abandoned the city, for instance, in order to regroup, and not until 12 August were Scherbatschev's forces strong enough to enter Monasterzyska. This allowed Kövess's forces to disengage and systematically destroy the crossings over the Bystryzyca before the Russians could put more than a few advance units into the area.

Though Brusilov did dispatch the 64th Infantry Division to supplement Letschitski's forces on 11 August, the Central Powers again moved more troops to the area in a shorter time. In addition to the German 1st Reserve Infantry Division, which joined the Carpathian Corps on 9 August, and the Turkish XV Corps (19th and 20th Infantry Divisions), which arrived on 11 August, Hindenburg and Falkenhayn directed three additional divisions to Army Group Archduke Karl: the Bavarian 10th Infantry Division, the German 2nd Cavalry Division, and the 2nd Bicycle Division from Breslau (Bratislava). Several German *Landsturm* units, including the 37th, had also been sent to support Group Kräwel during the initial stage of its retreat, and the German 103rd Reserve Infantry Brigade was detailed to the Austrian Third on 11 August.

While it is true that most of those troops were sent to South Army and that Kövess was eventually required to release the Austrian 55th Infantry Division and 44th Reserve Infantry Division in return for the German reinforcements, the Central Powers' strategy of infusing the front with German troops and German commanders worked. Though Russian advance parties did, on at least two occasions, set foot on Hungarian territory in August 1916, Letschitski's troops no longer had numbers and strength sufficient to overcome the Central Powers' defenses. Even an attempt to force the Bystryzyca using mounted artillery and a few armored vehicles on 12 August was deflected rather easily. The Russian threat in the Bukovina was essentially at an end.[10]

The Destruction of the Guards

This was due, at least in part, to Alekseev's increasing obsession with capturing Kovel and splitting the Central Powers' front, which he believed might lead to the collapse of Austria-Hungary. Realistically, there was no hope of splitting the front once Hindenburg's command had been extended. Since the beginning of August, reinforcements for the Habsburg armies had increasingly come from either Tirol or the Western Front, and not simply shifted from north to south. German troops were in any case already so thoroughly mixed in with the Habsburg units that preventing north-south movement was, at best, a secondary issue. Both Alekseev and Brusilov nonetheless remained committed to the battle around what became known as "the Kovel Pit." While they did not deprive the Ninth and Seventh armies of any units already there, they did not send any significant reinforcements southward either. The great Russian hope of course, since the beginning of the offensive, was that Romania would enter the war on the side of the Allies and provide the needed support. Men and materiel that might otherwise have been put to good use in support of Letschitski's drive on Hungary were thus expended in the fruitless battle for a target that no longer held great strategic significance.

According to Knox, Bezobrazov had asked once again for a change in tactics in his meeting with Brusilov on 3 August. The terrain was still highly unfavorable, with only three narrow causeways leading across the otherwise impassable marshes bordering the Stochod. Nearly seventy German aircraft patrolled the approaches constantly, little hindered by either the five slow planes or the single antiaircraft battery Brusilov possessed. The German aircraft bombarded the Russian lines on a regular basis. The Russians still had no accurate maps, and continuing German control of the air thus rendered artillery preparations almost useless. The swampy ground minimized the effect of shelling in any case. Alekseev had also argued for a different approach, asking Brusilov to forgo activity in other sectors in order to concentrate all available resources on the capture of Kovel. Brusilov contemptuously dismissed Bezobrazov as incompetent, and willfully misinterpreted Alekseev's instructions.[11] In plan, in practice, and in product, the Guards Army's second assault on Kovel therefore differed little from the first. Lesch's Third Army would concentrate its forces against the northern shoulder of the Stochod salient, holding three cavalry divisions in reserve in order to exploit the slightest breakthrough. Eighth Army would focus on the southern shoulder of the salient and strike west against the (presumably) weaker Habsburg units defending Vladimir-Volynsk. Eleventh Army would engage, again, in a pinning action. The main blow would be delivered directly against the Stochod salient by the three corps of the Guards Army (I, XXX, and I Guards). The II Guards Corps was to launch a secondary action against a bridgehead on the southern shoulder of the salient and attempt to flank the defenders.

On 5 August, the Guards Rifle Company (II Guards) correspondingly launched a probing attack against the southwestern sector of the Kovel Front. It was a disaster. Though the artillery had been brought to the front lines with great effort, the order to fire on the enemy's defenses was never given. When the Russian infantry went forward, therefore, there were neither gaps in the enemy wire nor holes in the forward obstacles for them to exploit. In Knox's view: "The section chosen [. . .] seems to have been about as ill-selected as can be imagined. The men had to ford a marsh wading up to their middles. The losses, which are estimated at 70 per cent, were greater owing to the ten months in the rear having been spent too much in close-order drill."[12]

Disgusted, Brusilov ordered Bezobrazov to dismount his cavalry divisions and add them to the weight of the infantry before the next attack. Brusilov then shifted the main focus of the operation to Third Army in the north, with I Guards making a complementary attack near Sokal. The change made little difference.

The Russian artillery opened up at 6:00 AM on 8 August, concentrating this time on destroying the enemy obstacles. After six hours, however, little progress had been made. "We had no plans of the enemy's defences and only the vaguest idea of the position of his batteries, for our airmen had been unable to venture over the enemy's lines on their inferior machines," Knox wrote later. "We were ignorant of the shape and extent of the wood the enemy occupied, for our maps were last corrected nineteen years ago."[13] Left to advance over relatively open ground against still-entrenched positions, I Guards nonetheless managed to reach the Central Powers' forward trenches with relatively few casualties. Company commanders comprised a good proportion of the losses suffered, however, and the leaderless Russian units retreated under cover of darkness. The main attack fared little better.

After shelling the Central Powers' positions throughout the day, I Siberian Corps (Third Army) had launched its attack just after midnight on 8 August. The first wave of Russian infantry managed to reach the forward line of the Austrian 53rd Infantry Division (Corps Fath), but a determined counterattack soon cleared the trenches, and the Russians resumed shelling. By 6:00 AM, the Central Powers' entire line from Brody to Pinsk was under fire. At noon, as their heavy artillery continued to pound away at the obstacles and forward trenches of the Austro-German position, Russian infantry began to fill the saps they had completed during the night. Only a few weak, probing attacks came the first time the artillery stopped, however, and when they were deflected by defensive artillery, the Russian guns resumed firing. Not until 5:00 PM did the Russian infantry attack in force.

Linsingen's forces were well prepared. Their aerial reconnaissance had revealed the locations of the Russian troop bunkers (*places d'armee*) during the relative calm of 2–6 August, and the German commander had redistributed his troops accordingly. The Austrian 75th Infantry Division, 7,300 men strong, was placed behind Corps Fath as an extra reserve, while elements from the 41st Honved Infantry Division were sent to supplement II Corps. A battalion from the 217th Reserve Infantry Regiment moved to the left wing of Corps Szurmay in order to ensure the connection to the 13th Guards Division of X Corps. Finally, Linsingen placed four German infantry battalions and a German cavalry regiment behind the lines of the unsteady Austrian Fourth Army to serve as a ready reserve. Troops all along the line were instructed to prepare their positions and to range their guns.

When the long, dense columns of Russian infantry finally emerged from their saps on the evening of 8 August, therefore, they met with withering defensive artillery fire at almost every turn. Lesch's I Siberian, which had a reputation for being particularly reliable and fierce, launched six separate attacks on the northern shoulder of the salient during the course of the night, yet they were forced to withdraw at dawn without having dented the enemy lines. The Guards Army fared no better. At one point, the 22nd Infantry Division of I Guards Corps managed to reach the forward trenches of the German 107th Infantry Division in the center of the salient and threatened to collapse the unit's left wing. Bernhardi immediately sent the German 46th Infantry Regiment forward to stem the tide, however, and the Russians were forced to withdraw just before dawn, having suffered heavy casualties to no gain. The II Guards Corps never came close to the bridgehead. Each wave of infantry that moved forward across the swampy terrain was easily shredded by well-directed artillery from the two German divisions holding the sector. In just over twelve hours' fighting the Guards Army lost another 7,000 men, some 20 percent of its operative force. When asked for a truce to bury the bodies, Marwitz refused; he wanted the bodies to remain there as a deterrent to future attacks.[14]

The single Russian success came, as might be expected, against the troops of the Austrian Fourth Army. The 13th Guards Division, positioned on the right wing of X Corps, crumbled under the very first attack by the Russian 4th Reserve Infantry Division, reinforced by elements of the Russian 53rd Infantry Division, at 6:00 AM, threatening the interior wing between X Corps and Corps Szurmay. The remaining divisions of the Habsburg Fourth—including the 11th Infantry Division—managed to hold their positions, however, and timely deployment of the local reserve restored the Habsburg line by noon. An ill-conceived attempt at a counterstroke that afternoon gave the Russians a second opportunity to breach the line when the 13th Guards Division scattered in confusion and left a 1,500-foot gap open, but again local reserves proved sufficient to stem the Russian tide. The action cost almost 1,500 men—the 13th Guards Division alone lost 1,200—but Linsingen and Hindenburg were satisfied that the new command system was working.[15]

When the pattern repeated itself the following day Brusilov called a halt to the offensive, ordering his forces around Kovel to go over to the defensive. Brusilov, naturally, blamed the artillery commanders. "The Duke of Mecklenburg is a very nice man," he told Knox, "but he knows absolutely nothing. Smislovski and Gilgenschmidt (the two corps inspectors of artillery) are no use. [. . .] The artillery was directed as it might

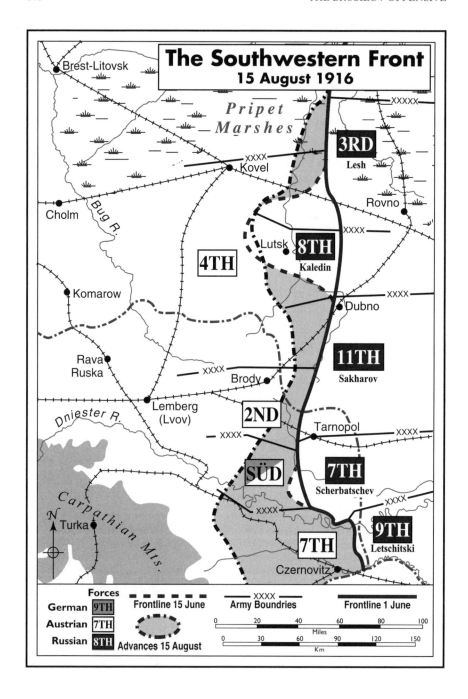

The Southwestern Front
15 August 1916

have been after two days of war instead of after two years."[16] The Guards Army was in any case broken, having lost more than 54,000 men and 500 officers since it was first deployed in the theater.[17] Rodzianko, the president of the Russian Duma, reported after an inspection that the Guards Army was angry and bitter over the seemingly useless casualties. "We are willing to give our lives for Russia, for our Motherland," one lieutenant had told him, "but not for the whims of generals."[18] Brusilov informed Alekseev of all of this in writing, and forwarded a copy of Rodzianko's report along with his request that Alekseev put the matter before the tsar. He found, however, that it was not so simple a matter.[19]

> Certainly it was very difficult for him [Alekseev] to alter such a procedural situation. I had the right [and the] powers of disposition of a front commander to appoint army commanders, corps commanders, and even all subordinate commanders to their positions, but the officers of the Guards were beyond my reach. The Tsar personally selected them, appointed them, and released them, and therefore it was practically unthinkable that the release of a great number of Guards officers would be attained in one stroke.[20]

In the end, Alekseev managed a fateful compromise. The Guards Army, now designated as the Special Army, was detailed to Evert's command on the Northwestern Front, along with Third Army. The attacks on Kovel would continue throughout August under Evert's direction, and were renewed periodically through November, always with the same result. At least seventeen separate charges by the Guards Army broke in the face of high-explosive artillery shells, traversing machine-gun fire, and massed rifle fire between 1 August and 16 September. The casualties were almost too many to count. "All we know," Hindenburg wrote later, "is that sometimes in our battles with the Russians we had to remove the mounds of enemy corpses from before our trenches in order to get a clear field of fire against fresh assaulting waves."[21]

On 21 September, Nicholas II finally wrote to Alekseev, asking him "to stop our hopeless attacks, so as to later pull the Guards and some other troops out of the front lines and give them some time to rest and be refilled."[22] The tsar also agreed to furlough Bezobrazov for at least two months, after which he intended to appoint him as a corps commander in the Guards Army again. To assuage Brusilov and, ostensibly, to allow him to concentrate on events in the Bukovina, the IV Siberian Corps was added permanently to his command.[23] Even before all of this worked its way through Stavka, however, Letschitski's drive had already begun to peter out, and by 15 August it was done. The Brusilov Offensive was over.

Enter Romania

The Allies had one more arrow in their quiver for the Eastern Front, however. Inspired, somewhat belatedly, by Brusilov's success in the Bukovina, the Romanian government declared war against Austria-Hungary on 27 August. This was what the Central Powers—particularly Austria-Hungary—had feared would happen for more than two years, and at the time it appeared to be a significant threat. If Romania entered the war, Conrad wrote, it "would decide [the war] against us."[24] The Romanian Army contained 623,000 men, and three-fourths of them were poised to strike against Austria-Hungary in Transylvania, while the remainder were to defend against a possible Bulgarian invasion. Most observers believed that this force, augmented by three Russian divisions (the 61st and the 115th Infantry Divisions, along with one cavalry division) under General A. M. Zaionchkovski, known as the Dobruja Detachment, would shift the balance of the war. "By making the necessary arrangement with Rumania to crush the Austrian army," French president Raymond Poincaré had written, "we should compel Germany to make an additional effort which may well be beyond her immediate resources."[25] For the Allies, it was a chance to drive Austria-Hungary from the war and perhaps force the Germans to make peace; for the Romanians, it offered the chance to lay claim to ethnically Romanian areas within the Habsburg Empire and complete the process of national unification.

Like Italy, Romania had been a member of the Triple Alliance in 1914, having signed on in 1883. In August 1914, however, King Carol, Romania's pro-German ruler, died under suspicious circumstances, and a new, pro-Russian dynasty was installed. Territorial interest in Transylvania, an area with a substantial ethnic Romanian population that belonged to the Hungarian half of the Habsburg Empire, and in Bessarabia, a similar territory held by the Russian tsar, thus persuaded Romania's new leaders to abjure the alliance in 1914. Negotiations with the Allies had ensued almost immediately, while the Central Powers also did their best to convince Romania at least to stay out of the conflict. Germany in fact signed a new treaty with Romania and received crucial shipments of oil and food from Romania in the winter of 1915–16, even though the treaty was never confirmed by the Romanian parliament. Romania's position, Falkenhayn wrote, "could not be regarded as less than benevolent to the Central Powers, but was nonetheless very questionable."[26]

It was at least clear to the Romanians that there was little point in joining the Allies unless or until victory was assured, since victory by the Central Powers might also have its rewards. Until August 1916, there had been little reason to think that the Allies would triumph on the Eastern Front. Serbia, after its initially successful resistance, had been crushed; neither the Salonika nor the Gallipoli campaign had succeeded in significantly weakening the Central Powers; and the Russians had met with nothing but defeat until Brusilov launched his offensive. With a strong and threatening Bulgarian force only thirty miles from Bucharest and ready to intervene on behalf of the Central Powers in order to advance its own territorial interests, the Romanian government had found it prudent to remain neutral through the first two years of the conflict.

The Austro-Hungarian collapse in the Bukovina in late June and early July 1916, however, presented an opportunity that seemed too good to pass up. Negotiations with the Allies, which had been rather lukewarm, began to heat up again. Russia began sending munitions to Romania as early as 14 July 1916, and dispatches intercepted by the Central Powers seemed to indicate that Romania had agreed in principle to enter the war in conjunction with an Allied offensive in the Balkans. No treaty had been concluded though, and the Romanians took no action, but negotiations continued to intensify. The only remaining issue, apparently, was timing. The Romanian military leadership wanted the French to launch an offensive in the Balkans ten days prior to any Romanian entry into the war, which they claimed could not reasonably take place until the middle of August. Russia, on the other hand, wanted Romania to make a supporting strike into the Bukovina no later than 7 August. To sway Romania to its way of thinking, Stavka promised to send 30,000 men and 400 machine guns to support the Romanian offensive; the 1st Serbian Volunteer Division, comprising Habsburg subjects who had switched sides and were now fighting under Russian command, was also—fatefully—detailed to Romania. England pledged to deliver materials as well, while France agreed to launch a diversionary strike in the Balkans.

Despite the Russian pressure, Romania was still not ready to take the final steps to war. Not until 8 August was a draft treaty completed, and even then the Romanians were dissatisfied with some of the details. The Habsburg High Command nonetheless expected a Romanian strike by 20

August and began to build a new operational group for the new theater. Conrad even asked Falkenhayn to order a preemptive strike on the part of Mackensen regardless of whether or not Romania declared war at that time, which the German commander naturally declined. Falkenhayn did not believe Romania was ready to strike; in his opinion, the threat of a Bulgarian counterattack on Bucharest remained sufficient to hold Romania in check. Even if it was not, he was convinced that the Romanians would not strike before the harvest was over, and he considered it entirely possible that the Austrians were falsifying information in order to force Germany to send additional troops south. "According to all incoming and reliable reports, " Falkenhayn wrote to Conrad on 13 August, "the Romanian attack, if it happens at all, will still be delayed for some time."[27] He advised the Habsburg commander to send the Austrian 51st Infantry Division, which had been designated for the defense of Siebenbürgen in case of a Romanian attack, to help relieve the latest Italian thrust on the Isonzo.

On the following day, just as the Russian drive in the Carpathians reached its peak, Bulgaria, which had also wavered for much of the war, seemingly removed the threat to Bucharest by launching a strike against Macedonia. Convinced that the time was ripe, the Romanians signed a military convention with the Allies on 17 August. "It was the moment, if ever, for Romania to march," Britain's ambassador to Bucharest wrote.[28] In return for the Dobruja Detachment, English supplies, and the promise of a favorable territorial settlement, Romania pledged itself to declare war on Austria-Hungary no later than 28 August, with an attack to follow immediately. To cover the mobilization, the French would launch a strike in the Balkans beginning on 18 August.

While Western, Allied diplomats were delighted with this turn of events, almost all parties on the Eastern Front were not. For Falkenhayn in particular it was a bitter pill to swallow; when combined with the failure at Verdun, it cost him his command. Romania's entry into the war would also bring Bulgaria into the war and make Turkey a full-fledged participant on the Eastern Front. Both states favored a unified command under German auspices. Falkenhayn, of course, had not been opposed to the idea, so long as he would be the commander. Accordingly, as Romania's declaration seemed imminent, he again opened a dialog on the subject with Conrad beginning on 21 August. The Habsburgs' chief of general staff, however, remained adamantly opposed to any such union. He argued that Germany could hardly assume command of the entire war effort when it was not even at war with Italy, as Austria-Hungary was, for it would almost certainly bargain away Habsburg lands in order to forward German interests. Unfortunately for Conrad, Italy not only declared war on Germany on 27 August 1916, but the Archduke Friedrich was working behind the scenes to oust him in favor of a German commander. Unfortunately for Falkenhayn, that commander would be Hindenburg.

Romania's declaration of war on 27 August (which was, ironically, 14 August under the older, Julian calendar used by both Russia and Romania at the time) had shaken the German emperor's faith in Falkenhayn, who had assured him that Romania was not about to enter the conflict. Wilhelm II did not, apparently, take the news well, and, worried that Falkenhayn's carelessness might cost Germany the war, he released him in favor of Hindenburg on 28 August. Conrad hoped the move might end talk of a unified command, but instead it accelerated. Influenced by Archduke Ferdinand, Franz Josef now took up the proposal. Thus outfoxed, Conrad could only play a defensive endgame, hoping to secure as much for Austria-Hungary as possible in any agreement. When the negotiations concluded on 9 September, however, Conrad found he was virtually powerless. The Habsburg emperor retained the right of consultation, but the power of command lay with Hindenburg. As part of the agreement, moreover, German officers were to be given command over Habsburg units, albeit under the auspices of an "officer exchange" and only in German-speaking units. Two days later, the Archduke Friedrich "suggested" that Pflanzer-Baltin report sick and ask to be relieved of duty because the Germans had doubts about his ability and refused to put soldiers under his command. For the Austrians therefore, and for Falkenhayn, the Romanian declaration had been a bitter disappointment.[29]

Brusilov and Alekseev were also rather nonplussed by Romania's entry. Brusilov was disappointed first of all at the paucity of Russian aid to the Romanians. "Unfortunately, Alekseev had underestimated my opinion regarding our assistance in Dobruja. One should have sent not just a single corps with two second-rate divisions of personnel in very weak condition," Brusilov wrote in his memoirs, "but an entire army with good divisions."[30] Alekseev would have none of it. "I have been all along opposed to the intervention of Rumania," he said, "but have been forced to agree to it by pressure from France and England. Now that the principle has been accepted, if the Emperor ordered me to send fifteen Russian wounded men there, I would not on any account send sixteen."[31] Though Brusilov later claimed that Alekseev misled him on this count, both men were certainly well aware that Romania was more a military liability than an asset.[32]

Despite its impressive size on paper, the Romanian Army was prepared for war in almost no meaningful way. Most of the Romanian divisions were poorly equipped; five divisions possessed no machine guns at all, and the remaining eighteen were woefully short of not only machine guns but also artillery and wheeled transportation. The army had stockpiled only a six-week supply of munitions, and any additions would have to come from outside, via Russia. The only possible routes, via either Archangelsk or Vladivostok and then across the rear of the Southwestern Front, were already clogged with traffic. Goods would also have to be transshipped at the border, since the Russian and Romanian railways used different gauges, and only two single-tracked lines connected the two states. Thirteen of the Romanian infantry divisions had been formed only recently, and thus the men had little training, if any. Most of the Romanian soldiers were in any case illiterate peasants, and the officers reportedly were not much better. According to Norman Stone, "British observers felt that the operations of the Romanian army would make a public-school field-day look like the execution of the Schlieffen Plan; while the comments of Russians who had to fight side-by-side with the Romanians were often unprintable."[33] One of those Russians who did put something in print, Major General Anton I. Denikin, said of the Romanian Army: "There were several capable Generals, the officers were effeminate, and the men were splendid. The artillery was adequate, but the infantry was untrained."[34] Lieutenant General Andrei M. Zaionchkovski, whom Brusilov had personally selected to command the Dobruja Detachment, was less enamored of his allies.[35] After his first encounter with the Romanians, Zaionchkovski begged to be released from what he termed "a punishment for some crime I did not even know I had committed. I have to fight with the Romanian troops more than with the enemy. I feel certain that when the first Bulgarian shell lands, the Romanians will scatter in all directions."[36]

The initial Romanian advance was carried out without event, however; some 370,000 soldiers marched into Hungary, where they faced Arz's hastily assembled Austrian First Army.[37] Because the Austrian First had only about 34,000 men, including the Austrian 61st Infantry Division and part of the 51st Infantry Division, as well as units drawn from the local Alpine militias, the customs police, and the reserves, the Romanians expected little resistance. The Romanian commanders failed to take advantage of the situation though, preferring instead to wait to see what would happen. "In the beginning of the campaign the Roumanian Army showed complete disregard of the experience of the World War," Denikin noted. "In matters of equipment and ammunition their levity was almost criminal."[38] The Romanians neither engaged the Austrians nor fortified the local towns. Hermannstadt, the capital of Hungarian Transylvania, was not occupied until 6 September, though it was defended only by the local gendarmerie. It looked, initially, as if Brusilov and the Russians might regain their momentum, but it was not to be.

The Carpathian Disaster

Almost nothing went right in the brief Romanian campaign. To begin with, the French diversion in the Balkans failed miserably. Letschitski's attempt to pin down, if not break, the Central Powers in the Carpathians misfired as well. His forces, with a large cavalry component and almost no howitzers, were almost completely unsuited to fighting in the mountains. With complete control of the air, the German artillery positioned itself on the reverse slopes of the foothills, where the Russians could not locate it, and bombarded the infantry as it climbed. Frequently it took the Russians, untrained and unfamiliar with mountain warfare, hours to reach positions they could see only a few hundred yards beyond. Forced onto the roads winding through the narrow valleys, the Russian advance quickly ground to a halt. After declaring war against Romania on 1 September, the Bulgarians launched a strike into Dobruja, which they had lost to Romania in 1913. Mackensen, perhaps the most consistently successful commander on the Eastern Front during the entire war, commanded the Central Powers' forces, which consisted of four Bulgarian divisions, two Turkish divisions, and a few Austrian and German units.[39]

The attack caught the Russians and the Romanians off guard, since they had convinced themselves that Bulgaria, traditionally Russophilic, would remain neutral. Mackensen's small force advanced quickly; the single Romanian division left to defend the border was practically destroyed in the opening engagement. Zaionchkovski's forces provided more resistance, but they were no match for Mackensen's forces either; the Bulgarians fought with a vengeance once they discovered the Serbs were fighting with the Russians. With two of his three corps reduced to about a seventh of their strength over the course of only three days (2–4 September), Zaionchkovski was forced to withdraw. Mackensen then established a siege against the Danubian fortress of Tutracaia, which the Romanian commander promptly declared would be "a Romanian Verdun." A classic nineteenth-century fortification, Tutracaia was surrounded by at least fifteen vast earthworks and defended by a garrison of nearly 40,000 men—almost three times the size of Mackensen's attacking army. After only one day's battle though, on 6 September, the Romanian commander surrendered the fortress to Mackensen. Two days later a second Danubian fortress, Silistria, capitulated without even the pretense of a fight. Mackensen had lost some 7,000 men; the Romanian casualties numbered only 7,000 as well, but more than 40,000 Romanian soldiers—including three generals—had surrendered.

It might have been better had they all surrendered, but some 12,000 Romanians had managed to flee the fortresses, only to surrender to what they thought were approaching Bulgarian units. When it turned out that the "attackers" were in reality part of Zaionchkovski's force, anarchy ensued. The Russians, who regarded the Romanians with contempt, sacked the countryside. Mackensen's force advanced steadily into the chaos, driving the brawling allies from Dobruja. His chief of staff summed up the campaign: "Bad roads, large herds of water buffalo, oxen, horses. Many buzzards. Dust, heat; then tropical rains."[40]

Determined to regain Dobruja, the Romanians adopted a defensive posture in Transylvania and shifted three divisions to the southeast to form the core of a new "South Army Group" tasked with retaking the area. By 15 September, the Allies had assembled some fifteen divisions—almost half again the number now commanded by Mackensen, who had been reinforced with units drawn from the northern portion of the Eastern Front. While Zaionchkovski was to carry out the main strike in Dobruja, Romanian forces would attempt to cross the Danube and catch Mackensen's force in the rear. The flanking attack was, in the words of Norman Stone, "a burlesque. Bridges were inadequate and broke down under the weight of guns and horses. Austro-Hungarian gunboats did much damage to the infantry as it tried to cross. Such initial success as the crossings had was owing almost entirely to the deduction made by Kosch, the German commander, from the Romanians' behavior that they were only there to defend Bucharest."[41]

It went no better for Zaionchkovski, who was about to be relieved of his command in any case. The Romanian elements on his right wing retreated almost immediately, without informing Zaionchkovski. With their flank exposed, the Russians in the center fell back, only to be overtaken by the Romanian elements on their left, which were fleeing the Bulgarian cavalry. Though Zaionchkovski had ordered his troops to destroy the port of

Constanza, no one bothered to do so. The Russian naval detachment that was guarding the installation simply sailed away, allowing the Bulgarians to capture huge stores of grain and oil. "Unfortunately, it is too late to save the situation," Knox noted in his diary on 25 October. "The allied line in the Dobruja is now many miles north of the Constanza railway. The Russian troops are reduced to nothing. The 61st and the Serb Division have about 3,000 bayonets each. The 115th Division was untried and has not distinguished itself. The 3rd Rifle Division was taken away at a critical moment to defend the approaches to Bucharest. [. . .] As things are, it seems likely that all Wallachia with its grain and oil will be lost to the enemy."[42]

Knox was a keen observer, if not exactly a prophet. By the end of October 1916 the Russian-Romanian counterattack had been thoroughly defeated, and the Central Powers held the territory south of the Danube River. To make matters worse, the Germans had also defeated the Romanian defensive force in Transylvania during that time. The new Ninth Army, commanded (ironically enough) by Falkenhayn, drove the Romanians out of Hungary with relative ease. The Romanians had left only ten divisions to face the combined twelve divisions of Arz's First Army and Falkenhayn's. Worse, these troops had dug shallow trenches well beyond their supply lines yet within easy reach of the Austro-Hungarian railheads. They were scattered across a wide front stretching from the Danube to the Maros, and often had no communications. Falkenhayn was therefore able to work his way methodically north, driving back first one unit and then another beginning from 18 September, while Arz performed a similar maneuver starting from the north. Hermannstadt fell on 25 September, and by 6 October the German Ninth Army had reached Kronstadt, which fell three days later. "The Romanians are in retreat along the whole line," Paléologue reported from Moscow. "The High Command is incapable and the troops are tired and dispirited."[43]

In order to prevent Falkenhayn and Arz from driving across to join with Mackensen, the Romanian High Command now decided to adopt a defensive position on the Danube and shift the bulk of its forces north to meet the threat. This, combined with the onset of winter in the mountain passes, sufficed to slow the German advance. In the Red Tower Pass, where the Bavarian Life Guards Regiment was advancing, bitter cold and wind forced the men into their tents for several days. Two weeks later, crossing yet another pass, the Life Guards found themselves slogging through snow and cold severe enough to kill numerous horses—which then provided the only steady supply of food. "It was somewhat tough, but it tasted absolutely delicious," one Bavarian soldier wrote in his diary.[44] By the end of October, all of Transylvania was in the hands of the Central Powers as well.

The relentless German advance threatened to rupture the Allies' lines on the Eastern Front. Arz's thrust had opened a gap between the Romanians and the south wing of Letschitski's Ninth Army that forced the Russian commander to forgo any further strikes at Hungary just to plug the gap. Mackensen's forces were poised to cut Bucharest off from the sea, and it was clear that only massive Russian aid could even forestall a Romanian collapse. As Evert's attacks on Vladimir-Volynsk were making no progress, Alekseev realized that he would have to call off the offensive to stave off disaster. The Guards Army—now properly called the Special Army and commanded by General Gurko—was once again given over to Brusilov's command and tasked with defending Lutsk. The Russian Third Army extended its front southward once again, and Eighth Army was shifted south to the Dniester, which allowed Letschitski and Sakharov to extend their fronts. Klembovski, whom Brusilov had originally nominated as his successor to command Eighth Army, now took command of the Russian Eleventh Army, while Sakharov replaced Zaionchkovski at the head of what was now called the Danube Army. The Russian Fourth Army, which had been held in reserve, was now sent to Romania as well. All told, thirty-six Russian infantry divisions and eleven cavalry divisions were moving south. It was not enough.

Because the Romanian railways in the area were capable of handling only 19 trains per day and each Russian corps required 130 trains to move, there was no means of getting the Russian troops into Romania. The Romanians had provided only 30 trains in any case, so many Russian units therefore had to make the journey from Czernovitz on foot.[45] Needless to say, they did not arrive either in a timely manner or in sufficient force to be effective. By 9 November, only the Russian IV Corps had reached its positions in Romania, which sufficed merely to hold the Bulgarians south of the Danube. By the time the remaining troops (one division from XXIV Corps and two divisions each from XL Corps and VIII Corps) had detrained between late November and mid-December, it was too late. The German 109th Infantry Division (Ninth Army) crossed the Alt River on 26 November, allowing Falkenhayn and Mackensen to join forces. Protected by the Austrian Danube Fleet, Mackensen's troops shifted across the Danube, and the Germans launched a drive on Bucharest. The Romanian Fourth Army, commanded by General Constantin Prezan, had only eighteen battalions facing forty German battalions. A French military mission, dispatched to

Bucharest in an attempt to create "a Balkan Marne," was decisively defeated on 6 December. The depleted Romanian forces abandoned Bucharest the following day, fleeing under cover of huge smoke clouds caused by British agents setting fire to the oil fields of Plöesti.

All told, the Romanians had lost more than 73,000 men killed or wounded, 147,000 captured, and some 90,000 missing in action. The action, which many had thought would rekindle the Brusilov Offensive and doom the Central Powers, had had exactly the opposite effect. Stavka had been forced to shift so many troops south—not so much to defend Romania, for which Alekseev cared little, but to guard its newly exposed right flank—that all offensive movement on the part of the Russians had come to an end. Russia's offensive power and its army were in fact broken, though it was not entirely evident at the time. The Central Powers, on the other hand, reaped a bonanza with the defeat of Romania. Over 2 million tons of grain, 250,000 head of livestock, 200,000 tons of timber, and Romania's annual output of a million tons of oil came into their hands with the fall of Romania, without which neither Austria-Hungary nor Germany might have been able to fight through the winter of 1916–17.[46]

CHAPTER SEVEN

CONSEQUENCES

The Romanian debacle marked, in many ways, the beginning of the end for Russia. Whatever slight hopes Brusilov might have had for the renewal of his offensive in September and October of 1916 were dashed as the reserves of the Southwestern Front—twenty-seven divisions in all—were drawn off to prevent a complete collapse in Romania. This additional front of nearly 320 kilometers, coupled with the loss of nearly 2 million men during the summer of 1916 (including an estimated 1 million dead), left the "Russian steamroller" without sufficient forces to move forward.[1] Many of the infantry units on the Southwestern and Romanian fronts were reportedly at between 50 and 60 percent of full strength in the autumn of 1916, and there was sincere doubt in official circles that Russia could make good the losses. According to Stavka estimates of 15 October 1916, the army needed at least 300,000 new soldiers every month for six months in order to fill the ranks in time for a new offensive in 1917. Yet calculations revealed that even if the second-class reserves (men between the ages of thirty-seven and forty), the 1919 cadre, and some 200,000 men who had previously been discharged were all called up, the numbers would be insufficient.[2] Just as worrisome though were reports that the troops already at the front were showing signs of unrest.

Disaffection with the war had long been a problem on the Russian home front, but by autumn 1916 it was reaching crisis proportions.[3] One police report of the time noted that "the ever-growing disorder in the rear, or in other words in the entire country, which is chronic and cumulative, has now attained such an extraordinarily rapid rate of growth that it now [. . .] menaces shortly to throw the country into catastrophically destructive chaos and spontaneous anarchy."[4] Aleksandr Konovalov, who later served as minister of trade and industry in the Russian Provisional Government, told the historian Bernard Pares that "it was in October [1916] that living conditions became really alarming, and it was from this time that the revolutionary mood must be dated."[5] A report of the *Okhrana* (secret police) from October 1916 confirms this view, reading in part: "There is a marked increase in hostile feelings among the peasants, not only against the government, but against all other social groups."[6]

The sheer number of losses suffered by the Russian army—one historian has estimated that Russia lost at least 2 million dead and between 8 and 10 million wounded in the first twenty-nine months of the war—increasingly brought these estranged elements into the ranks.[7] General Ruzski, for instance, noted that reserves sent to the front during the winter of 1916–17 were "increasingly poisoned by propaganda."[8] Perhaps more importantly, the losses significantly reduced the stabilizing influence of the aristocratic officer class. In the first two-plus years of the war, while the Russian Army grew from 1.2 million men to 6.6 million men, the size of the Russian officer corps went from 41,000 to nearly 150,000. Taking into account the 63,000 officers killed during that time means that nearly 170,000 men had entered the Russian officer corps during the war. The majority of these men, even in elite units, stemmed from non-noble families and received remarkably little training.[9] At the end of the Brusilov Offensive, for example, the vaunted Imperial Russian Life Guards Grenadier Regiment consisted of "young officers whose graduation had been hastened, army officers transferred to the regiment, soldiers called up from the older classes of reserves, and badly trained recruits."[10] Fully 70 percent of the junior officers in the Russian Army were of "peasant origin" by the end of 1916, and fewer than 10 percent of all officers had been fully trained in a military academy.[11]

Though officers such as Anton Denikin have argued that the army remained a bastion of the monarchy until the Provisional Government took over, it seems clear that morale had already begun to crumble long before that.[12] During the celebration of Orthodox Easter in 1916, for instance, there were instances of fraternization among the units of XXXX Corps, and desertion rates on the Southwestern Front during the Brusilov Offensive were remarkably high.[13] The massive losses suffered during the later attempts to take Kovel undoubtedly lowered the morale of the troops even further, and by autumn the "disease" of revolution was beginning to infect the front. On the night of 1–2 October 1916, for example, units of the VII Siberian Corps balked when ordered to take up positions for an attack. One week later, two regiments in the Special (Guards) Army forced soldiers from a neighboring unit to halt work on the trenches in their sector, and there were reports of threats against any soldiers who launched an attack. Brusilov believed that these were isolated incidents, but he nevertheless asked Alekseev to investigate the source of the disruptions.[14] As autumn gave way to winter, the number of incidents mounted. More than a dozen regiments mutinied in December 1916. "Take us and have us shot," one company telegraphed to the tsar, "but we just aren't going to fight any more."[15]

Few in the Russian High Command, however, believed that there were serious problems brewing in the army. Both Brusilov and Aleksandr Dukhonin, the quartermaster general for the Southwestern Front, thought that a quiet winter of training and rebuilding the Russian defensive positions, along with the return of the regular officers wounded during the summer, would restore order and discipline at the front.[16] Dukhonin blamed the Romanian misadventure for most of the Russians' morale problems, as did many others. Many Russian officers, in fact, held negative attitudes toward Romania but were generally positive about the prospects for the war. Both Kaledin and General Abram Dragomirov, for example, told Knox in early November 1916 that they expected the Germans to be retreating before the Russian cavalry soon enough.[17] Stavka obviously agreed with this assessment. At a conference in Chantilly, France, held on 15 November 1916, Russian representatives agreed to coordinate pressure on the Central Powers across all fronts in 1917 and launch an offensive that spring. With an estimated superiority of at least 60 percent in guns and troops on every front, Stone notes, "[e]arly in 1917, Russian generals were full of fight. [. . .] Even Evert's mouth watered, as he contemplated the great amounts of shell with which he would plaster a few square kilometers of German line in the coming spring offensives."[18]

From an administrative standpoint, there was certainly some cause for optimism. The success of the Brusilov Offensive validated the extensive reforms carried out under Polivanov and demonstrated that the shell shortage and supply problems of 1914–15 had been overcome.[19] "This offensive also proved," Brusilov wrote in his memoirs, "that the opinion that the Russian Army had already given up after the mishaps of 1915, which had for one reason or another spread across Russia, was false."[20] Not only had the offensive demonstrated the vigor of the Imperial Russian Army, it had also exposed the weakness of the Austro-Hungarian Empire in particular and of the Central Powers' position in general. In a span of three months, the Russians had pushed the front lines westward by nearly 50 kilometers on the central sectors of the Eastern Front and by as much as 125 kilometers in the south. Brusilov's forces captured some 400,000 prisoners of war and inflicted nearly 1.5 million casualties on the enemy. The Habsburgs had been driven from Galicia and from the Bukovina, their armies devastated, demoralized, brought to the point of collapse, and forced to accept German control of the entire front as the price of even temporary salvation. As Soviet Lieutenant General P. A. Shilin noted (inaccurately) in the introduction to Brusilov's memoirs: "In order to prevent a breakthrough the enemy was forced to bring some thirty divisions from the West, from Italy, and from the Balkans."[21] While the Brusilov Offensive may not have achieved a strategic breakthrough, many historians therefore still credited it with saving Italy in the face of the Habsburg offensive in Tirol, relieving German pressure on Verdun, and putting the Entente in position to make a decisive strike in 1917.[22] Walther Hubatsch, in his 1963 history of the Central Powers during the First World War, went so far as to call the Brusilov Offensive "one of the greatest victories of world history."[23]

Brusilov, however, was not willing to go that far. He did indeed claim that his 1916 campaign had prevented a major Italian defeat, alleviated the strain on the British and French positions on the Western Front, brought Romania into the war, negated all of the Central Powers' plans for that year, and "completely altered" the general situation. He also noted, however, that "[t]hese operations brought no strategic results. [. . .] The Southwestern Front did everything that it could in line with the possibilities. It was not in a position to do more—I at least could do no more. Perhaps in my place a military genius like Julius Caesar or Napoleon could have realized more, but I had no such ambitions and I could not have had them."[24] Later and more specialized historians have tended to agree with this view, seeing the Brusilov Offensive as a piece of tactical genius that had limited strategic results.[25]

The historian who has most closely examined the myths and actuality of the Brusilov Offensive is undoubtedly Rudolf Jerabek. Through extensive work in the Austrian War Archive Jerabek has challenged, among other things, the notion that the Brusilov Offensive saved the Italians from disaster on the Tirolean Front in May 1916. He argues that the offensive had ground to a halt already on 20 May and thus, "even before the start of Brusilov's relief offensive it had become clear that there could be no more thought of a victorious battle in the area around Venezia."[26] This view, which has since won the support of other historians, holds that it was Conrad's ineffective planning and intra-command squabbling that combined to halt the Tirolean campaign, not any action on the part of the Russians.[27]

Conrad, who considered Italy to be "the real enemy" in the war, had been planning to strike in the south Tirol area since late 1915 at the very latest. His initial plan called for sixteen divisions, with eight mountain divisions tabbed to spearhead the invasion and eight to follow up the initial breakthroughs. Conrad's intent was to take only three divisions from the Russian Front (the 22nd, 34th, and 43rd infantry divisions, all from Second Army); two additional divisions would come from the Balkan Front, and Germany was to supply three or four divisions as well. Falkenhayn, who had not been consulted in the initial planning stages, refused to go along with the plan when Conrad informed him of it at the end of January 1916. The German commander had already decided to shift his focus to the west, and was in fact already withdrawing German forces from the southern (Habsburg) sectors of the front in order to strike the French at Verdun. Where there had been twenty German divisions on the front south of the Pripet in August 1915, by April 1916 there were only two.

Conrad nevertheless decided in March to go ahead with fewer forces, but also to draw fifteen batteries of heavy artillery and a fourth division (the 10th, from Fourth Army) from the Russian Front. When the Russian offensive at Lake Narotch failed miserably that month, however, Conrad and his staff were encouraged to draw yet another division (the 3rd Infantry Division, from Seventh Army) from the Russian Front to the Tirol. The heavy guns had been replaced by a greater number of smaller batteries, and the influx of new recruits had actually swollen the number of men under arms on the Russian Front from 560,000 to 620,000.[28] The Habsburg commander simply did not believe that the Russians could attack in either Galicia or the Bukovina without shifting additional forces south. "A Russian attack under this relation [of forces]," Conrad wrote, "is unforeseeable from any perspective."[29]

What Conrad had done, in fact, was make a Russian attack not only more likely, but also more likely to succeed. The movement of Habsburg troops on the Russian Front did not go unnoticed by the Russians; Brusilov's intelligence network in particular had reported the withdrawal of seasoned units from the front as early as March 1916. This information, relayed of course to the Italians, had largely deprived the Austro-Hungarian forces of the element of surprise. Snow and ice along the mountainous roads to the front—which Conrad had not, unbelievably, planned for—slowed the Austrian preparations by five weeks, moreover, giving the Italians additional notice and even more time to prepare. The Italians, however, planned even more poorly than Conrad had; they based their defenses in the mountains while the Austrians proceeded through the valleys, cutting off one post after another. Encouraged by this initial advance but well aware that the Italians had already called on Russia to launch a relief strike, on 25 May Conrad reluctantly agreed to draw still more troops from the Russian Front. Rather than send more experienced troops though, he dispatched the relatively untested 11th Infantry Division (Fourth Army). Conrad also asked Falkenhayn to release the two divisions of the Habsburg XII Corps serving under General Woyrsch's command north of the Pripet, and even when the German commander refused, Conrad preferred to draw troops from the Balkan and Isonzo fronts rather than weaken his defenses further in the east.

Even before those troops could arrive though, rain and snow combined to halt the Habsburg offensive. Supply trains could not reach the troops, and the artillery could not move forward. General Count Luigi Cadorna, the Italian commander in chief, managed to reinforce the Italian First Army in the interval and quickly raised the Italian Fifth Army to supplement his forces. On 2 June—still two days before Brusilov launched his offensive—Paléologue recorded in his diary that the Italians had stemmed the Austrian tide in the Tirol.[30] On the following day, Conrad's chief planner for Italian operations admitted that the offensive had failed.[31] "I have spoken to many officers who fought in Tirol," a member of the Italian operations staff wrote later, "and they told me in all honesty that they were not going to advance further, even if they also asserted that one should not have halted the offensive just to supply the necessary forces against the Russians."[32] Falkenhayn also, in his memoirs, notes that the Habsburg advance in the Tirol was over by early June.[33] Clearly, the Brusilov Offensive had done little to halt the Habsburg advance; in fact, Conrad's weakening of the Russian Front in order to carry out his Tirolean adventure contributed greatly to Brusilov's success.

A similar case, if perhaps not quite as strong, can be made with regard to Verdun. If, for instance, it was the insertion of German troops into the front south of the Pripet as "corset stays" that staved off collapse in June and

July 1916, then certainly it was the withdrawal of German forces in February and March 1916 that helped create the conditions for the success of the Brusilov Offensive. Stone, in fact, cites the German departure as far more important than the Austrian dispositions.[34] And while the claim that the Russian campaign of June 1916 lightened the burden on the French and English is not without some truth, it is clear both that Falkenhayn's strategy was a failure long before Brusilov launched his attack and that the German attacks were hardly diminished in strength until mid-July. Even Falkenhayn, who had every reason to cite the Brusilov Offensive as the reason for the failure at Verdun, noted in his memoirs simply that the withdrawal of units from the Western Front to reinforce the Austrians in Galicia made the German position in the west "less favorable." He complained only that the Germans were thus unable to preempt the Somme Offensive.[35]

It was not until 8 June 1916, after all, that Falkenhayn even agreed to send the first divisions from the Western Front to reinforce the crumbling Habsburg armies. The German operation at Verdun, code-named "Judgment" (*Gericht*) had opened on 21 February, and at the time the Germans possessed a strategic reserve of over twenty-five divisions on the Western Front. The Germans deployed phosgene gas, flamethrowers, rifle grenades, and storm troopers. Aerial battles augmented the artillery barrages on a regular basis. Yet by mid-March Kaiser Wilhelm was convinced the operation was a failure, and several leading German generals quickly chimed in with their own opinions of the disaster; Crown Prince William even asked that the campaign be halted. It went on. The German Fifth Army was virtually destroyed by early May, and German casualties continued to mount. Yet even as Conrad was bombarding the German High Command with requests for assistance in early June 1916, the Germans launched another attack at Verdun.

Falkenhayn finally dispatched three German divisions to Galicia from the Western Front on 9 June 1916, but he also initiated major strikes against Verdun on 23 June and 11 July. Both came very near to capturing key French positions, but it is doubtful that three German divisions would have made the difference. In the course of the 22 June attack alone, the Germans committed over 70,000 reserves.[36] Each side, moreover, still possessed additional reserves that it might have thrown into the fray. Of the twenty-five divisions diverted to aid the Habsburg forces in Galicia and in the Bukovina during the Brusilov Offensive, only eight came directly from the Western Front, and only two of those were withdrawn before major operations at Verdun were concluded. Of the rest, two came from Macedonia, two were Turkish, one was released from the Austrian XII Corps, and one came from Army Group Prince Leopold near Pinsk. Eight were Habsburg divisions sent back from the Italian Front, and six were either reserve divisions or divisions newly created by dividing formations already on the German sectors of the Eastern Front. According to Hindenburg and Ludendorff, Germany created thirty-three new divisions during the summer of 1916; at least two-thirds of them saw action in the west.[37]

Falkenhayn was careful to keep most of the elite German units in the west, moreover, since the Central Powers were well aware of the impending offensive on the Somme. Those divisions sent east from France tended to be reserves, or units that had already been withdrawn from the line to be refilled. In the end, he claimed, it made no difference. "[T]he most dangerous moment of the Russian Offensive had passed before the first shot of the Battle of the Somme was fired. The events that followed, in any case, had no decisive influence on the numbers of reinforcements sent East. [. . .] It is improbable that the decision only to withdraw just sufficient forces from the West for the work in hand would have been altered if the Battle of the Somme had not taken place."[38] For Falkenhayn the key to a decision lay, in 1916, in France, and he would not be diverted. As Falkenhayn reminded his commanders, after all, seizing the fortresses of Verdun was not the object of the operation—inflicting casualties upon the French was. The battles at Verdun certainly absorbed a far greater proportion of the German reserve than either the Brusilov Offensive or the Somme Offensive, and the Germans still held one division in their strategic reserve at the beginning of August.[39]

It was in any case the Austro-Hungarian armies that absorbed the brunt of the Brusilov Offensive. The losses during the first sixteen months of the war had been staggering. Between August 1914 and January 1915, the Habsburg forces suffered more than 1.1 million casualties; they recorded another 2 million dead, wounded, or captured in 1915.[40] So great was the carnage that the Austrian High Command calculated in October 1915 that they had manpower reserves sufficient only to carry on operations for another eight months—or precisely until June 1916.[41] The massive casualties inflicted by the Brusilov Offensive thus constituted a virtual death sentence for the Austro-Hungarian armies. During the first two months of the campaign, in June and July 1916, more than 7,000 Habsburg officers and 400,000 enlisted men were killed, wounded, or captured by the Russians. Another 70,000 reported sick and were transported to the rear. Before the offensive petered out in November 1916, the Austro-Hungarian armies had lost another 300,000 men. Well over two-thirds of the Habsburg armies' fighting strength of 900,000—counting all fronts—had been lost.[42]

Even more devastating, however, was the speed and manner in which they were lost. On the day the Brusilov Offensive opened, for instance, the Austrian Fourth Army numbered some 117,800 men; four days later, only 35,800 remained. The Austrian Seventh Army lost 76,200 men during that same period from its original strength of 194,200. By 16 June, the Seventh had been reduced by more than half; its casualty rate stood at 57 percent. Many units were almost completely destroyed. The 1st Vienna Reserve Infantry Regiment (Seventh Army), for example, lost 77 percent of its men dead on the first day of the offensive. The 7th Infantry Division (Fourth Army) lost 7,700 out of 17,600 men, most of them taken captive. In fact, nearly one-third of the Austro-Hungarian forces on the Russian Front—almost 193,000 men, including 2,992 officers—were either taken prisoner by or simply surrendered to the Russians within the first week of the campaign. Half of the casualties suffered by Seventh Army in the opening week were prisoners of war. Of the 82,000 men lost by Fourth Army, more than 76,000—almost 93 percent—had been taken captive.[43] "The whole of Fourth Army has really been taken prisoner," Kundmann wrote on 10 June.[44] The 1st Vienna Reserve Infantry Regiment, which stood and fought, was the exception rather than the rule among the Austro-Hungarian troops during the first days of the Brusilov Offensive. Fully 60 percent of the Habsburg casualties during the offensive reportedly consisted of deserters.[45]

A common explanation for the panicked collapse of the Habsburg forces rests upon the general premise that the Slavs within the Austro-Hungarian armies had been won over to pan-Slavism and simply refused to fight their "Russian brothers."[46] In planning for the offensive, Brusilov and his staff had taken some care to target sectors they knew to be manned by ethnically Slavic troops with just this idea in mind. In some cases, it appeared to be borne out. The 79th Infantry Regiment, composed mostly of Croats and Serbs, possessed one of the best unit records on the Italian Front, for instance. In its first action on the Russian Front, however, on 7 June, the regiment saw 2,060 men and 42 officers taken prisoner by the Russians.[47] There were, Jerabek admits, "not just a few nations [sic] whose motivation was lacking against the Russians."[48] According to the record left by the English journalist Stanley Washburn, many Habsburg soldiers actually seemed more content in Russian captivity: "I visited many places

[. . .] where Austrians were working in droves, and where one had to look closely for any Russians at all, and then probably discovered the guard sitting under a tree smoking a cigarette with an Austrian. Great is the contrast between this picture and that of the small columns of the heavily guarded German captives, of sullen, lowering countenance, and sulky expression, whom one passes on the highways."[49]

The overall results of the offensive, however, clearly demonstrate that the ethnicity of the Habsburg troops bore little relation to their performance. Units drawn from the territory around Vienna were as likely to collapse as those comprising Polish and Ruthenian troops. Almost 60 percent of the 70th Honved Infantry Division—clearly a non-Slavic unit—surrendered on 4 June. The Czech 8th Infantry Regiment surrendered to the Russians almost intact on 5 June. The Viennese 13th Infantry Division (Seventh Army) simply broke and fled during the battle for Olyka on 27 July. The Austrian Seventh Army, for instance, comprised mainly Croatian and Hungarian units; it was considered the most solid of the Habsburg armies, and the loyalties of the troops had been unquestioned since the outbreak of the war.[50] Yet it crumbled as readily as any other Habsburg unit during the Brusilov Offensive. On 17 June Letschitski's Ninth Army seized a bridgehead across the Pruth held by Seventh Army, for example; the Russians captured 1,500 Austrian soldiers and suffered only a single man wounded in the process.[51] Even the Habsburg artillery, long considered among the elite elements of the army, was prone to panic. During a fighting retreat on 23 July, for example, the 46th Infantry Division (Fourth Army) lost 12,000 men but only two guns out of sixteen batteries.[52] "Although the artillerists know their business well," a Russian observer wrote, "they did not now have the courage to do their duty by the infantry. Batteries made off to the rear much earlier and more rapidly than they should have done, and left the infantry to its fate."[53]

Much of the blame for the poor performance of the Austro-Hungarian troops throughout the Brusilov Offensive must be laid at the feet of the Habsburg officers, up to and including Conrad himself. The Habsburg officer corps fought at the front in 1914—Conrad had, famously, established his headquarters first in the border fortress of Przemysl—but the price had been heavy. Between August 1914 and January 1915, Austria-Hungary counted almost one-third of the officers in its regular army as casualties; 3,200 of them were killed and 7,800 were wounded. Another 8,000 though, were "missing." Many of the Habsburg officers were killed leading "glorious" bayonet charges; specially detailed Russian sniper units picked off others. Junior officers and reserve officers suffered disproportionately. Three of every four officers lost held the rank of lieutenant or captain; subaltern officers became casualties at a rate four times that of regular officers.[54] As early as December 1914, the German plenipotentiary at Austrian headquarters warned Falkenhayn that the Habsburg armies were unreliable. "The lack of officers is a calamity," he wrote.[55] Conrad admitted as much himself in a brief to the Austrian prime minister on 21 December: "The best officers and non-commissioned officers have died or been removed from service, likewise the core of the rank and file."[56] Revealingly, the official Austrian history of the conflict denotes the army after February 1915 as a "*Landstürm* [reserve] and militia army."[57]

Conrad's response was to remove himself and his officers from the front. Already in November 1914 he had shifted the Austro-Hungarian High Command to Teschen, well behind the lines. Soon he brought his new wife there as well, and other staff officers followed suit. The town quickly took on a distinctly nonmartial air, as did the Habsburg chief of staff himself. "Conrad almost never appears at headquarters before 11:00 a.m.," one of his aides wrote, "and almost never in the afternoons before 8:00 p.m. In between he's not available [*ist er nicht zu sprechen*], or he has to be disturbed in his home, which I naturally often cannot bear to do."[58] Conrad met his army commanders infrequently and seldom spoke to them about military matters in person; he visited the troops in the front lines even more rarely. Once an energetic and imaginative commander, Conrad increasingly sank into despondency and inactivity, with only a tenuous connection to his generals and almost none to the soldiers.[59]

This attitude carried over rather naturally to Conrad's subordinates. The staffs charged with coordinating each front, left without oversight, often fell to squabbling amongst themselves about the disposition of men and materiel. Front commanders established their headquarters so far behind the lines that they nearly lost touch with their armies; army commanders remained far enough to the rear that their posts took on the atmosphere of a garrison town, particularly after the Central Powers' successful offensive in the summer of 1915. Where thirty-nine officers holding the rank of colonel or higher had been killed in the first four months of the war, only thirty-one died in combat over the remaining thirty-five months of the war.[60] Even the front lines, according to Washburn, had the look and feel of a peaceful village rather than a combat zone.

One glance at the line suggests that the Austrians never dreamed of being turned out of these positions, while ten minutes behind the line confirms that conclusion.

[. . . T]heir trenches were constructed most elaborately from great unhewn logs, heavily covered over, and so connected up with the reserve and supporting trenches winding in every direction through the woodland, that the occupants must have considered themselves absolutely safe.

At a safe distance from rifle fire behind the lines one came on the officers' quarters, with elaborate provisions for comfort and what seemed like a veritable park in the heart of the forest. Here one found a beer garden, with buildings beautifully constructed from logs and decorated with rustic tracery, while chairs and tables made of birch still stood in lonely groups about the garden, just as they were left when the occupants of the place suddenly found they had business elsewhere. In a sylvan bower was a beautiful altar of birch trimmed with rustic traceries, while the whole was surrounded by a fence through which one passed under an arch nearly made of birch branches, above which were the words "Honved Tabor," which I believe means Honved Regiment. The Austrians must have had an extremely comfortable time here.

[. . .] One of the advancing [Russian] corps captured a trench with a piano in it, and if the stories of large quantities of miscellaneous lingerie (not included in the list of official trophies) that fell into Russian hands are to be believed, one feels that the Austrians did not spend a desolate or lonely winter on this front.[61]

The Austro-Hungarian reserves spent more time establishing—and presumably beautifying—their positions than they did training to defend them, even though the High Command was perfectly aware that a Russian strike was in the offing. "Most [of the reserves] were put into the positions immediately upon arrival," Tersztyanszky wrote of the 11th Infantry Division, for example, "and there weeks of ditch digging [*Schanzarbeit*] soon reduced them to the level of mere work battalions."[62] Most reserves had been called up so quickly, moreover, that they received a mere eight weeks of training. The reserve officers were thus almost completely lacking in technical instruction and consequently panicked in the face of the Russian assault. Many surrendered to the enemy at the beginning of a battle, while others removed themselves from the lines on grounds of illness or simply deserted. In the first half of July 1916, for instance, the sick rolls list one officer for every thirteen men—far above the normal ratio in the Austro-Hungarian armies at the time.[63] Frontline units therefore naturally suffered from a lack of leadership and repeatedly blundered at the tactical level.

It was the Habsburg commanders, however, whose failures were most telling. Though they blamed everything from "drumming fire" to dust stirred up by the Russian artillery, it was their own ineptitude that truly caused the collapse of the Austro-Hungarian armies. Despite all signs to the contrary, for instance, the Habsburg High Command continually either ignored or dismissed the possibility of a Russian offensive in the summer of 1916, even when the army commanders brought the facts to their attention. Conrad and his generals remained supremely confident in the strength of their defensive positions, and both corps and divisional commanders ignored the Russian preparations and allowed the troops to concentrate on construction to the detriment of training. When the offensive opened, they found themselves trapped, with the greater proportion of the troops—including the reserves—in the front lines of the forward positions. Communications at all levels were sporadic even before the attack, and oftentimes ignored. Archduke Josef Ferdinand blatantly disregarded instructions from Linsingen on more than one occasion, while both Pflanzer-Baltin and Böhm-Ermolli committed the fatal error of throwing what few reserves they disposed of into battles piecemeal despite orders to the contrary. Most of the Austrian reserves, however, disposed of no artillery. The heavy guns had long ago been sent to the Italian Front, and the Austro-Hungarian defensive doctrine dictated that large numbers of guns be placed in the forward lines. No Habsburg commander demonstrated any proficiency in executing a flexible defense, and many simply panicked under fire. "The first clashes and battles brought the voluntary or—in most cases—forced departure of incompetent leaders and chiefs of staff," Jerabek notes.[64] Feldmarschalleutnant von Sellner, Lieutenant General Benigni, and Pflanzer-Baltin all reported themselves as ill in the early days of the offensive, for instance. Reports from the front also overstated the damages severely, and commanders at every level withdrew both unnecessarily and without notifying either their superiors or their neighbors. "Just how far the military incompetence of the commanders appears to have affected them," Jerabek writes, "reveals itself in the course of the catastrophe at Lutsk. Already on 7 June [. . .] not only most of the troops but also the leadership with the exception of II Corps was just pitiful (*geradezu kläglich*)."[65]

Where Conrad had been reluctant to replace his failed commanders in 1914, he found himself under severe pressure from the Germans to do so in June 1916. Martigny, the commander of X Corps, was relieved on 7 June, and many other corps and divisional commanders followed. Benigni and the Archduke Josef Ferdinand were respectively demoted and relieved of command as well. Pflanzer-Baltin was essentially forced to cede all of his command functions to von Seeckt in July 1916, and then reported himself ill and relinquished his command in August under intense German pressure. Even Conrad was essentially relieved of duty due to his poor performance during the Brusilov Offensive. First Hindenburg's front was extended south to Lemberg in July and then, when Falkenhayn was dismissed following the Romanian entry in late August, Hindenburg took command of the entire Eastern Front. Franz Josef considered firing his chief of staff outright, but eventually the emperor was convinced he should allow Conrad to carry on, if only because there was no suitable replacement. The Habsburg commander was, however, a mere figurehead.[66]

By September 1916, the Austrians had been forced to accept almost total German control over the forces on the Eastern Front. Only Army Group Archduke Karl remained even nominally independent, and there Seeckt held the real power in his role as chief of staff to the Habsburg heir. The blending of German and Austro-Hungarian units, which had begun in late July 1916, had become increasingly pervasive throughout August. German staff and line officers, along with batteries of German artillery, German machine gun units, and German sergeants-major, were inserted into virtually every Austro-Hungarian unit.[67] By 9 October, there were only five purely Austro-Hungarian battalions remaining in the Austrian Fourth Army, and 106 of the army's 116.5 battalions were actually German.[68] Though the agreement technically left Conrad in command of an Austro-Hungarian army, Habsburg soldiers wore German field-gray uniforms and German spiked helmets. Berlin even subsidized the Habsburg war effort to the tune of 100,000,000 *Kronen* per month. It was, as one historian has suggested, as if the Habsburg Empire had become Bavaria, just another state in the German Empire, and it promised only to get worse.[69] "If the Allies win," Conrad lamented, "we have lost. If Germany wins, we are lost."

For once, Conrad had gotten it right. The Brusilov Offensive effectively put an end to whatever slim hopes of victory, or even survival, the Habsburg leadership might have had. The Austro-Hungarian military had, for all intents and purposes, ceased to exist, and thus the monarchy lost a fundamental pillar of its existence. The mood of the populace, already doubtful, now took a turn for the worse as war-weariness turned to defeatism. A few politicians in Vienna hoped that Austria might still find "its own Bismarck" and survive in an altered form, but these were pipe dreams. Where once the Habsburgs had dreamed of adding Congress Poland to the empire, they were forced in November 1916 to fall in with a joint declaration written in Berlin calling for an independent Polish constitutional monarchy.[70] The Russian gains of June-November 1916 had given Germany the

The Southwestern Front
31 December 1916

Frontline 31 December

upper hand in central Europe and brought the Austro-Hungarian Empire to the brink of extinction.

That it had not done more was only partially Brusilov's fault. He had accomplished more than any other Russian commander would throughout the war, with far less in the way of men and materiel. He alone among the Russian commanders had learned the lessons of 1914 and 1915, and was willing to apply them. His work in coordinating infantry and artillery, including the use of aircraft, may well merit the claim of Soviet military historians that Brusilov was among the founders of modern combined-arms doctrine. Accurate fire from the Russian guns severely disrupted communication between the Austro-Hungarian artillery and the front, and pinned the Habsburg troops in their bunkers, thus enabling the Russian infantry to reach the enemy's lines virtually unmolested. Diligent sapping and innovative engineering techniques such as tunneling under obstacles aided the attacks as well. By dint of energetic leadership, hard work, thorough preparation, and a willingness to embrace new tactics and technologies, he had very nearly decided the war on the Eastern Front. If Evert had launched an attack in mid- or even late June 1916 as he had promised, the Germans might not have been able to move enough troops south fast enough to hold the line. If Alekseev had been quicker to shift resources away from the Northern and Western fronts to Brusilov's offensive, Letschitski and Scherbatschev might have been able to carry the war into Hungary and deal the Habsburgs a decisive blow. As it was, at the critical moment when the Austrians were reeling and the Germans had not yet come to their aid, Brusilov found himself with only a single cavalry division in reserve—hardly enough to exploit the situation.[71]

Brusilov, in his memoirs, issues scathing indictments of the Russian commanders for their failure to support him. "We had no Supreme Commander," he writes; "[and] his chief of staff [Alekseev] was in any case not a man of strong action despite his knowledge."[72] Yet, as Norman Stone writes, "In this case, failure to exploit the break through was almost a direct consequence of breaking through in the first place."[73] Neither Brusilov nor Stavka had ever intended the advance on the Southwestern Front to be anything more than an auxiliary attack, and the method he chose—dispersing his forces along a broad front—mitigated against decisive penetration. Brusilov himself, moreover, must bear some of the blame, for once Alekseev did begin to shift resources to the Southwestern Front, Brusilov abandoned the very methods that had brought his initial success. Though he criticizes Kaledin for advancing north against the Germans holding

Kovel instead of directly west against the Austro-Hungarians at Vladi-mir-Volynsk, it seems clear that this was in fact Brusilov's decision.[74] His subsequent concentration on Kovel, at the expense of the advances in the Bukovina, also proved costly. Rather than continue to plan, prepare, and "tap along the wall" as he had in June and early July, Brusilov reverted to the more traditional and usually disastrous Russian method of massed infantry assaults across the swamps surrounding the Stochod River. "The Russian Command," Knox observed glumly, "for some unknown reason seems always to choose a bog to drown in."[75]

The dismal ending to the Brusilov Offensive, where even the small successes of late July and early August brought only the bitter fruit of Romanian intervention, doubtless contributes to the historical neglect of the campaign. Western historians, while crediting Brusilov with "the great-est Russian achievement of the war," quickly note that the overall results included massive casualties, the destruction of the "old Russian Army," and the establishment of the preconditions for revolution. And while Soviet his-torians held Brusilov up as a model, this was more due to his service—both real and supposed—to the Red Army; for the same reason, officers who served with Brusilov and who went on to publish their memoirs in the West hold him in contempt. General Aleksei A. Brusilov has thus become something of a "lost" personage in the history of the First World War.

The Brusilov Offensive nonetheless deserves a place among the most important campaigns of the 1914–18 conflict. While it may not have achieved precisely what Brusilov set out to accomplish in the short run—relieve Italy, ease the pressure on Verdun, and provide a distraction that would enable the Russians to break through against the Germans in the north—it was nonetheless a decisive turning point in the war. The Russian attacks at Lutsk, Okna, and Czernovitz destroyed once and for all the military capacity of the Habsburg Empire. Austria-Hungary was forced to accept German domination within the alliance, and driven to explore a separate peace. Brusilov's success also drew Romania into the war, and though this proved hurtful to the Russian cause, it was still significant. In combination with the casualties incurred during the Brusilov Offensive, the Romanian adventure effectively curtailed Russia's capacity to launch further attacks. The Brusilov Offensive thus marked the height of Russia's wartime achievement, in June and July 1916, and at the same time set the Russian Army on the path to revolution. It was truly, as Brusilov wrote, "one of the greatest crises of the Eastern Front."[76]

NOTES

INTRODUCTION

1. Information on the Western Front Association can be found at: http://web.western frontassociation.com (accessed 29 December 2006).

2. The literature of the Western Front is far too extensive to list here, but includes, for instance: Alistair Horne, *The Price of Glory: Verdun, 1916* (New York: Penguin, 1962); Martin Middlebrook, *The First Day on the Somme: 1 July 1916* (London: Penguin, 1980); Tim Travers, *How the War Was Won: Command and Technology in the British Army on the Western Front, 1917–1918* (London: Routledge, 1992); Robin Prior and Trevor Wilson, *The Somme* (New Haven: Yale University Press, 2005); Lyn Macdonald, *The Somme* (London: Penguin, 1993); Ian Beckett, *Ypres: The First Battle 1914* (New York: Longman, 2006); and Lyn Macdonald, *They Called It Passchendale: The Story of the Third Battle of Ypres and the Men Who Fought in It* (London: Atheneum, 1989).

3. Winston Churchill, *The Unknown War: The Eastern Front* (New York: Charles Scribner's Sons, 1931); Norman Stone, *The Eastern Front 1914–1917* (New York: Charles Scribner's Sons, 1975). Several general studies of the First World War, most notably Basil Liddell Hart's *The Real War 1914–1918* (Boston: Little and Brown, 1930) and Hans Herzfield's *Der Erste Weltkrieg* (Munich: Deutsches Taschenbuch, 1968), included substantial analysis of the Eastern Front, but still focused on developments in the west. There is also a good body of work on events in the east in German, including Manfried Rauchensteiner's *Tod des Doppeladlers* (Vienna: Styria Verlag, 1993) and much of Rudolf Jerabek's work, that has simply not been translated.

4. Dennis Showalter, *Tannenberg: Clash of Empires* (Hamden, Conn.: Archon Books, 1991).

5. Österreichisches Bundesministerium für Landesverteidigung, *Österreich-Ungarns Letzter Krieg 1914–1918*, 7 vols., ed. Edmund Glaise von Horstenau and Rudolf Kizling (Vienna: Verlag der Militärwissenschaftlichen Mitteilungen, 1931–38); Deutsches Reichsarchiv, *Der Weltkrieg 1914–1918. Die militärischen Operationen zu Lande*, 14 vols. (Berlin: E. S. Mittler and Sohn, 1925–44). See also: Graydon A. Tunstall Jr. "The Habsburg Command Conspiracy: The Falsification of Historiography on the Outbreak of World War I," in *Austrian History Yearbook* 271 (Houston: Rice University, 1996), 181–98.

6. Holger Herwig, *The First World War: Germany and Austria-Hungary, 1914–1918*

(London: Arnold, 1997). Herwig's work, of course, is not solely concerned with the Eastern Front. Stone's survey remains the only work in English dealing solely with the Eastern Front, but Herwig adds a great deal from the German and Austro-Hungarian perspectives.

7. John Reed, *The War in Eastern Europe* (London: Eveleigh Nash, 1916); Stanley Washburn, *The Russian Campaign, April to August 1915: Being the Second Volume of "Field Notes from the Russian Front"* (London: Andrew Melrose, n.d. [1915]); Stanley Washburn, *Victory in Defeat: The Agony of Warsaw and the Russian Retreat* (New York: Doubleday, Page, 1916); Stanley Washburn, *The Russian Advance: Being the Third Volume of "Field Notes from the Russian Front," Embracing the Period from June 5th to September 1st, 1916* (New York: Doubleday, Page, 1917); Maurice Paléologue, *An Ambassador's Memoirs*, 3 vols., trans. F. A. Holt (New York: George H. Doran, 1931).

8. Major-General Alfred W. F. Knox, *With the Russian Army 1914–1917*, 2 vols. (New York: Arno Press and *New York Times*, 1971).

9. Stone, *Eastern Front*, 305n3. Lt. Gen. Nikolas N. Golovine, *The Russian Army in the World War* (Yale: New Haven, 1931).

10. *Komissiya po isseledovaniyu i ispol'zovaniyu opyta mirovoi i grazhdanskoi voiny*, 7 vols. (Moscow: Vysshii Voennyi Redaktsionnyi Sovet, 1920–23).

11. Andrei Medardovich Zaionchkovskii, *Mirovaia voina 1914–1918 gg.: obshchii strategicheskii ocherk* (Moscow: Gosudarstvenii voennoe izdatelnostovo, 1924). The 1931 version lists Jukims I. Vacietis as a coauthor; he was the head of the editorial board of the Frunze Academy (the RKKA Academy was renamed after Frunze in 1926), which reissued the work as a two-volume set. The 1938 edition, which came out as three volumes, makes no mention of Vacietis. It was published by the state military publishing entity within the People's Commissariat for Defense of the U.S.S.R. (Gosudarstvenni voennoe izdatelstvo Narkomata oborony Soiuza SSR). The accompanying maps were also reprinted in 1938–39.

12. A. M. Zaionchkovskii and A. N. De-Lazari, *Miorvaia voina 1914–1918: atlas skhem k trudu A. Zaoinchkovskovo* (Moscow: Gosudarstvenii voennoe izdatelnostvo, 1924).

13. A. M. Zaionchkovskii, *Podgotovka Rossii k Mirovoi voine v mezhdunarodnom otnoshenii* (Leningrad: Izdatel voennoe, 1926), and A. M. Zaionchkovskii, *Podgotovka Rossii k imperialisticheskoi voine: ocherki voennoi podgotovki i pervonachal'nykh planov: po arkivnym dokumaentam* (Moscow: Gosudarstvenii voennoe izdatelstvo, 1926). Both of these volumes were reprinted in 1974. See also: A. M. Zaionchkovskii, *Mirovaya Voyna. Manevrennii period 1914–1915 godov na russkom (evropayskom) teatre* (Moscow and Leningrad: Gosudarstvennoye Izdatelstvo, 1929); G. Khmelevski, *Mirovaya imperialisticheskaya voyna . . . sistematicheski ukazatel knizhnoy i statenoy voennoe-istoricheskoy literaturi* (Moscow: Gosudarstvennii voennoe izdatelstvo, 1936); D. Verzhkhovski and V. Lyakhov, *Pervaya Mirovaya Voina* (Moscow: Gosudarstvennii voennoe izdatelstvo, 1964); and M. Lyons, comp., *The Russian Imperial Army. A Bibliography of Regimental Histories and Related Works* (Stanford: Hoover Institution on War, Revolution, and Peace, 1968).

14. There are several memoirs by Russian participants—mostly officers and politicians—in the conflict, but most stem from opponents of the revolutions, and thus must be treated with some care. See, for instance: Anton I. Denikin, *The Russian Turmoil; Memoirs: Military, Social, and Political* (Westport, Conn.: Hyperion, 1920); Basil Gourko, *Memoirs and Impressions of War and Revolution in Russia, 1914–1917* (London: John Murray, 1918); A. G. Lukomsky, *Vospominaniia* (Berlin: Otto Kirkhner, 1922); Peter A. Polovtsov, *Glory and Downfall* (London: G. Bell, 1935). There is even a suggestion, for instance, that Brusilov's memoirs were tampered with—his anti-Bolshevik second wife

is said to have forged the latter part of the work while in exile in Czechoslovakia during the 1930s. Ivan Rostunov, *Brusilov* (Moscow: Voennoe Izdatelstvo Ministerstva Obronii CCCP, 1964), 9–12.

15. W. Bruce Lincoln, *Passage through Armageddon* (New York: Simon and Schuster, 1986).

16. Nikolai N. Smirnov, ed., *Rossiia i Pervaia mirovaia voina: materialy mezdunarodnovo kollokviuma* (St. Petersburg: D. Bulanin, 1999).

17. Geoffrey Jukes, *Carpathian Disaster: The Death of an Army* (New York: Ballantine, 1971), 143.

18. According to Matitiahu Mayzel, graduates of the General Staff Academy commanded approximately 30 percent of the Russian Imperial Army's infantry regiments, 68 percent of the infantry divisions, 77 percent of the cavalry divisions, and 62 percent of the army corps. Twenty of the twenty-two front commanders during the First World War, moreover, were graduates of the Academy, with Brusilov and Ivanov—two of the most highly regarded commanders—being the exceptions. Mayzel, *Generals and Revolutionaries: The Russian General Staff during the Revolution: A Study in the Transformation of a Military Elite* (Osnabrück: Biblio, 1979), 40–41.

19. Until February 1917 Russia followed the older Julian calendar, which was thirteen days behind the Gregorian calendar commonly used in Western Europe and the United States. In this "New Style" or Gregorian system, the tsar's abdication occurred on 15 March 1917. Unless otherwise noted, all dates in this text follow the Gregorian system.

20. Robert S. Feldman, *Between War and Revolution: The Russian General Staff, February–July 1917* (Ann Arbor: University Microfilms, 1968), 8, 54, and 56n23; Mayzel, *Generals and Revolutionaries*, 70; Brian Taylor, *Politics and the Russian Army: Civil-Military Relations, 1689–2000* (Cambridge: Cambridge University Press, 2003), 92–93

21. Feldman, *Between War and Revolution*, 134.

22. Denikin, *Russian Turmoil*, 149.

23. Taylor, *Politics and the Russian Army*, 88 and 92–95; Feldman, *Between War and Revolution*, 81.

24. Feldman, "The General Staff in June," in *Between War and Revolution*, 360–61; George Katkov, *The Kornilov Affair: Kerensky and the Break-up of the Russian Army* (New York: Longman, 1980), 8; Allan Wildman, "The February Revolution in the Russian Army," in *The Russian Imperial Army, 1796–1917*, ed. Roger Reese (Burlington, Vt.: Ashgate, 2003), 317 and 325.

25. Denikin, *Russian Turmoil*, 161.

26. Rostunov, *Brusilov*, 167–70; Lincoln, *Armageddon*, 405–408; Richard Abraham, *Alexander Kerensky: The First Love of the Revolution* (New York: Columbia University Press, 1987), 202–203.

27. Feldman, *Between War and Revolution*, 144.

28. Ibid., 193; Alexander Kerensky, *The Kerensky Memoirs: Russia and History's Turning Point* (London: Cassell, 1966), 276–77.

29. Denikin, *Russian Turmoil*, 175–76. See also: Feldman, *Between War and Revolution*, 220–22; and Mayzel, *Generals and Revolutionaries*, 104–106.

30. Mayzel, *Generals and Revolutionaries*, 105–107; Abraham, *Alexander Kerensky*, 201–202; Feldman, *Between War and Revolution*, 277–78.

31. Lincoln, *Armageddon*, 408.

32. Kerensky, *Memoirs*, 285.

33. Katkov, *Kornilov Affair*, 30–31; W. Bruce Lincoln, *Red Victory: A History of the Russian Civil War* (New York: Simon and Schuster, 1989), 41; David R. Jones, "The

Imperial Russian Life Guards Grenadier Regiment, 1906–1917: The Disintegration of an Elite Unit," in *The Russian Imperial Army, 1796–1917*, ed. Roger Reese (Burlington, Vt.: Ashgate, 2003), 303.

34. Lincoln, *Red Victory*, 41.

35. Lincoln, *Armageddon*, 411; Feldman, *Between War and Revolution*, 310. Taylor, *Politics and the Russian Army*, 102, gives the date as 13 July.

36. Mayzel, *Generals and Revolutionaries*, 113–14; Abraham, *Kerensky*, 231–33; Katkov, *Kornilov Affair*, 52–53. Denikin, as might be expected, denies that Brusilov did anything but demur and allow others (Denikin himself, most notably) to make the case in clear, strong terms. Denikin, *Russian Turmoil*, 281–94.

37. Rostunov, *Brusilov*, 161. Lincoln notes that there was a "general longing for a general on a white horse" (i.e., a dictator) in Russia at the end of the summer of 1917, but he mentions only Kornilov in this context. Denikin notes that people were bandying about the names of Kornilov and Brusilov in mid-June, while Katkov says that Alekseev—who was brought back as supreme commander for a few days at the end of the Kornilov Affair—was the prime candidate to head a military dictatorship. Kerensky, on the other hand, says that while there were conspiracies to create a military dictatorship swirling about in the summer of 1917, he believes that Brusilov was unaware of them. Lincoln, *Red Victory*, 41; Denikin, *Russian Turmoil*, 103–104; Katkov, *Kornilov Affair*, 100–102; Kerensky, *Memoirs*, 364.

38. Mayzel, *Revolutionaries*, 113–14; Rostunov, *Brusilov*, 187–88; Abraham, *Kerensky*, 234; .

39. Rostunov, *Brusilov*, 189.

40. Taylor, *Politics and the Russian Army*, 131–32.

41. Rostunov, *Brusilov*, 194.

42. Taylor, *Politics and the Russian Army*, 133–34.

43. Lincoln, *Red Victory*, 83.

44. It is unclear exactly how many former tsarist officers ever served in the Red Army, but the best guess, based upon a number of sources, is around 600. Most of these officers, of course, served in planning and advisory posts, and not in the field. Mayzel, *Revolutionaries*, 266n65; Lincoln, *Red Victory*, 84.

45. David R. Jones, "The Officers and the October Revolution," in *The Russian Imperial Army, 1796–1917*, ed. Roger Reese (Burlington, Vt.: Ashgate, 2003), 393.

46. Richard Luckett, *The White Generals: An Account of the White Movement and the Russian Civil War* (London: Longman, 1971), 55.

1. RUSSIA IN THE FIRST WORLD WAR

1. Rank equivalencies are listed on page 47.

2. Stone, *Eastern Front*, 234, gives the number as more than 745,000; the official Austrian history of the war, *Das Kriegsjahr 1916, erster Teil; die Ereignisse von Jänner bis Ende Juli* (vol. 4 in the series *Österreich-Ungarns Letzter Krieg, 1914–1918*, ed. Österreichischen Bundesministerium für Landesverteidigung and Österreichischer Kriegsarchiv, [Vienna: Verlag der Militärwissenschaftlichen Mitteilungen, 1933], hereafter ÖULK), 360, says the Russians already had 675,000 men on the Northern Front in April and expected the number to rise to 877,000-plus by summer. Russian sources, on the other hand, list the numbers as 754,000 on the Western Front and 466,000 on the Northern Front (Sergei N. Semanov, *Brusilov* (Moscow: Molodaya Gvardaya, 1980), 176; Rostunov, *Brusilov*, 112.)

3. Lincoln, *Armageddon*, 240.

4. ÖULK, 360–61; Aleksei A. Brusilov, *Meine Erinnerungen* (Berlin: Militaerverlag der DDR, 1983), 198–99; Rostunov, *Brusilov*, 115.

5. Stone, *Eastern Front*, 235 and 239; Rostunov, *Brusilov*, 116. Semanov gives a much more detailed picture of the discussion during and after the meeting, to the point where it seems impossible to have been documented (Semanov, *Brusilov*, 176–81).

6. Brusilov, *Erinnerungen*, 210.

7. Lincoln, *Armageddon*, 174.

8. Stone, *Eastern Front*, 239; *Russischer Operationsplan und Durchbruch von Luck, 1916* (ÖKA, Ms-Wk: Russ. 13 [1916]), 4; Brusilov, *Erinnerungen*, 201. Letschitski, commander of Ninth Army, did not attend the briefing due to illness.

9. George H.Allen, Admiral F. E. Chadwick, and Henry C. Whitehead, *The Great War* (Philadelphia: George Barrie's Sons, 1916), 343.

10. William C. Fuller Jr. *Civil-Military Conflict in Imperial Russia, 1881–1914* (Princeton: Princeton University Press, 1985), particularly 196–207, and 220–30. See also: Bruce Menning, *Bayonets before Bullets: The Imperial Russian Army 1861–1914* (Bloomington: Indiana University Press, 1992), 200–271; and David Alan Rich, *The Tsar's Colonels: Professionalism, Strategy, and Subversion in Late Imperial Russia* (Cambridge, Mass.: Harvard University Press, 1998).

11. Fuller, *Civil-Military Conflict*, 220–21.

12. Allan K. Wildman, *The Road to Soviet Power and Peace*, vol. 2 of *The End of the Russian Imperial Army* (Princeton, N.J.: Princeton University Press, 1987), 20–23; David G. Herrmann, *The Arming of Europe and the Making of the First World War* (Princeton: Princeton University Press, 1996), 131–32 and 204–205; Menning, *Bayonets*, 200–271. Fuller offers a good historiography of Sukhomlinov and his tenure as war minister in *Civil-Military Conflict*, 237–44, and renders an overall positive judgment of his professionalism, if not of his personal conduct.

13. Wildman, *Road to Soviet Power and Peace*, 66–67.

14. Herrmann, *Arming of Europe*, 63 and 201–210; Menning, *Bayonets*, 229–32; Fuller, *Civil-Military Conflict*, 222; Knox, *With the Russian Army*, xxiii; Lawrence Sondhaus, *Franz Conrad von Hoetzendorf: Architect of the Apocalypse* (Boston: Humanities Press, 2000), 158.

15. Herrmann, *Arming of Europe*, 27–29; Lincoln, *Armageddon*, 24, 61, and 90; Knox, *With the Russian Army*, xxiv and 220; Wildman, *Road to Soviet Power and Peace*, 85–86.

16. Wildman, *Road to Soviet Power and Peace*, 17 and 73–74; Allen, Whitehead, and Chadwick, *Great War*, 219, 24, and 333–37; Knox, *With the Russian Army*, xxii–xxiii.

17. Stone, *Eastern Front*, 146; Golovine, *Russian Army*, 128; Michael Florinsky, *The End of the Russian Empire* (New Haven: Yale University Press, 1931), 208; Lincoln, *Armageddon*, 24.

18. Lincoln, *Armageddon*, 89.

19. Florinsky, *Russian Empire*, 218–19; Lincoln, *Armageddon*, 89 and 121.

20. Paléologue, *Ambassador's Memoirs*, 2:157.

21. Menning, *Bayonets*, 255–56; Lincoln, *Armageddon*, 90.

22. Stone, *Eastern Front*, 51 and 148.

23. Herrmann, *Arming of Europe*, 205; Menning, *Bayonets*, 232; Knox, *With the Russian Army*, xxxii; Golovine, *Russian Army*, 34; Stone, *Eastern Front*, 51.

24. Menning, *Bayonets*, 232.

25. Stone, *Eastern Front*, 51.

26. Herrmann, *Arming of Europe*, 205; Lincoln, *Armageddon*, 24.

27. Golovine, *Russian Army*, 17.

28. Knox, *With the Russian Army*, xxxiv.

29. Hermann, *Arming of Europe*, 233–35; Allen, Whitehead, and Chadwick, *Great War*, 217–27, 237–43, 333–38; Golovine, *Russian Army*, 45–46; Wildman, *Road to Soviet Power and Peace*, 73.

30. Menning, *Bayonets*, 204.

31. Hermann, *The Arming of Europe*, 27–28.

32. Sondhaus, *Architect*, 53. *Zum Studium der Taktik* was published in 1891 but, as Sondhaus effectively demonstrates, Conrad's thinking changed little in the time leading up to the First World War.

33. Sondhaus, *Architect*, 52–53; Herrmann, *Arming of Europe*, 25–26.

34. Knox, *With the Russian Army*, xxv.

35. Florinsky, *Russian Empire*, 217.

36. Menning, *Bayonets*, 277.

37. Fuller, *Civil-Military Conflict*, 195.

38. John W. Steinberg, "The Challenge of Reforming Imperial Russian General Staff Education, 1905–1909," in *Reforming the Tsar's Army: Military Innovation in Imperial Russia from Peter the Great to the Revolution*, ed. David Schimmelpfennig van der Oye and Bruce W. Menning, 232–49 (Washington, D.C.: Woodrow Wilson Press Center and Cambridge University Press, 2004), 237–38.

39. Herrmann, *Arming of Europe*, 93.

40. Menning, *Bayonets*, 236.

41. Knox, *With the Russian Army*, xxvi–xxvii.

42. Fuller, *Civil-Military Conflict*, 231–32; Katkov, *Kornilov Affair*, 1; and Taylor, *Politics and the Russian Army*, 52.

43. Steinberg, "Challenge," 248–49; Menning, *Bayonets*, 234–36. See also: Wildman, *Road to Soviet Power and Peace*, 8–9 and 22–23; Allen, Whitehead, and Chadwick, *Great War*, 333–34; Knox, *With the Russian Army*, xxv–xxx, and 264; and Florinsky, *Russian Empire*, 208.

44. Spencer C. Tucker, ed., *The European Powers in the First World War: An Encyclopedia* (New York: Garland, 1996), 673.

45. Florinsky, *Russian Empire*, 208.

46. Knox, *With the Russian Army*, 331.

47. Menning, *Bayonets*, 250; Knox, *With the Russian Army*, 42. Florinsky, *Russian Empire*, 209–10.

48. Rich, *Tsar's Colonels*, 3. Menning gives a much more generous picture of the field commanders, including Kuropatkin, than most historians, calling them "far from an incompetent or inexperienced group." Menning, *Bayonets*, 249. See also: Roger Reese, ed., *The Russian Imperial Army, 1796–1917* (Burlington, Vt.: Ashgate, 2003), xiii.

49. Knox, *With the Russian Army*, 394.

50. Ibid., 332. In fairness, Menning calls Alekseev "extraordinarily capable" (*Bayonets*, 249), and Knox's report gives a fairly balanced picture overall of "a man fifty-eight years of age, of simple, unassuming manners and a tremendous worker," who happened to have some faults.

51. Stone, *Eastern Front*, 192.

52. Lincoln, *Red Victory*, 77.

53. Knox, *With the Russian Army*, 205.

54. Ibid., xxx. See also: Herrmann, *Arming of Europe*, 93–94, 205–206, and Menning, *Bayonets*, 215–21.

55. See, for instance: Herrmann, *Arming of Europe*, 93 and 204; Knox, *With the Russian Army*, xxv–xxxii; and Wildman, *Road to Soviet Power and Peace*, 80–82.

56. Allen, Whitehead, and Chadwick, *Great War*, 343.

57. Golovine, *Russian Army*, 18–23; Knox, *With the Russian Army*, xxv; Florinsky, *Russian Empire*, 222; Allen, Whitehead, and Chadwick, *Great War*, 342–43; Menning, *Bayonets*, 226.

58. Allen, Whitehead, and Chadwick, *Great War*, 343.

59. Ibid., 342.

60. Lincoln, *Armageddon*, 79; Knox, *With the Russian Army* 49; Menning, *Bayonets*, 249.

61. Herwig, *First World War*, 91; Lincoln, *Armageddon*, 80–81.

62. Lincoln, *Armageddon*, 82. See also: Knox, *With the Russian Army*, 95–96.

63. Herwig, *First World War*, 92–93.

64. Rostunov, *Brusilov*, 78; Sondhaus, *Architect*, 158.

65. Menning, *Bayonets*, 242.

66. L. C. F. Turner, "The Russian Mobilization in 1914," 261–84, in *The Russian Imperial Army, 1796–1917*, ed. Roger Reese (Burlington, Vt.: Ashgate, 2006), 274.

67. Lincoln, *Armageddon*, 72. For details on the Russian war planning and troop dispositions, see: Menning, *Bayonets*, 238–48.

68. Lincoln, *Passage through Armageddon*, 75.

69. Knox, *With the Russian Army*, 204.

70. Lincoln, *Passage through Armageddon*, 83.

71. John Keegan, *The First World War* (New York: Alfred A. Knopf, 1999), 169.

72. Herwig, *First World War*, 110.

73. Keegan, *First World War*, 170; Herwig, *First World War*, 112 and 119–20.

74. Herwig, *First World War*, 135–36; Stone, *Eastern Front*, 111–17; Lincoln, *Armageddon*, 118–21.

75. Lincoln, *Armageddon*, 121.

76. Herwig, *First World War*, 136.

77. Ibid., 136–39; Stone, *Eastern Front*, 113–16; Lincoln, *Armageddon*, 121; Sondhaus, *Architect*, 163.

78. Herwig, *First World War*, 110 and 139.

79. Ibid., 139 and 147–48; Jukes, *Carpathian Disaster*, 48; Lincoln, *Armageddon*, 122–23.

80. Sondhaus, *Architect*, 166.

81. Herwig, *First World War*, 78, 87–88, 111–12.

82. Sondhaus, *Architect*, 166.

83. Herwig, *First World War*, 78–79, 94–95, 108–109, and 139–40. See also: Sondhaus, *Architect*, 162–66, and 180–82.

84. Lincoln, *Armageddon*, 121.

85. Ibid., 123.

86. Ibid., 123–25; Stone, *Eastern Front*, 120; Herwig, *First World War*, 139.

87. Knox, *With the Russian Army*, 253.

88. Stone, *Eastern Front*, 127–30; Lincoln, *Armageddon*, 123–25; Herwig, *First World War*, 140–41.

89. Lincoln, *Armageddon*, 123–24.

90. Rostunov, *Brusilov*, 78.

91. Herwig, *First World War*, 139.

92. See, for instance, Alon Rachmáninov, "Did Austria-Hungary Fall Victim to Conflicting Nationalisms?" in *History in Dispute*, vol. 9—World War I, Second Series; series ed. Anthony J. Scotti Jr., 134–41 (Detroit: St. James Press, 2003), 136–37.

93. Stone, *Eastern Front*, 113, 120, and 122. Stone discusses the general issue of morale on 125–27.

94. Herwig, *First World War*, 140–42; Stone, *Eastern Front*, 128–30; Lincoln, *Armageddon*, 124–25. The exact figures for the artillery and machine guns are taken from Lincoln; Herwig merely notes that the Germans possessed 1,500 medium and heavy guns, while Stone calculates the totals as 905 light-to-medium guns and only 24 heavy guns. Interestingly, Stone includes the artillery of the Austrian Third and Fourth armies in his calculations.

95. Herwig, *First World War*, 141–42.

96. Lincoln, *Armageddon*, 127.

97. Ibid.

98. Stone, *Eastern Front*, 138; Lincoln, *Armageddon*, 128.

99. Herwig, First World War, 141–46; Knox, With the Russian Army, 269 and 283; Stone, Eastern Front, 128–43; Lincoln, Armageddon, 125–63. It is not clear on precisely which day the fortress fell. Lincoln (128–29) gives the date as 2 June, Herwig (142) opts for 3 June, and Stone (141) says it was 4 June.

100. Golovine, *Russian Army*, 162.

101. Knox, *With the Russian Army*, 301.

102. Lincoln, *Armageddon*, 152.

103. Knox, *With the Russian Army*, 309.

104. Stone, *Eastern Front*, 183.

105. Herwig, *First World War*, 145.

106. Stone, *Eastern Front*, 184.

107. Erich Ludendorff, *My War Memories, 1914–1918* (London: Hutchinson, 1919), 146–48.

108. Lincoln, *Armageddon*, 238.

109. Stone, *Eastern Front*, 165–93; Herwig, *First World War*, 144–49; Lincoln, *Armageddon*, 129–32 and 136–64.

110. Knox, *With the Russian Army* 330.

111. Ibid., 333.

112. Brusilov, *Erinnerungen*, 176.

113. Lincoln, *Armageddon*, 160.

114. Ibid., 160.

115. Ibid.

2. MAKING PREPARATIONS

1. Erich von Falkenhayn, *The German General Staff and Its Decisions* (New York: Dodd, Mead, 1920), 239–40 and 248.

2. Rudolf Jerabek, *Die Brussilowoffensive*, manuscript in the holdings of the Oesterreichisches Staats- und Kriegsarchiv library, 119–20 and 126.

3. Ludendorff, *War Memories*, 210.

4. Falkenhayn, *German General Staff*, 274.

5. Lincoln, *Armageddon*, 240–41.

6. Paléologue, *Memoirs*, 2:157. See also: Stone, *Eastern Front*, 212.

7. Knox, *With the Russian Army*, 421. See also: Lincoln, *Armageddon*, 241.

8. Lincoln, *Passage through Armageddon*, 240.

9. Jukes, *Carpathian Disaster*, 104; Lincoln, *Passage through Armageddon*, 242–43.

10. Wildman, *Road to Soviet Power and Peace*, 8.

11. Stone, *Eastern Front*, 166 and 191–93.

12. Stone, *Eastern Front*, 227, 233, and 239; Washburn, *Russian Advance*, 9–10; Lincoln, *Armageddon*, 239–40.

13. Stone, *Eastern Front*, 234.

14. Lincoln, *Armageddon*, 240.

15. Herwig, *First World War*, 208.

16. Rostunov, *Brusilov*, 19.

17. Washburn, *Russian Advance*, 11.

18. Rostunov, *Brusilov*, 42.

19. Ibid., 45.

20. Lincoln, *Armageddon*, 240. See also: Rostunov, *Brusilov*, 55.

21. Golovine, *Russian Army*, 195.

22. Denikin, *Russian Turmoil*.

23. Washburn, *Russian Advance*, 8.

24. For a more detailed breakdown of Russian doctrine as it stood in 1914, see Menning, *Bayonets*, 256–66.

25. Stone, *Eastern Front*, 237.

26. Jerabek, *Brussilowoffensive*, 207–208.

27. Lincoln, *Armageddon*, 246.

28. Stone, *Eastern Front*, 239. Jerabek, *Brussilowoffensive* (203), gives the figures as 40.5 infantry divisions and 16 cavalry divisions for the Russians against 38.5 and 11.5 for the Austro-Hungarian forces, while Jukes (*Carpathian Disaster*, 113) gives slightly lower figures for each side: 36 Russian infantry divisions and 12.5 cavalry divisions facing 37 infantry divisions and 9 cavalry divisions of the Central Powers.

29. ÖKA, Ms-Wk: NFA 2.Armee.165, report from the *Südarmee* of 18 March 1916.

30. Jerabek, *Brussilowoffensive*, 197.

31. ÖKA, Ms-Wk:Russ. 5 (1916), 1.

32. Herwig, *First World War*, 207; Semanov, *Brusilov*, 190–91.

33. Brusilov, *Erinnerungen*, 221; Semanov, *Brusilov*, 185.

34. Jerabek, *Brussilowoffensive*, 201; see also Semanov, *Brusilov*, 172 and 190.

35. Lincoln, *Armageddon*, 246.

36. General information on the Russian preparations for the Brusilov Offensive can be found in: Stone, *Eastern Front*, 238; Jukes, *Carpathian Disaster*, 114; ÖULK, IV, 365–66; Jerabek, *Brussilowoffensive*, 193–205; Semanov, *Brusilov*, 190–204; Polkovnik Bazarevskii, *Nastupatelnaya Operatsiia 9-i russkoi armii, Yun 1916 goda* (Moscow: Gosudarstvennoy Voennoye Izdatelstvo, 1937), 43–73 and 34–60; Knox, *With the Russian Army*, 437–44; Lincoln, *Armageddon*, 246–48; and.

37. Falkenhayn, *German General Staff*, 275–78.

38. Jerabek, *Brussilowoffensive*, 9.

39. Nachlass Kundmann, ÖKA, Ms-Wk: B/15, 264.

40. Ibid., 389 and 398.

41. Jerabek, *Brussilowoffensive*, 116; Falkenhayn, *German General Staff*, 279.

42. Herwig, *First World War*, 149–54; Jerabek, *Brussilowoffensive*, 113–17; Stone, *Eastern Front*, 243.

43. Jerabek, *Brussilowoffensive*, 139.

44. For information on the Austro-Hungarian preparations for the Tirol offensive, see: Herwig, *First World War*, 180–205; and Jerabek, *Brussilowoffensive*, 128–42.

45. Jerabek, *Brussilowoffensive*, 145–48.

46. ÖKA, Ms-Wk: NFA 2.Armee.160, *Tagebuch* 68, 2–4.

47. Malcolm C. Grow, *Surgeon Grow: An American in the Russian Fighting* (New York: Frederick A. Stokes, 1918), 223.

48. Jerabek, *Brussilowoffensive*, 149–72; Stone, *Eastern Front*, 240–42.

49. Jerabek, *Brussilowoffensive*, 178. See also: ÖULK, IV, 373.

50. ÖKA, Ms-Wk: AOK 2700 4. Armee, Q.Op. 15800 B.5c, Brückenkopf Luck u. Styr.

51. ÖULK, IV, 373.

52. See, for instance: ÖKA, Ms-Wk:Russ.5 (1916), 2.

53. ÖKA, Ms-Wk: Russ.15 (1916), 13–14.

54. Jerabek, *Brussilowoffensive*, 234–36; ÖULK, IV, 372–374; Stone, *Eastern Front*, 247; Edmund Glaise von Horsetnau, *Die Kriegsführung in Russland und Ostgalizien in den Jahren 1916 und 1917*, ÖKA, Ms-Wk: Russ 2 (1916), 4–6.

55. See, for instance: ÖKA, Ms-Wk: AOK 2683, 1.A: Mat. Sit. 1. AK 1916, Q.Op. 14500, Beilage 13: Bekleidung u. Ausrüstung; and Beilage 8: Sanitaire Situation; ÖKA, Ms-Wk: AOK 2700, 4. A: Q.Op. 20600, Sanitäre Situation 1.5.1916, Q.Op. 23500, Zur matiereller Situation am 15. Juni 1916, and Q.Op. 15800, Bekleidung u. Ausrüstung 1.5.1916.

56. ÖKA, Ms-Wk: Russ.13 (1916), 11.

57. Jerabek, *Brussilowoffensive*, 180–88; ÖKA, Ms-Wk: Russ.15 (1916), 14.

58. Jerabek, *Brussilowoffensive*, 238.

59. Jerabek, *Brussilowoffensive*, 230–32.

60. AK Befehl #12, *Tagebuch* No. 67, 13 May 1916, ÖKA, NFA 2.A.160

61. Stone, *Eastern Front*, 242. See also: Herwig, *First World War*, 211–12.

62. Graydon Tunstall, "German and Austro-Hungarian War Planning and War Aims and the Concept of *Mitteleuropa*," in *20th Century Hungary and the Great Powers*, vol. 33 of *War and Society in Central Europe*, ed. Ignac Romsics (Boulder: Social Science Monographs, 1995), 22; George Shanafelt, *The Secret Enemy: Austria-Hungary and the German Alliance, 1914–1918* (Boulder: East European Monographs, 1985), 63 and 84; Herwig, *First World War*, 209–11; Nachlass Kundmann, 391–94.

63. Stone, *Eastern Front*, 242.

64. Jerabek, *Brussilowoffensive*, 164.

65. Herwig, *First World War*, 210–11; Stone, *Eastern Front*, 240–43; Jerabek, *Brussilowoffensive*, 159–69.

66. ÖKA, Ms-Wk: NFA 2. Armee.165

67. ÖKA, Ms-Wk: B-1466, Nachlass Böhm-Ermolli, 525.

68. Jerabek, *Brussilowoffensive*, 173 and 200.

69. ÖKA, Ms-Wk: NFA 2. Armee.160: *Tagebuch* 67, Op. 1909, 13 May 1916.

70. ÖKA, Ms-Wk: NFA 4. Armee.115: *Tagebuch* 10 (2.2.1916–8.8.1916)

71. ÖKA, Ms-Wk: NFA 2.Armee.160, *Tagebuch* 68, 25–27.

72. ÖKA, Ms-Wk: Russ.15 (1916), 16.

73. ÖKA, Ms-Wk: NFA 2.Armee.160, *Tagebuch* 68, 118–28.

74. ÖULK, IV, 369–75.

75. Jerabek, *Brussilowoffensive*, 209.

76. Jerabek, *Brussilowoffensive*, 210–15; see also, for instance: ÖKA, Ms-Wk: AOK 2683 1. Armee, Q.Op. 1300, Verluste der 1. Armee in der Zeit vom 1. Bis 15. Mai 1916, and Q.Op. 14500, Verluste der 1. Armee in der Zeit vom 15. bis 31. Mai 1916.

77. See, for instance, Stone, *Eastern Front*, 241 (though his casualty figures are too low), and Jerabek, *Brussilowoffensive*, 237–42.

78. Jerabek, *Brussilowoffensive*, 217.

79. Ibid., 240; ÖULK, IV, 373.

80. Jerabek, *Brussilowoffensive*, 242.

81. ÖULK, IV, 370.

82. ÖKA, Ms-Wk: NFA 4. Armee.115: *Tagebuch 10* (2.2.1916–8.8–1916); Jerabek, *Brussilowoffensive*, 210.

83. Falkenhayn, *German General Staff*, 278–79; Jerabek, *Brussilowoffensive*, 253.

84. Stone, *Eastern Front*, 246–47; Jukes, *Carpathian Disaster*, 113–15; ÖULK, IV, 362–63 and 366–68; Lincoln, *Armageddon*, 246–47.

3. THE OFFENSIVE BEGINS

1. ÖULK, IV, 375.

2. A. M. Zaionchkovski, *Russischer Kriegsplan für das Sommer 1916 (Durchbruch von Luzk)*. ÖKA, Ms-Wk: Russ 13 (1916), 1–6. Zaionchkovski had been the commander of the Russian XXX Corps (Eighth Army) during the Brusilov Offensive. The manuscript is a summary of remarks made at a conference in Moscow with his Austrian counterparts on 17 August 1920.

3. Many Austrian sources, including Jerabek—who is usually critical of the official reports, claim that the Russian artillery shelled the Habsburg positions with "drumming fire" (*Trommelfeuer*). Brusilov's orders, however, specifically forbade this. Stone, whose numerical assessments of Russian forces seem most accurate, does not mention *Trommelfeuer* at all. He attributes the Russian success to accuracy (Stone, *Eastern Front*, 248–49). The reports of British Major General Alfred Knox, a liaison to the Russian forces, make no mention of drumming fire but emphasize the methodical approach taken by the Russian artillery. Likewise an April 1928 article by an Austrian veteran in *Der 94er*, a veterans' journal, says that given the Russian artillery numbers, it is unlikely that they engaged in "drumming fire." Lt. Berndt, "Das Wunder der Brussilow-Offensive," in ÖKA, Ms-Wk.

4. Nachlass Kundmann, 405.

5. Ludendorff, *War Memories*, 219.

6. Falkenhayn, *German General Staff*, 280.

7. ÖULK, IV, 375.

8. Jerabek, *Brussilowoffensive*, 255–56; ÖULK, IV, 375–377.

9. ÖULK, IV, 377.

10. Stone, *Eastern Front*, 247. Austrian sources generally give higher numbers both here and on other sectors of the front. See: ÖULK, IV, 365–375.

11. Ernst Wisshaupt, *Die Krise der 7. Armee nach der Schlacht bei Okna (4–10. Juni 1916)—Wodurch wurde sie verursacht?* ÖKA, Ms-Wk: Russ. 12 (1916), 6. Wisshaupt was a captain in the Austrian army; he wrote the study in 1925.

12. Rudolf Kiszling, *Der Feldzug von Luck im Sommer 1916* ÖKA, Ms-Wk: Russ. 5 (1916), 5.

13. ÖKA, *Die Kämpfe der Heeresgruppe G. O. Böhm-Ermolli bzw. d. 2. Armee im Sommer 1916, inkl. Der Schlacht bei Brody*. Ms-Wk: Russ (1916):3, 4; Jerabek, *Brussilowoffensive*, 256; Kiszling, *Der Feldzug von Luck im Sommer 1916*, 2–5. Kiszling was chief of staff for the 70th HID in June 1916.

14. ÖULK, IV, 379–380; *Feldzug von Luck*, 5; Stone, *Eastern Front*, 249; ÖKA, Ms-Wk: B-1466, Nachlass Böhm-Ermolli, 532.

15. Jerabek, *Brussilowoffensive*, 286–87.

16. ÖULK, IV, 421.

17. Jerabek, *Brussilowoffensive*, 294–95; ÖKA, Ms-Wk: Russ. 15 (1916): Cavalry Lt. Alphons Bernhard, *Die Schlacht bei Okna, 4. Bis 10. Juni 1916*, 20; Stone, *Eastern Front*, 251–53; Nachlass Kundmann, 410.

18. Nachlass Kundmann, 405; Bernhard, *Die Schlacht bei Okna*, 20; Knox, *With the Russian Army*, 443–44.

19. *ÖULK*, IV, 423–424; Jerabek, *Brussilowoffensive*, 295–96; Stone, *Eastern Front*, 253; Jukes, *Carpathian Disaster*, 120–25.

20. Wisshaupt, *Krise der 7. Armee*, 7–8; Bernhard, *Schlacht bei Okna*, 23–26; Jerabek, *Brussilowoffensive*, 296–98.

21. Knox, *With the Russian Army*, 441.

22. Bernhard, *Schlacht bei Okna*, 33.

23. Wisshaupt, *Krise der 7. Armee*, 15.

24. *ÖULK*, IV, 445.

25. Wisshaupt, *Krise der 7. Armee*, 20.

26. Jerabek, *Brussilowoffensive*, 349

27. Ibid., 310–11; *ÖULK*, IV, 444. Brusilov's figures for Austro-Hungarian POWs are somewhat higher; he estimated that the Russian Seventh Army had captured 34,000 prisoners—716 of them officers—while the Russian Ninth took an additional 55,000. Stone, *Eastern Front*, 254. Knox (*With the Russian Army*, 443) gives figures more in line with those in Stone, reporting that Scherbatschev captured over 16,000 men—including 415 officers—between 4 and 10 June, as well as 10,000 captured from 14 to 21 June. Knox's figures for prisoners taken by XI Corps—over 24,000 men between 4 and 12 June (*With the Russian Army*, 445)—also seem to agree with Stone's.

28. For details of the offensive on the southern half of the front from 4–29 June, see: Jerabek, *Brussilowoffensive*, 290–310 and 346–51; *ÖULK*, IV, 425–55; Stone, *Eastern Front*, 251–55; Kiszling, *Feldzug von Luck*, 9; Wisshaupt, *Krise der 7. Armee*, 8–28; Bernhard, *Schlacht bei Okna*, 23–47; Knox, *With the Russian Army*, 443–47; and Jukes, *Carpathian Disaster*, 123–25.

29. Gen. Kralowitz, chief of general staff for Fourth Army, in Jerabek, *Brussilowoffensive*, 258.

30. Kiszling, *Feldzug von Luck*, 6–7; *ÖULK*, IV, 382–83;

31. Jerabek, *Brussilowoffensive*, 259.

32. Kiszling, *Feldzug von Luck*, 6–7; *ÖULK*, IV, 383–88; Jerabek, *Brussilowoffensive*, 261–63; Stone, *Eastern Front*, 249–50.

33. *ÖULK*, IV, 386.

34. Kiszling, *Feldzug von Luck*, 7–8; Stone, *Eastern Front*, 248–49; Jerabek, *Brussilowoffensive*, 259–63; *ÖULK*, IV, 387–88.

35. Nachlass Kundmann, 407.

36. Jerabek, *Brussilowoffensive*, 311–13; Stone, *Eastern Front*, 250; Kiszling, *Feldzug von Luck*, 8; Falkenhayn, *German General Staff*, 280.

37. Jerabek, *Brussilowoffensive*, 264–65; *ÖULK*, IV, 388–89; Stone, *Eastern Front*, 250; Nachlass Kundmann, 407–408; Kiszling, *Feldzug von Luck*, 8.

38. Jerabek, *Brussilowoffensive*, 264–72; *ÖULK*, IV, 388–93.

39. Jerabek, *Brussilowoffensive*, 272–74, and 312–14; Nachlass Kundmann, 408; *ÖULK*, IV, 392–95; ÖKA, Ms-Wk: *Die Kämpfe der Heeresgruppe G. O. Böhm-Ermolli bzw. d. 2. Armee im Sommer 1916, inkl. der Schlacht bei Brody*, Ms-Wk: Russ. 3 (1916), 7; Stone, *Eastern Front*, 250.

40. *ÖULK*, IV, 394–98; Jerabek, *Brussilowoffensive*, 273–78; Kiszling, *Feldzug von Luck*, 8.

41. *ÖULK*, IV, 400.

42. Jerabek, *Brussilowoffensive*, 280–81.

43. *ÖULK*, IV, 399–403; Jerabek, *Brussilowoffensive*, 281–85.

44. Nachlass Böhm-Ermolli, 538.

45. ÖULK, IV, 403–411; Zaionchkovski, *Russischer Kriegsplan*, 8–9; Jerabek, *Brussilowoffensive*, 322–23; Kiszling, *Feldzug vom Luck*, 8–9; Stone, *Eastern Front*, 257; Nachlass Böhm-Ermolli, 546.

46. Zaionchkovski, *Russischer Kriegsplan*, 9; Ludendorff, *War Memories*, 220–22; Falkenhayn, *German General Staff*, 282; and ÖULK, IV, 403–405.

47. Nachlass Böhm-Ermolli, 548–49.

48. Nachlass Kundmann, 426.

49. ÖULK, IV, 411–415; Stone, *Eastern Front*, 255–57; Jukes, *Carpathian Disaster*, 124–25.

4. STALEMATE AND RENEWAL

1. Nachlass Kundmann, 412.

2. Falkenhayn, *German General Staff*, 281–82.

3. Nachlass Kundmann, 410

4. Ibid., 410.

5. Ibid., 411.

6. Falkenhayn, *German General Staff*, 281–85; Jerabek, *Brussilowoffensive*, 319–21.

7. Falkenhayn, *German General Staff*, 284.

8. Ibid., 286–88.

9. Nachlass Kundmann, 422.

10. Ibid., 420–23; Jerabek, *Brussilowoffensive*, 321–27.

11. ÖULK, IV, 488 and 570–57; Lincoln, *Armageddon*, 253.

12. Jukes, *Carpathian Disaster*, 124–25;

13. Joseph T. Furhmann, ed., *The Complete Wartime Correspondence of Tsar Nicholas II and the Empress Alexandra: April 1914–March 1917* (Westport, Conn.: Greenwood Press, 1999), 491.

14. Stone, *Eastern Front*, 257; Jukes, *Carpathian Disaster*, 125; Jerabek, *Brussilowoffensive*, 369–72; Brusilov, *Erinnerungen*, 217–18.

15. Brusilov, *Erinnerungen*, 218–22.

16. Edmund Glaise von Horstenau, *Die Kriegsführung im Russland und Ostgalizien in den Jh. 1916 und 1917*, ÖKA, Ms-Wk: Russ (1916) 2, 7; Jerabek, *Brussilowoffensive*, 327–34; ÖULK, IV, 473–87; Stone, *Eastern Front*, 255–56; ÖKA, Ms-Wk: *Kämpfe der Heeresgruppe Böhm-Ermolli*, 28–30; Kiszling, *Feldzug von Luck*, 14; Falkenhayn, *German General Staff*, 289.

17. Jerabek, *Brussilowoffensive*, 368.

18. ÖKA, Ms-Wk: *Die Kämpfe des deutschen 10. Armeekorps in Wolhynien, 16.VI-31. VII.16*; Ms-Wk: Russ. 14 (1916), 1; ÖKA, Ms-Wk: *Die Kämpfe der Heeresgruppe G. O. Böhm-Ermolli bzw. der 2. Armee im Sommer 1916, inkl. der Schlacht bei Brody*, ÖKA, Ms-Wk: Russ (1916):3, 32–34; ÖULK IV, 488–98; ÖKA, Ms-Wk: *Der Feldzug von Luck im Sommer 1916*, ÖKA, Ms-Wk: Russ (1916):5, 14–15.

19. Nachlass Kundmann, 433.

20. ÖULK, IV, 493–99; Stone, *Eastern Front*, 257; Jerabek, *Brussilowoffensive*, 240–41.

21. Jerabek, *Brussilowoffensive*, 365.

22. ÖULK, IV, 537.

23. Jerabek, *Brussilowoffensive*, 365.

24. Jerabek, *Brussilowoffensive*, 351–52 and 364–65; ÖULK, IV, 539–45.

25. ÖULK, IV, 495–530; Jerabek, *Brussilowoffensive*, 351–52; ÖKA, Ms-Wk: *Der Feldzug von Luck*, 17–18.

26. Knox, *With the Russian Army*, 472.

27. Stone, *Eastern Front*, 262.

28. Brusilov, *Erinnerungen*, 226–27.

29. Lincoln, *Armageddon*, 256; Knox, *With the Russian Army*, 473.

30. Lincoln, *Armageddon*, 255.

31. Lincoln, *Armageddon*, 255–56; ÖULK, IV 522–23.

32. Brusilov, *Erinnerungen*, 221–24; Lincoln, *Armageddon*, 254–55; ÖULK, IV, 523 and 535; Jukes, *Carpathian Disaster*, 125.

33. Brusilov, *Erinnerungen*, 221.

34. Stone, *Eastern Front*, 256.

35. Lincoln, *Armageddon*, 255.

36. Lincoln, *Armageddon*, 255; Fuhrmann, *Complete Wartime Correspondence*, 515–16. The Austro-Hungarian estimates are only slightly higher: about 300,000 killed and as many wounded or captured; ÖULK, IV, 568.

37. Brusilov, *Erinnerungen*, 222.

38. Stone, *Eastern Front*, 260.

39. Jerabek, *Brussilowoffensive*, 341–44; ÖULK, IV, 499.

40. Nachlass Kundmann, 434.

41. ÖULK, IV, 502 and 509; Jerabek, *Brussilowoffensive*, 343–44.

42. ÖULK, IV, 502.

43. ÖULK, IV, 517–18.

44. ÖULK, IV, 521.

45. Ludendorff, *War Memories*, 224.

46. Jerabek, *Brussilowoffensive*, 356.

47. Spencer Tucker, *The Great War, 1914–1918* (London: UCL Press, 1998), 104.

48. Jerabek, *Brussilowoffensive*, 357.

49. Jerabek, *Brussilowoffensive*, 358.

50. Nachlass Kundmann, 453.

51. Ibid., 450–53; Jerabek, *Brussilowoffensive*, 359–63 and 366–67; Falkenhayn, *German General Staff*, 289–91.

52. Cited in Jerabek, *Brussilowoffensive*, 389–390n83. Jerabek disputes entirely Stone's version—and the official Austrian version—of the encounter, wherein the Russians failed entirely to prepare the assault.

53. ÖULK, IV, 571–575; Lincoln, *Armageddon*, 253–54; Stone, *Eastern Front*, 260–61.

54. Fuhrmann, *Complete Wartime Correspondence*, 514.

55. Lincoln, *Armageddon*, 254; Stone, *Eastern Front*, 261; Jerabek, *Brussilowoffensive*, 387–91.

56. Stone, *Eastern Front*, 260. Brusilov, in his memoirs, notes that Eleventh Army alone took over 34,000 prisoners and seized 45 guns, but his time frame is 1–14 July, so it is difficult to compare the figures. Brusilov, *Erinnerungen*, 223.

57. ÖULK, IV, 578–613; Lincoln, *Armageddon*, 253; Jerabek, *Brussilowoffensive*, 376–77.

58. ÖULK, IV, 541, 564, 609, and 642; Jerabek, *Brussilowoffensive*, 375.

5. A TALE OF NORTH AND SOUTH

1. ÖULK, IV, 486 and 608–609.

2. Falkenhayn, *German General Staff*, 304.

3. Herwig, *First World War*, 213.

4. Ibid., 214–15; Jerabek, *Brussilowoffensive*, 353; Paleologue, *Memoirs*, 3:286.

5. ÖKA, Ms-Wk: AOK 2720, *Materielle Situation d. 2. AK,* Qu. Op. 1060, "Materielle Sit. f. den 15. Juni 1916."

6. Stone, *Eastern Front,* 260.

7. ÖKA, Ms-Wk: *Die Kämpfe der 11. Korps in der Südbukovina und den angrenzenden Teilen Rumäniens von Anfang Juli bis Mitte November 1916,* von Feldzugsmeister Hugo Habermann, ÖKA, Ms-Wk: Russ (1916):10, 2–3;ÖKA, Ms-Wk: NFA *der 7. Armee.89,* Op. No. 1316/11 and 1316/12; Jerabek, *Brussilowoffensive,* 367.

8. ÖULK, IV, 560–567,

9. Jerabek, *Brussilowoffensive,* 362 and 367.

10. Nachlass Kundmann, 470.

11. Stone, *Eastern Front,* 261.

12. ÖULK, IV, 596–608; Jerabek, *Brussilowoffensive,* 381–83; Herwig, *First World War,* 158.

13. Nachlass Böhm-Ermolli, 552; Jukes, *Carpathian Disaster,* 125–26; ÖULK, IV, 612–615; ÖKA, *Die Kämpfe der Heeresgruppe G. O. Böhm-Ermolli bzw. der 2. Armee im Sommer 1916, inkl. der Schlacht bei Brody,* Ms-Wk: Russ (1916): 3, 39–40.

14. Brusilov, *Erinnerungen,* 223.

15. ÖKA, Ms-Wk: NFA 2.Armee.160, *Tagebuch 68,* 103–107, and *Tagebuch 71,* 6–7; ÖKA, Ms-Wk: Mat. Sit. 2. AK, AOK 2691: Qu. Op. 5525—Beilage B, *Verluste der 2. Armee, 1–15.VII.1916;* ÖKA, Ms-Wk: 2. Armee, AOK 2690: Qu. Op. 4966—Beilage A, *Summarische Standesnachweisung der 2. Armee 15.VI.1916,* Qu. Op. 4966 B-B, *Verluste der 2. Armee, 1–15.VI.1916* .

16. Jerabek, *Brussilowoffensive,* 377; ÖULK, *Kriegsjahr 1916,* 627–33.

17. Nachlass Böhm-Ermolli, 564.

18. ÖULK, IV, 633–34 and 651–58; ÖKA, Ms-Wk: *Die Kämpfe der Heeresgruppe G. O. Böhm-Ermolli,* 46–51; ÖKA, Ms-Wk: 1. Armee AOK 2683: QOP 16,500, B. 8b, *Verluste der 1. Armee, 1–16.VI.1916;* QOP 19,500, B. 8b, *Verluste der 1. Armee, 15–30.VI.1916;* QOP 21,000, B. 8b, *Verluste der ö-u Truppen der Armeegruppe Marwitz/1. Armee, 1–15. VII.1916;* Nachlass Böhm-Ermolli, 561–566; Jukes, *Carpathian Disaster,* 126; Jerabek, *Brussilowoffensive,* 378–81; ÖKA, Ms-Wk: Russ (1916) 5, *Der Feldzug von Luck,* 25–27; Ludwig Eberhard Freiherr von Schlotheim, *Die kaiserlich deustsche Südarmee in den Kämpfen während der Brussilow-Offensive vom 4. Juni bis 14. August 1916* (Munich: C. H. Beck, 1936), 62–65.

19. Nachlass Kundmann, 490.

20. ÖKA, Ms-Wk: Russ. (1916) 3, *Die Kämpfe der Heeresgruppe G. O. Böhm-Ermolli,* 67–68, citing Order 91 of the Russian Eleventh Army command

21. Jerabek, *Brussilowoffensive,* 423.

22. Herwig, *First World War,* 214.

23. ÖULK, V, 117.

24. Jerabek, *Brussilowoffensive,* 378.

25. ÖULK, *Kriegsjahr 1916,* 643–45; Jerabek, *Brussilowoffensive,* 385.

26. Jerabek, *Brussilowoffensive,* 380.

27. Nachlass Kundmann, 488–90.

28. Jerabek, *Brussilowoffensive,* 394–95. Wilhelm II apparently did not wish to be seen acquiescing to the "will of the people" in choosing Hindenburg; Conrad was more concerned with personal and imperial prestige.

29. Ludendorff, *War Memories,* 229.

30. Nachlass Kundmann, 475.

31. Jerabek, *Brussilowoffensive,* 388–420; ÖULK, V, 117–21 and 148–49; Herwig, *First World War,* 215.

32. Jukes, *Carpathian Disaster*, 126–27; Brusilov, *Erinnerungen*, 223–24; ÖULK, *Kriegsjahr 1916*, 658–60; ÖULK, V, 122 and 133–34; Knox, *With the Russian Army*, 461–62.

33. Schlotheim, *Die kaiserlich deustsche Südarmee*, 62–64; ÖULK, V, 152–53; Jerabek, *Brussilowoffensive*, 428–30; ÖKA, Ms-Wk: Russ (1916) 5, *Der Feldzug von Luck im Sommer 1916*, 29–31; Jukes, *Carpathian Disaster*, 129; Brusilov, *Erinnerungen*, 225.

34. ÖULK, V, 141; ÖKA, Ms-Wk: B203.2–1, Beilage IX, *Auszug aus dem Tagebuch des 4. AK über die Kämpfe am 28. Juli 1916*, 1–17.

35. Jerabek, *Brussilowoffensive*, 421.

36. Jerabek, *Brussilowoffensive*, 421; ÖULK, V, 141. Brusilov himself gives the numbers as "more than 8,000 prisoners and 46 guns captured." Brusilov, *Erinnerungen*, 224.

37. ÖULK, V, 141.

38. Jerabek, *Brussilowoffensive*, 421n7; Jerabek's source is cited as: Freiherr Ludwig von Vogelsang, *Das steirische Infantriergiment Nr. 47 im Weltkrieg* (Graz, 1932), 450.

39. Nachlass Kundmann, 485–89; ÖULK, V, 138–41; Jerabek, *Brussilowoffensive*, 420–22; ÖKA, Ms-Wk: Russ (1916) 5, *Der Feldzug von Luck im Sommer 1916*, 28–29.

40. Jerabek, *Brussilowoffensive*, 425.

41. Knox, *With the Russian Army*, 389.

42. Jukes, *Carpathian Disaster*, 127–29; Lincoln, *Armageddon*, 256–57; Jerabek, *Brussilowoffensive*, 424–29; ÖULK, V, 124–36; Brusilov, *Erinnerungen*, 226–27.

43. Falkenhayn, *German General Staff*, 307.

44. Ludendorff, *War Memories*, 231.

45. Furhman, *Complete War Correspondence*, 537.

46. ÖULK, V, 126–32; Jerabek, *Brussilowoffensive*, 423; Jukes, *Carpathian Disaster*, 127.

47. Jerabek, *Brussilowoffensive*, 422–23.

48. ÖULK, V, 124–25; Jerabek, *Brussilowoffensive*, 423–24.

49. Nachlass Böhm-Ermolli, 572–74; ÖULK, V, 145–55.

6. THE OFFENSIVE SHATTERS

1. ÖULK, V, 155–57 and 179–80; ÖKA, Ms-Wk: Russ 10 (1916), FZM Hugo Habermann, *Die Kämpfe des 11. Korps in der Südbukovina und den angrenzenden Teilen Rumäniens von Anfang Juli bis Mitte November 1916*, 39–52.

2. ÖULK, V, 158–64; Jerabek, *Brussilowoffensive*, 425–28; Jukes, *Carpathian Disaster*, 127–29; Knox, *With the Russian Army*, 469. According to Knox, I Corps and XXX Corps were significantly under strength as a result of the initial battle for Kovel. He reports a total strength of only 19,000 men for the two corps, as opposed to the 25,000 accepted by both Jerabek and the official Austrian version. Jukes counts only twenty-five battalions—nine German and sixteen Hungarian—defending the sector for the Central Powers. The numerical superiority of the Russian forces was, regardless of the exact numbers, still overwhelming.

3. ÖULK, V, 160–74.

4. Nachlass Kundmann, 497.

5. Ludendorff, *War Memories*, 236.

6. ÖKA, Ms-Wk: AOK 2691, Material Situation d. 2. AK, Qu. Op. 6521, Beilage A, *Summarische Standesnachweisung 15.VIII* and Beilage B, *Verluste*.

7. ÖULK, V, 173–76; Nachlass Böhm-Ermolli, 575–78; Jerabek, *Brussilowoffensive*, 427–428; Schlotheim, *Südarmee*, 69–75; ÖKA, Ms-Wk: Russ 5 (1916), *Der Feldzug vom Luck*, 30–31.

8. Jerabek, *Brussilowoffensive*, 429.

9. Schlotheim, *Südarmee*, 77.

10. Schlotheim, *Südarmee*, 70–78; ÖULK, V, 182–89; Jerabek, *Brussilowoffensive*, 428–30; ÖKA, Ms-Wk: Russ 5 (1916), *Der Feldzug von Luck*, 30–31; Jukes, *Carpathian Disaster*, 128–30.

11. Knox, *With the Russian Army*, 459–64; ÖULK, V, 159–60; Jukes, *Carpathian Disaster*, 127–28; Jerabek, *Brussilowoffensive*, 425–26.

12. Knox, *With the Russian Army*, 466.

13. Ibid., 470.

14. Stone, *Eastern Front*, 272.

15. ÖULK, V, 161–71; Jukes, *Carpathian Disaster*, 129; Lincoln, *Armageddon*, 256–57; Brusilov, *Erinnerungen*, 227–28; ÖKA, Ms-Wk: AOK 2701, Mat. Sit. 4. AK, Qu. Op. 33000, Beilage 7, *Verlustrapport 25.VII-10.VIII 1916*.

16. Knox, *With the Russian Army*, 476.

17. Jerabek, *Brussilowoffensive*, 425.

18. Lincoln, *Armageddon*, 256.

19. Jukes, *Carpathian Disaster*, 129; Lincoln, *Armageddon*, 256–57; Brusilov, *Erinnerungen*, 228.

20. Brusilov, *Erinnerungen*, 228.

21. Lincoln, *Armageddon*, 259.

22. Fuhrmann, *Complete Wartime Correspondence*, 596.

23. Jukes, *Carpathian Disaster*, 129; Lincoln, *Armageddon*, 256–57; ÖULK, V, 197–98; Herwig, *First World War*, 219; Stone, *Eastern Front*, 271–72.

24. Jerabek, *Brussilowoffensive*, 439.

25. Lincoln, *Armageddon*, 258.

26. Falkenhayn, *German General Staff*, 232.

27. Jerabek, *Brussilowoffensive*, 454.

28. Lincoln, *Passage through Armageddon*, 257.

29. Jerabek, *Brussilowoffensive*, 456–86.

30. Brusilov, *Erinnerungen*, 229.

31. Knox, *With the Russian Army*, 484.

32. Brusilov, *Erinnerungen*, 229. Stone, *Eastern Front*, 273–74, details Alekseev's long-standing opposition to the Romanian venture.

33. Stone, *Eastern Front*, 265.

34. Denikin, *Russian Turmoil*, 134–35.

35. Brusilov, *Erinnerungen*, 229.

36. Lincoln, *Armageddon*, 258.

37. Stone, *Eastern Front*, 218, gives the Romanian strength as 369,000; Herwig, *First World War*, 274, notes that "nearly 400,000 Romanians crossed the Hungarian borders."

38. Denikin, *Russian Turmoil*, 134–35.

39. Falkenhayn, *German General Staff*, 319.

40. Herwig, *First World War*, 219.

41. Stone, *Eastern Front*, 277.

42. Knox, *With the Russian Army*, 487.

43. Paleologue, *Memoirs*, 3:52.

44. Herwig, *First World War*, 221.

45. Knox, *With the Russian Army*, 497–503.

46. General information on Romania's position and negotiations for entry into the war may be found in: Knox, *With the Russian Army*, 482–88; Jerabek, *Brussilowoffensive*,

432–55; Brusilov, *Erinnerungen*, 229–32; Stone, *Eastern Front*, 264–81; Herwig, *First World War*, 217–22; Jukes, *Carpathian Disaster*, 130–39; Falkenhayn, *German General Staff*, 231–37.

7. CONSEQUENCES

1. Lincoln, *Red Victory*, 26; Knox, *With the Russian Army*, 504; Jukes, *Carpathian Disaster*, 144.

2. Jukes, *Carpathian Disaster*, 149–51. The second-class reserves contained some 350,000 men, while the 1919 cadre was estimated at 700,000.

3. See, for instance, Lionel Kochan, *Russia in Revolution, 1890–1918* (New York: New American Library, 1966), 180–83; Lincoln, *Armageddon*, 92–113, 147, 181–82, and 215–37.

4. Taylor, *Politics and the Russian Army*, 68.

5. Raymond Pearson, *The Russian Moderates and the Crisis of Tsarism, 1914–1917* (New York: Barnes and Noble Books, 1979), 107.

6. Lincoln, *Red Victory*, 29.

7. Wildman, *Road to Soviet Power and Peace*, 8. Jukes, by way of comparison, estimates that by October 1916 the Russian Army had suffered 4,670,000 casualties, lost an additional 2,078,000 men as prisoners of war, and had more than 1,000,000 simply go "missing." *Carpathian Disaster*, 144.

8. Kochan, *Russia in Revolution*, 184.

9. See, for instance: Peter Kenez, "Changes in the Social Composition of the Officer Corps during World War I," in *The Russian Imperial Army, 1796–1917*, ed. Roger Reese, 285–92 (Burlington, Vt.: Ashgate, 2006).

10. David R. Jones, "The Imperial Russian Life Guards Grenadier Regiment, 1906–1917: The Disintegration of an Elite Unit," in *The Russian Imperial Army, 1796–1917*, ed. Roger Reese, 293–306 (Burlington, Vt.: Ashgate, 2006), 301.

11. Taylor, *Politics and the Russian Army*, 73; Kenez, "Changes in the Social Composition," 285 and 290.

12. Denikin, *Russian Turmoil*, 31–32; Kochan, *Russia*, 183–84; Lincoln, *Armageddon*, 259–60; Jukes, *Carpathian Disaster*, 144–49.

13. Jukes, *Carpathian Disaster*, 144–45.

14. Ibid., 145–48.

15. Lincoln, *Armageddon*, 259–60.

16. Jukes, *Carpathian Disaster*, 145.

17. Knox, *With the Russian Army*, 487–508.

18. Stone, *Eastern Front*, 282.

19. Florinsky, *Russian Empire*, 139 and 207.

20. Brusilov, *Erinnerungen*, 226.

21. Brusilov, *Erinnerungen*, 9.

22. See, for instance: Richard Charques, *The Twilight of Imperial Russia* (London: Oxford University Press, 1965), 229; Rostunov, *Brusilov*, 156; Tucker, *Great War*, 119; Golovine, *Russian Army*, 241–42; Shneer M. Levin, *Brusilovski proryo* (Moscow: Gospolizdat, 1941), 13–15; Robert P. Browder and Alexander Kerensky, eds., *The Russian Provisional Government, 1917: Documents*, 3 vols. (Stanford: Stanford University Press, 1961), 1:9; Gordon Brook-Shepherd, *The Austrians: A Thousand-Year Odyssey* (London: HarperCollins, 1996), 181; Jukes, *Carpathian Disaster*, 17; and Roger Chickering, *Imperial Germany and the Great War, 1914–1918* (Cambridge: Cambridge University Press, 2004), 70.

23. Walther Hubatsch, *Germany and the Central Powers in the World War 1914–1918* (Lawrence, Kans.: University of Kansas Publications, 1963), 72.

24. Brusilov, *Erinnerungen*, 234.

25. See, for instance: Wildman, *Road to Soviet Power and Peace*, 3–4 and 94–96; Jukes, *Carpathian Disaster*, 158–59.

26. Jerabek, *Brussilowoffensive*, 247.

27. Sondhaus, *Architect*, 189n65.

28. Jerabek, *Brussilowoffensive*, 125–43, 156–59, 592–97; Stone, *Eastern Front*, 243–44.

29. Jerabek, *Brussilowoffensive*, 139.

30. Paleologue, *Memoirs*, 2:268.

31. Sondhaus, *Architect*, 184–88; Stone, *Eastern Front*, 244–47; Jerabek, *Brussilowoffensive*, 248–50; Herwig, *First World War*, 205–206.

32. Jerabek, *Brussilowoffensive*, 595.

33. Falkenhayn, *German General Staff*, 278.

34. Stone, *Eastern Front*, 244.

35. Falkenhayn, *German General Staff*, 285 and 325–26.

36. Herwig, *First World War*, 213.

37. Ibid., 231.

38. Falkenhayn, *German General Staff*, 304.

39. Tucker, *Great War*, 99–105; Herwig, *First World War*, 181–95; Falkenhayn, *German General Staff*, 285–87 and 325–26.

40. Sondhaus, *Architect*, 183.

41. Jerabek, *Brussilowoffensive*, 529.

42. Ibid., 524 and 527; Sondhaus, *Architect*, 188–89; Herwig, *First World War*, 213; Stone, *Eastern Front*, 261; Brusilov, *Erinnerungen*, 220 and 232.

43. Jerabek, *Brussilowoffensive*, 522–23; Sondhaus, *Architect*, 188; Stone, *Eastern Front*, 253–54; Brusilov, *Erinnerungen*, 220 and 225. Brusilov, as Stone notes, underestimated the number of Austro-Hungarian POWs, claiming only 190,000 by 12 June and only 379,000 in the first two months.

44. Stone, *Eastern Front*, 250.

45. Herwig, *First World War*, 217.

46. See, for instance: Rostunov, *Brusilov*, 78; Jukes, *Carpathian Disaster*, 112.

47. Jerabek, *Brussilowoffensive*, 540.

48. Jerabek, *Brussilowoffensive*, 539. By way of contrast, see Stone, *Eastern Front*, 126.

49. Washburn, *Russian Advance*, 28.

50. Stone, *Eastern Front*, 251; Jerabek, *Brussilowoffensive*, 539–41.

51. Stone, *Eastern Front*, 253.

52. Jerabek, *Brussilowoffensive*, 537–42; Herwig, *First World War*, 212.

53. Stone, *Eastern Front*, 253.

54. Sondhaus, *Architect*, 166; Herwig, *First World War*, 139.

55. Herwig, *First World War*, 110.

56. Ibid., 113.

57. *ÖULK*, II, 271.

58. Jerabek, *Brussilowoffensive*, 516.

59. Ibid., 498–518; Herwig, *First World War*, 139–40.

60. Sondhaus, *Architect*, 166.

61. Washburn, *Russian Offensive*, 24–25.

62. Jerabek, *Brussilowoffensive*, 528.

63. Ibid., 527–29, 536–39, and 557–62.

64. Ibid., 548.

65. Ibid., 550.

66. For details of the negotiations leading to the unified command on the Eastern Front, see: Jerabek, *Brussilowoffensive*, 456–97; Sondhaus, *Architect*, 191–97; Stone, *Eastern Front*, 269–70; and Herwig, *First World War*, 214–16.

67. Herwig, *First World War*, 215.

68. Jerabek, *Brussilowoffensive*, 481.

69. Sondhaus, *Architect*, 191–92. See also: Herwig, *First World War*, 213–17.

70. Jerabek, *Brussilowoffensive*, 605–10; Herwig, *First World War*, 215–16.

71. Stone, *Eastern Front*, 255.

72. Brusilov, *Erinnerungen*, 233.

73. Stone, *Eastern Front*, 255.

74. Brusilov, *Erinnerungen*, 221; Stone, *Eastern Front*, 256; Lincoln, *Armageddon*, 252–53.

75. Knox, *With the Russian Army*, 470.

76. Brusilov, *Erinnerungen*, 236.

BIBLIOGRAPHY

FROM THE AUSTRIAN STATE ARCHIVE, WAR ARCHIVE (ÖKA)

Armeeoberkommando, Operationsbüro; AOK Akten

475: *Krieg gegen Rumänien*
789: *Einteilungsliste der Armee im Felde 27.9.1915–31.5.1916*
790: *Einteilungsliste der Armee im Felde 29.6–3.10.1916*
2263: *Ranglisten des Generalstabes 1915–1918*
2672: *Tagebücher—11. Buch von 12.4–4.7.1916*
2673: *Tagebücher—11.Buch von 12.4–4.7.1916*
2674: *Tagebücher—12.Buch von 5.7–2.10.1916*
2675: *Tagebücher—12.Buch von 5.7–2.10.1916*
2683: *Materialsituation d. 1. Armeekommandos 15.5–15.9.1916*
2690: *Materialsituation d. 2. Armeekommandos 1.1–2.7.1916*
2691: *Materialsituation d. 2. Armeekommandos 1.7–30.11.1916*
2695: *Materialsituation d. 3. Armeekommandos 1.1–1.7.1916*
2696: *Materialsituation d. 3. Armeekommandos 1.8–1.12–1916*
2700: *Materialsituation d. 4. Armeekommandos 1.1–1.7.1916*
2701: *Materialsituation d. 4. Armeekommandos 15.7–1.12–1916*
2720: *Materialsituation d. 7. Armeekommandos 1.1–1.7.1916*
2721: *Materialsituation d. 7. Armeekommandos 15.7–1.12.1916*

Nachlässe

B/15, *Nachlass Rudolf Kundmann*
B/203, *Nachlass Otto Berndt, Ritter von*
B/557, *Nachlass Karl Pflanzer-Baltin, Freiherr von*
B/892, *Nachlass Hans von Seeckt*
B/1000, *Nachlass Kövess von Kovesshaza*
B/1284, *Nachlass Paul Puhallo von Brlog, Freiherr von*
B/1466, *Nachlass Eduard Josef Adolf Böhm-Ermolli, Freiherr von*

Neue Feldakten; NFA

Hohe Kommanden 16: *Tagebücher 4.7–12.10–1916*
1. Operierendes Armeekommando, Karton 255: *Situationskarten 1916*
1. Armeekommando 22: *Kartenevidenzen der eigenen u. feindliche Lage 8.8.1916–1.4.1917*
1. Armeekommando 23: *Lagekarten*
2. Armeekommando, Karton 741: *Lagekarten 1916*
2. Armeekommando, Karton 742: *Lagekarten 1916*
2. Armee 159: *Lagekarten, Mai 1916*
2. Armee 160: *Tagebücher 1916*
2. Armee 161: *Karten 1916*
2. Armee 165: *Fliegermeldungen u. Bilder, 21.4–2.8.1916*
4. Armeekommando 115: *Tagebücher*
4. Armeekommando 128: *Eigenen u. feindliche Situationskarte*
7. Armeekommando 89: *Tagebücher 1916 (Abschrift)*
7. Armeekommando 90: *Lagekarten*
7. Armeekommando 91: *Lagekarten*
7. Armeekommando 92: *Lagekarten*
7. Armeekommando 93: *Lagekarten*
7. Armeekommando 122: *Gefangenenberichte*
7. Armeekommando 123: *Gefangenenberichte*
7. Armeekommando 124: *Gefangenenberichte*
7. Armeekommando 125: *Gefangenenberichte*

Manuscripts and Articles

Ms-Wk: Rus 2 (1916): *Die Kriegsführung im Russland u. Ostgalizien in den Jh. 1916 u. 1917.* by Staatsarchivar Generalstabmajor a. D. Edmund Glaise v. Horstenau.
Ms-Wk: Russ 3 (1916): *Die Kämpfe der Heeresgruppe G.O. Böhm-Ermolli bzw. d. 2. Armee im Sommer 1916, inkl. der Schlacht bei Brody.*
Ms-Wk: Rus 5 (1916): *Der Feldzug von Luck im Sommer 1916.* [by Rudolf Kiszling?]
Ms-Wk: Rus 10 (1916): *Die Kämpfe d. 11. Korps in der Südbukovina und den angrenzenden Teilen Rumäniens von Anfang Juli bis Mitte November 1916.* by Feldzugmeister Hugo Habermann.
Ms-Wk: Rus 12 (1916): *Die Krise der 7. Armee nach der Schlacht bei Okna (4–10. Juni 1916)—wodurch wurde sie verursacht?* by Ernst Wisshaupt, Hptm. im Ost. Bundesheer [1925?]
Ms-Wk: Rus 13 (1916): *Russischer Kriegsplan f.d. Sommer 1916 (Durchbruch von Luzk).* by A.M. Zaionchkovski [Kmdt d. XXX Korps].
Ms-Wk: Rus 13 (1916): *Russischer Operationsplan und Durchbruch von Luck, 1916.*
Ms-Wk: Rus 14 (1916): *Die kämpfe des deutschen 10. Armee-korps in Wolhynian, 16.VI—31. VII.16.* [newspaper article]
Ms-Wk: Rus 15 (1916): *Die Schlacht bei Okna 4. bis 10. Juni 1916,* by Oberst d. R. Alphons Bernhard.
"Das Wunder der Brussilow-Offensive." by Berndt. *Der 94er,* April 1928, 6/4.

SECONDARY SOURCES

Abraham, Richard. *Alexander Kerensky: the First Love of the Revolution*. New York: Columbia University Press, 1987.

Allen, George H., Admiral F.E. Chadwick, and Henry C. Whitehead. *The Great War, Second Volume: The Mobilization of the Moral and Physical Forces*. Philadelphia: George Barrie's Sons, 1916.

Balayev, Polkovnik. *Die 8. Armee beim Durchbruch von Luck*. [Russian] Moscow: n.p., 1924.

Bazarevski, Polkovnik. *Nastupatelnaya Operatsiya 9-i russkoi armii, Yun 1916 goda*. Moscow: Gosudarstvennoi Voennoye Izdatelstvo, 1937.

Black, Jeremy. *Warfare in the Western World, 1882–1975*. Bloomington: Indiana University Press, 2002.

Brook-Shepherd, Gordon. *The Austrian Odyssey*. New York: St. Martin's Press, 1957.

———. *The Austrians: A Thousand-year Odyssey*. New York: HarperCollins, 1997.

Browder, Robert P. and Alexander F. Kerensky, eds. *The Russian Provisional Government 1917. Documents* (3 vols.). Stanford: Stanford University Press, 1961.

Brusilov, Aleksei Alekseyevich. *A Soldier's Notebook, 1914–1918*. Westport, CT: Greenwood Press, 1971.

Brussilow, A.A. *Meine Errinerungen*. [Berlin]: Militärverlag der DDR, no date. (Original version, Moscow: Voennizdat, 1983).

Bubnov, Aleksandr. *V Tsarkoi Stavka. Vospominnania admirala Bubnova*. New York: Izdatelstvo Imenii Chekova, 1955.

Charques, Richard. *The Twilight of Imperial Russia*. London: Oxford University Press, 1965.

Cherkasov, P.V. *Der Durchbruch bei Luck*. Moscow: n.p., 1927.

———. *Der Durchbruch der 11. Armee in Mai (alt) 1916*. Moscow: n.p., 1924.

Cherkasov, P.V., ed. *Mirovaya Voiyna 1914—1918 "Lutskii Proriv." Trudi i materiali k operatsii yugo-zapadnovo fronta v mai—yunye 1916 goda*. Moscow: Vizschii Voiyennii Redaktsionii Soviet, 1924.

Chickering, Roger. *Imperial Germany and the Great War, 1914–1918*. (New Approaches to European History). Cambridge: Cambridge University Press, 1998.

Churchill, Winston S. *The Unknown War: The Eastern Front*. New York: Scribner, 1931.

Cornish, Nik. *The Russian Army 1914–18*. Oxford: Osprey, 2001.

Cowley, Robert and Geoffrey Parker, eds. *The Reader's Companion to Military History*. Boston and New York: Houghton Mifflin Company, 1996.

Cramon, August von. *Unser österreichisch-ungarischer Beundesgenosse im Weltkriege: Errinerungen aus meiner vierjährigen Tätigkeit als bevollmächtiger deutscher General beim k.u.k Armeeoberkommando*. Berlin: E.S. Mittler & Sohn, 1922.

Deak, Istvan. *Beyond Nationalism: A Social and Political History of the Habsburg Officer Corps, 1848–1918*. New York: Oxford University Press, 1990.

Denikin, Anton I. *The Russian Turmoil. Memoirs: Military, Social, and Political*. Westport, CT: Hyperion Press, 1920.

De Lazari, A. N., and Andrei M. Zaionchkovski. *Mirovaia voina 1914–1918: Atlas skhem k trudu A. Zaionchkovskovo*. Moscow: Gosudarstvenny Voennoye Izdatelstvo, 1924.

Diakov. *Wie es im Sommer 1916 zur Brusilov-Offensive kam*. Vienna: n.p. 1923.

Falkenhayn, General Erich von. *The German General Staff and Its Decisions, 1914–1916*. New York: Dodd, Mead and Company, 1920.

Feldman, Robert S. *Between War and Revolution: the Russian General Staff, February-July 1917*. Ann Arbor: University Microfilms, 1968.

Florinsky, Michael T. *The End of the Russian Empire*. New Haven: Yale University Press, 1931.

Forty, Simon. *Historical Maps of World War I*. London: Public Records Office; and New York: Sterling Publications, 2002.

Furhmann, Joseph T., ed. *The Complete Wartime Correspondence of Tsar Nicholas II and the Empress Alexandra, April 1914–March 1917*. Westport, CT: Greenwood Press, 1999.

Gatrell, Peter. *Government, Industry, and Rearmament in Russia, 1900–1914*. Cambridge: Cambridge University Press, 1994.

Golovine, Lt. Gen. Nicholas N. *The Russian Army in the World War*. New Haven: Yale University Press, 1931.

——. *The Russian Campaign of 1914. The Beginning of the War and Operations in East Prussia*. (Capt. A.G.S. Muntz, trans.) Fort Leavenworth, KS: The Command and General Staff School Press, 1933.

Graham, Stephen. *Russia in 1916*. London, Toronto, and Melbourne: Cassell & Company, Ltd., 1917.

Grow, Malcolm C. *Surgeon Grow. An American in the Russian Fighting*. New York: Frederick A. Stokes Company, 1918.

Herrmann, David G. *The Arming of Europe and the Making of the First World War*. Princeton, NJ: Princeton University Press, 1996.

Herwig, Holger H. *The First World War. Germany and Austria Hungary 1914–1918*. Oxford: Oxford University Press, 1996.

Hubatsch, Walther. *Germany and the Central Powers in the World War 1914–1918*. Lawrence, KS: University of Kansas Publications, 1963.

Imperial War Museum, Department of Printed Books. *Trench Fortifications 1914–1918. A Reference Manual*. Nashville: Battery Press, 1998.

Jerabek, Rudolf. *Die Brussilowoffensive 1916. Ein Wendepunkt der Koalitionskriegführung der Mittelmächte*. Dissertation zur Erlangung des Doktorgrades an der geistwissenshaftlichen Fakultät der Universität Wien, Vienna, 1982. (In the library collection of the Austrian State Archive, War Archive.)

Johnson, Douglas Wilson. *Topography and Strategy in the War*. New York: Henry Holt and Company, 1917.

Jones, Archer. *The Art of War in the Western World*. Urbana: University of Illinois Press, 1987.

Jung, Peter. *The Austro-Hungarian Forces in World War I (1), 1914–16*. Oxford: Osprey, 2003.

Jukes, Geoffrey. *Carpathian Disaster: Death of an Army*. New York: Ballantine Books, 1971.

Katkov, George. *The Kornilov Affair. Kerensky and the Break-up of the Russian Army*. New York: Longman, 1980.

Keegan, John. *The First World War*. New York: Alfred A. Knopf, 1999.

Kerensky, Alexander. *The Kerensky Memoirs. Russia and History's Turning Point*. London: Cassell, 1966.

Kitchen, Martin. *The Silent Dictatorship: The Politics of the German High Command under Hindenburg and Ludendorff, 1916–1918*. London: Croom Helm, 1976.

Knox, Major-General Alfred W. F. *With the Russian Army 1914–1917* (2 vols.). New York: Arno Press and *The New York Times*, 1971.

Kochan, Lionel. *Russia in Revolution, 1890–1918*. New York: New American Library, 1966.

Levin, S. *Brusilovskii proriy*. Oguz: Gospolitizdat, 1941.

Lincoln, W. Bruce. *Passage through Armageddon. The Russians in War and Revolution, 1914–1918*. New York: Simon & Schuster, 1986.

——. *Red Victory. A History of the Russian Civil War*. New York: Simon and Schuster, 1989.

Luckett, Richard. *The White Generals. An Account of the White Movement and the Russian Civil War*. New York: Viking, 1971.

Ludendorff, General Erich. *My War Memories, 1914–1918*. (2 vols.) London: Hutchinson & Co., no date [1920].

Mayzel, Matitiahu. *Generals and Revolutionaries. The Russian General Staff during the Revolution: A Study in the Transformation of Military Elite*. Osnabrück: Biblio, 1979.

Manning, Roberta Thompson. *The Crisis of the Old Order in Russia: Gentry and Government*. Princeton: Princeton University Press, 1982.

Menning, Bruce W. *Bayonets before Bullets: The Imperial Russian Army, 1861–1914*. Bloomington: Indiana University Press, 1992.

Österreichischer Bundesministerium für Landesverteidigung; Österreichischer Kreigsarchiv, eds. *Österriech-Ungarns Letzter Krieg, 1914–1918* (6 vols.). Vienna: Verlag der Militärwissenschaftlichen Mitteilungen, 1933.

Paléologue, Maurice. *An Ambassador's Memoirs*. (3 vols., F.A. Holt, trans.) New York: George H. Doran Co., 1931.

Pearson, Raymond. *The Russian Moderates and the Crisis of Tsarism, 1914–1917*. New York: Barnes & Noble Books, 1979.

Rauchensteiner, Manfried. *Der Tod des Doppeladlers: Österreich-Ungarn und der Erste Weltkrieg*. Vienna: Styria Verlag, 1993.

Reed, John. *The Collected Works of John Reed*. New York: The Modern Library, 1995.

——. *The War in Eastern Europe*. London: Eveleigh Nash Company, Limited, 1916.

Reese, Roger, ed. *The Russian Imperial Army, 1796–1917*. Burlington, VT: Ashgate, 2006.

Rich, David Alan. *The Tsar's Colonels: Professionalism, Strategy, and Subversion in Late Imperial Russia*. Cambridge, MA: Harvard University Press, 1999.

Rothenberg, Gunther E. *The Army of Francis Joseph*. West Lafayette: Purdue University Press, 1976.

Ruffkey, David L. "The Brusilov Offensive" in *History in Dispute: World War I: First Series—History in Dispute, vol. 8*, Dennis Showalter, ed. London: St. James Press, 2002.

Schimmelpenninck van der Oye, David and Bruce W. Menning, eds. *Reforming the Tsar's Army. Military Innovation in Imperial Russia from Peter the Great to the Revolution*. Cambridge and Washington, D.C.: Cambridge University Press and Woodrow Wilson Center Press, 2004.

Schlotheim, Ludwig Eberhard, *Freiherr* von. *Die kaiserlich deutsche Südarmee in den Kämpfen während der Brussilow-Offensive vom 4. Juni bis 14. August 1916. Ein Beitrag zur Geschichte der Kaiserlich Deutschen Südarmee*. Munich: C.H. Beck, 1936.

Semanov, Sergei. *General Brusilov. Dokumentalnoye Povestvovannie*. Moscow: Voyennoye Izdatelstvo, 1986.

Sergeyev-Tsensky, S. *Brusilov's Breakthrough. A Novel of the First World War*. (Helen Altschuler, trans.) London: Hutchinson & Co., Ltd., n.d.

Shanafelt, George W. *The Secret Enemy: Austria-Hungary and the German Alliance, 1914–1918.* Boulder: Eastern European Monographs, 1985.

Silberstein, Gerard E. *The Troubled Alliance: German-Austrian Relations 1914 to 1917.* Lexington, KY: University Press of Kentucky, 1970.

Smirnov, Nikolas N., ed. *Rossi'a ii pervaya mirovaya voina. (Materialii mezhdurodnovo naiuchnovo collokviuma.* St. Petersburg: St. Petersburg Branch of the Institute of Russian History of the Russian Academy of Science, 1999.

Sondhaus, Lawrence. *Franz Conrad von Hötzendorf: Architect of the Apocalypse.* Studies in Central European History. Boston: Humanities Press, 2000.

Stevenson, David. *Armaments and the Coming of War. Europe, 1904–1914.* Oxford: Clarendon Press, 1996.

Stone, Norman. *The Eastern Front 1914–1917.* New York: Charles Scribner's Sons, 1975.

Sukiennicki, Wiktor. *East Central Europe during World War I: From Foreign Domination to National Independence.* Boulder: East European Monographs, 1984.

Taylor, Brian D. *Politics and the Russian Army: Civil-Military Relations, 1689–2000.* Cambridge: Cambridge University Press, 2003.

Tucker, Spencer C. *The Great War, 1914–1918.* Bloomington: Indiana University Press, 1998.

Tucker, Spencer C., ed. *The European Powers in the First World War: an encyclopedia.* New York: Garland, 1996.

Tunstall, Graydon A., Jr. "German and Austro-Hungarian War Planning and War Aims and the Concept of *Mitteleuropa,*" in *20th Century Hungary and the Great Powers* (*War and Society in East Central Europe,* vol. XXXIII), Ignac Romsics, ed. Boulder: Social Science Monographs, 1995.

———. "The Habsburg Command Conspiracy: The Falsification of Historiography on the Outbreak of World War I," in *Austrian History Yearbook,* v. 27, 1996, pp. 181–198.

———. "Austria-Hungary: A Great or Balkan Power?" in *History in Dispute: World War I: First Series—History in Dispute, vol. 9,* Dennis Showalter, ed. London: St. James Press, 2002.

———. "The Brusilov Offensive" in *History in Dispute: World War I: First Series—History in Dispute, vol. 8,* Dennis Showalter, ed. London: St. James Press, 2002.

Vulliamy, C. E., ed., *The Red Archives. Russian State Papers and Other Documents Relating to the Years 1915–1918.* A. L. Hines, translator. London: Geoffrey Bles, 1922.

Washburn, Stanley. *The Russian Campaign, April to August 1915, being the Second Volume of "Field Notes from the Russian Front."* London: Andrew Melrose, Ltd., n.d. [1915]

———. *Victory in Defeat. The Agony of Warsaw and the Russian Retreat.* Garden City, NJ, and New York: Doubleday, Page & Company, 1916.

———. *The Russian Advance; being the Third volume of Field Notes from the Russian Front, embracing the period from June 5th to September 1st, 1916.* Garden City, NJ, and New York: Doubleday, Page & Company, 1917.

Wheatley, John. "Austria-Hungary: A Great or Balkan Power?" in *History in Dispute: World War I: First Series—History in Dispute, vol. 9,* Dennis Showalter, ed. London: St. James Press, 2002.

Wildman, Allan K. *The End of the Russian Imperial Army. The Old Army and the Soldiers' Revolt (March-April 1917).* Princeton: Princeton University Press, 1980.

———. *The End of the Russian Imperial Army. The Road to Soviet Power and Peace.* Princeton: Princeton University Press, 1987.

Zaionchkovski, Andrei M. *Strategic Skizzen.* Moscow: n.p., 1923.

———. *Podgotovka Rossii k Mirovoi voine v mezhdunarodnom otnoshenii.* Leningrad: Voennoye Izdatelstvo, 1926.

———. *Mirovaya Voina. Manevrennii period 1914–1915 godov na russkom (evropayskom) teatre.* Moscow and Leningrad: Gosudarstvennoye Izdatelstvo, 1929.

———. *Mirovaya Voina, 1914–1918 gg.* (2nd edition). Moscow: Gosudarstvennoe Voennoe Izdatelstvo, 1931.

WEBSITES

"The Brusilov Offensive," http://www.worldwar1.com/tlbruoff.htm

First World War.com, http://www.firstworldwar.com

Photos of the Great War, WWI Image Archive, http://www.gwpda.org/photos/greatwar.htm#TOP

"Solving Problems through Force; The Leadership of the Empire of Austria-Hungary during World War I," http://www.geocities.com/veldes1/index.html

The Western Front Association, http://www.westernfrontassociation.com

"Why Brusilov Must Return," http://www.greatwardifferent.com/Great_War/Russian_Soldier/Brusilov_Return_01.htm

INDEX

After working at the U.S. Embassy in Moscow, TIMOTHY C. DOWLING earned his doctorate from Tulane University in 1999. He taught at the Vienna International School in Austria before taking an appointment at the Virginia Military Institute in 2001. A specialist in modern German and Russian history, Dowling is the editor of two volumes of personal perspectives on the world wars.